Dedicated to
My Grandfather
Late Sh. Ram Krishan Gupta

Parag Gupta

20 SAMPLE PAPERS IN Economics

As per the latest Design of Question Paper for 2020 Examinations

Class XII CBSE Syllabus

This book contains

- **Fast Track Notes for Revision**
- **Ten Sample Papers** (with Solutions) including
  - CBSE Latest Sample Paper 2019–20
- **Ten Sample Papers–For Practice (With Hints and Answers)**

ARYA PUBLICATIONS
(AVICHAL PUBLISHING COMPANY)
Industrial Area, Trilokpur Road, Kala Amb 173 030, Distt. Sirmour (HP)
Delhi Office : **1002 Faiz Road (opp. Hanumanji Murti), Karol Bagh, New Delhi 110 005**

Published by:

ARYA PUBLICATIONS
(Avichal Publishing Company)
Industrial Area, Trilokpur Road
Kala Amb 173 030, Distt. Sirmour (HP)
Phone: 01702-238688, 238832

Delhi Office:
1002 Faiz Road (opp. Hanumanji Murti)
Karol Bagh, New Delhi 110 005 (India)
Ph.: 011-28752745, 28752604
Fax: 011-28756921
Email: info@apcbooks.co.in
Website: www.apcbooks.co.in

ISBN–978–81–7855–797-7

First Edition: November 2015
Second Edition: October 2016
Third Edition: November 2017
Fourth Edition: August 2018
Fifth Edition: October 2019

Price: ₹ 250.00

Laser Typesetting at:

Laser Tech Prints (D)

Printed at:
Deepak Offset Printers
Bawana Industrial Area, Delhi

Preface

I would like to express my gratitude to my loving parents, for their dedication, devotion and constant support towards the preparation of this book. It is a great pleasure in presenting the fifth edition of this book.

The book has been prepared according to the latest CBSE question paper pattern (2019-20) for class XII students. Salient features of this book:

1. It contains the **complete summary** of all chapter's topic wise which will definitely help students in the last moment revision and quickly grasping all the key points.
2. **Flowcharts and other important formulae** have been complied for better memorization.
3. **HOTS** questions and **MCQs** have been incorporated in all the sample papers and practice papers.
4. **Analytical** questions are given in each sample paper for complete preparation of the exams.
5. **Solved sample papers** will provide the students a glimpse of how to write the answers in CBSE exams to score the maximum marks.
6. **Unsolved practice papers** will give the students a real check of their preparations and also help them in proper time management.

I am heartedly thankful to **Sh. Naveen Gupta** and **Sh. Tushar Gupta** of Arya Publications for their encouragement, coordination and dedication in bringing out this book. I would like to thank my wife **Anjali Gupta** for her constant help and support in preparing the book. Also, I sincerely thank all my respected teachers and elders for their constant guidance and blessings and I am also thankful to my student **Kriti Sinha** for her efforts in improvising the book.

Last but not least, any suggestion for further improvement will be gladly acknowledged and appreciated.

CA Parag Gupta
caparaggupta@gmail.com

Syllabus

Economics

Theory: 80 Marks **Project: 20 Marks**

UNITS	MARKS	PERIODS
Part A—Introductory Macroeconomics		
1. National Income and Related Aggregates	10	28
2. Money and Banking	6	15
3. Determination of Income and Employment	12	27
4. Government Budget and the Economy	6	15
5. Balance of Payments	6	15
	40	**100**
Part B—Indian Economic Development		
6. Development Experience (1947-90) and Economic Reforms Since 1991	12	28
7. Current Challenges Facing Indian Economy	22	60
8. Development Experience Of India: A Comparison with Neighbours	6	12
	40	**100**

PART A—INTRODUCTORY MACROECONOMICS

UNIT 1: NATIONAL INCOME AND RELATED AGGREGATES (28 PERIODS)

What is Macroeconomics?

Basic concepts in macroeconomics: consumption goods, capital goods, final goods, intermediate goods; stocks and flows; gross investment and depreciation.

Circular flow of income (two sector model); Methods of calculating National Income – Value Added or Product method, Expenditure method, Income method.

Aggregates related to National Income: Gross National Product (GNP), Net National Product (NNP), Gross and Net Domestic Product (GDP and NDP) - at market price, at factor cost; Real and Nominal GDP.

GDP and Welfare

UNIT 2: MONEY AND BANKING (15 PERIODS)

Money — meaning and supply of money — Currency held by the public and net demand deposits held by commercial banks.

Money creation by the commercial banking system.

Central bank and its functions (example of the Reserve Bank of India): Bank of issue, Govt. bank, Banker's bank, Control of credit through Bank Rate, CRR, SLR, Repo Rate and Reverse Repo Rate, Open market operations, Margin requirement.

UNIT 3: DETERMINATION OF INCOME AND EMPLOYMENT (27 PERIODS)

Aggregate demand and its components.

Propensity to consume and propensity to save (average and marginal).

Short-run equilibrium output; investment multiplier and its mechanism.

Meaning of full employment and involuntary unemployment.

Problems of excess demand and deficient demand; measures to correct them - changes in government spending, taxes and money supply.

UNIT 4: GOVERNMENT BUDGET AND THE ECONOMY (15 PERIODS)

Government budget—meaning, objectives and components.

Classification of receipts—revenue receipts and capital receipts; classification of expenditure - revenue expenditure and capital expenditure.

Measures of government deficit - revenue deficit, fiscal deficit, primary deficit and their meanings.

UNIT 5: BALANCE OF PAYMENTS (15 PERIODS)

Balance of payments account - meaning and components; balance of payments deficit-meaning.

Foreign exchange rate – meaning of fixed and flexible rates and managed floating.

Determination of exchange rate in a free market.

PART B—INDIAN ECONOMIC DEVELOPMENT

UNIT 6: DEVELOPMENT EXPERIENCE (1947-90) AND ECONOMIC REFORMS SINCE 1991 (28 PERIODS)

A brief introduction of the state of Indian economy on the eve of independence.

Common goals of Five Year Plans.

Main features, problems and policies of agriculture (institutional aspects and new agricultural strategy, etc.), industry (industrial licensing, etc.) and foreign trade.

Economic Reforms Since 1991

Features and appraisals of liberalisation, globalisation and privatisation (LPG policies); Concepts of demonetization and GST.

UNIT 7: CURRENT CHALLENGES FACING INDIAN ECONOMY (60 PERIODS)

Poverty — absolute and relative; Main programmes for poverty alleviation: A critical assessment.

Rural development: Key issues — credit and marketing — role of cooperatives; agricultural diversification; alternative farming — organic farming.

Human Capital Formation: How people become resource; Role of human capital in economic development; Growth of Education Sector in India.

Employment: Formal and informal growth, problems and policies.

Infrastructure: Meaning and Types; Case Studies; Energy and Health; Problems and Policies — A critical assessment.

Sustainable Economic Development: Meaning, Effects of Economic Development on Resources and Environment, Including Global Warming.

UNIT 8: DEVELOPMENT EXPERIENCE OF INDIA: A COMPARISON WITH NEIGHBOURS (12 PERIODS)

India and Pakistan

India and China

Issues: growth, population, sectoral development and other human developmental indicators.

Suggested Question Paper Design

Marks: 80 **Duration: 3 hrs**

S. No.	Typology of Questions	Objective Type/ MCQ 1 Mark	Short Answer I 3 Marks	Short Answer II 4 Marks	Long Answer 6 Marks	Marks
1.	**Remembering**: Exhibit memory of previously learned material by recalling facts, terms, basic concepts and answers.	5	1	2	1	22
2.	**Understanding:** Demonstrate understanding of facts and ideas by organizing, comparing, translating, interpreting, giving descriptions and stating main ideas.	5	1	2	1	22
3.	**Applying:** Solve problems to new situations by applying acquired knowledge, facts, techniques and rules in a different way.	5	1	1	1	18
4.	**Analysing and Evaluating:** Examine and break information into parts by identifying motives or causes. Make inferences and find evidence to support generalizations. Present and defend opinions by making judgements about information, validity of ideas, or quality of work based on a set of criteria. **Creating:** Compile information together in a different way by combining elements in a new pattern or proposing alternative solutions.	5	1	1	1	18
	Total	20 × 1 = 20	4 × 3 = 12	6 × 4 = 24	4 × 6 = 24	80 (24)

Note. There will be **Internal Choice** in questions of 1 mark, 3 marks, 4 marks and 6 marks in both sections (A and B). In all, total 8 internal choices.

Contents

FAST TRACK NOTES FOR REVISION

MACROECONOMICS

UNIT 1: NATIONAL INCOME AND RELATED AGGREGATES

1. **Basic activities in an economy/ Phases in an economy**	• **Production**: Any activity which produces material goods and services or which increases the value of commodities already produced. • **Consumption:** Consuming goods and services for the satisfaction of human wants is known as consumption. • **Investment:** The net addition to capital, *i.e.* capital formation or in other words, the excess of production over consumption is known as investment.
2. **Final goods**	• These goods are meant for final consumption by consumers or for investment by firms and no further transformation takes place. These are included in the estimation of the national income.
3. **Intermediate goods**	• These are used as raw materials for the production of other goods or for resale purposes in the same year. These are not included in the estimation of national income since these are further transformed.
4. **Consumption (Consumer) goods**	• These are the goods which are consumed by the ultimate consumer for the satisfaction of his wants. For example, milk used by a household.
5. **Capital goods**	• These are the goods which are used for producing other goods. For example, machinery, equipment, etc.
6. **Circular flow of income**	• It refers to the continuous circular movement of money and goods and services in an economy.
7. **Real flow**	• Under real flow, households render factor services to the firms and the firms produce goods and services to pay for the services.

8. **Money flow**	• It includes all monetary payments by firms to households for their factor services and by households to the firm for the purchase of goods and services.
9. **Leakages**	• The amount of money withdrawn from the flow of income is known as leakages. For example, savings, taxes and imports.
10. **Injections**	• The amount of money added to the flow of income is known as injections. For example, investment, government expenditure like subsidies and exports.
11. **Flow**	• It is the quantity which is measured **over a period** of time. It has a time dimension. Eg.: capital formation, income, savings, etc.
12. **Stock**	• It is the quantity which is measured **at a particular** point of time. It has no time dimension. Eg.: capital, money supply, closing inventory, capital, etc.
13. **Factor payments**	• These are the payments received against factor services (land, labour, capital and entrepreneur) *i.e.* rent, wages, interest and profit. These are included while estimating the national income.
14. **Transfer payments**	• These payments are received without rendering any service and are unilateral in nature. Eg.: gifts, donations, old age pensions, national debt interest, etc. These are not included while estimating the national income.
15. **Resident**	• An individual is said to be a resident if his period of stay in a country exceeds one year and his **economic interest** lies in that country.
16. **Citizen**	• A person who resides in a country according to the legal provisions of that country is known as a citizen.
17. **Depreciation**	• It is the loss in the value of an asset due to normal wear and tear or expected obsolescence. It is also known as the **consumption of fixed capital.**
18. **Net factor income from abroad (NFIA)**	• Factor income (earned by normal residents) from abroad (–) Factor income (paid to non-residents) in domestic territory
19. **Net indirect taxes**	• Indirect taxes (–) Subsidy
20. **Domestic (economic) territory**	• It is the geographical territory administered by the government within which persons, goods and capital circulate freely.
21. **Domestic income**	• It is the total factor income generated within the domestic territory of a country.

22. **National income**	• It is the money value of all the final goods and services produced in an economy including net factor income from abroad but excluding depreciation.
23. **Nominal national income**	• In this case, national income is calculated at **current prices**.
24. **Real national income**	• In this case, national income is calculated at **constant prices**. It is a better measure of development of an economy as compared to nominal national income.
25. **GDP deflator**	$\text{GDP deflator} = \frac{\text{Nominal GDP}}{\text{Real GDP}} \times 100$

National Income (Formulae List)

1.	Net	=	Gross (–) Depreciation
2.	Domestic	=	National (–) NFIA
3.	Factor Cost	=	Market price(MP) (–) Net indirect taxes (NIT) ***Or*** Market price(MP) (–) Indirect taxes (+) Subsidies

** National Income = NNP_{FC}
** Domestic Income = NDP_{FC} (*i.e.* National income (–) NFIA)
** Depreciation = Consumption of fixed capital

<u>NFIA</u> = Net compensation of employees
(+)
Net income from property and entrepreneurship (*i.e.* operating surplus)
→ <u>Rent</u> (+) <u>Interest</u> (+) <u>Profit</u>
(+)
Net retained earnings of resident company abroad
(Undistributed Profits)

Measurement of National Income

Three methods of measurement:

1. Value Added Method (Production Method)
2. Income Method
3. Expenditure Method

1. **Value added method** measures national income by estimating the value added at factor cost.

Steps involved:

1.	Calculate the value of output	=	Sales (+) Closing Stock (–) Opening Stock ***Or*** Sales (+) Change in Stock
2.	Calculate the value of intermediate consumption (*i.e.* the cost of raw materials/ inputs)		
3.	GVA_{MP} (*i.e.* GDP_{MP})	=	Step(1) – Step(2)
4.	NVA_{FC}	=	GVA_{MP} (–) Depreciation (–) Net Indirect Taxes (NIT)
5.	Take the sum total of all NVA_{FC} from the three sectors (*i.e.* Primary, Secondary and Tertiary) and we get NDP_{FC} (*i.e.* Domestic Income)		
6.	Finally, NNP_{FC} (*i.e.* National Income)	=	NDP_{FC} (+) NFIA

2. **Income method** measures the national income from the side of payments made in the form of factor payments (*i.e.* rent, wages, interest and profits).

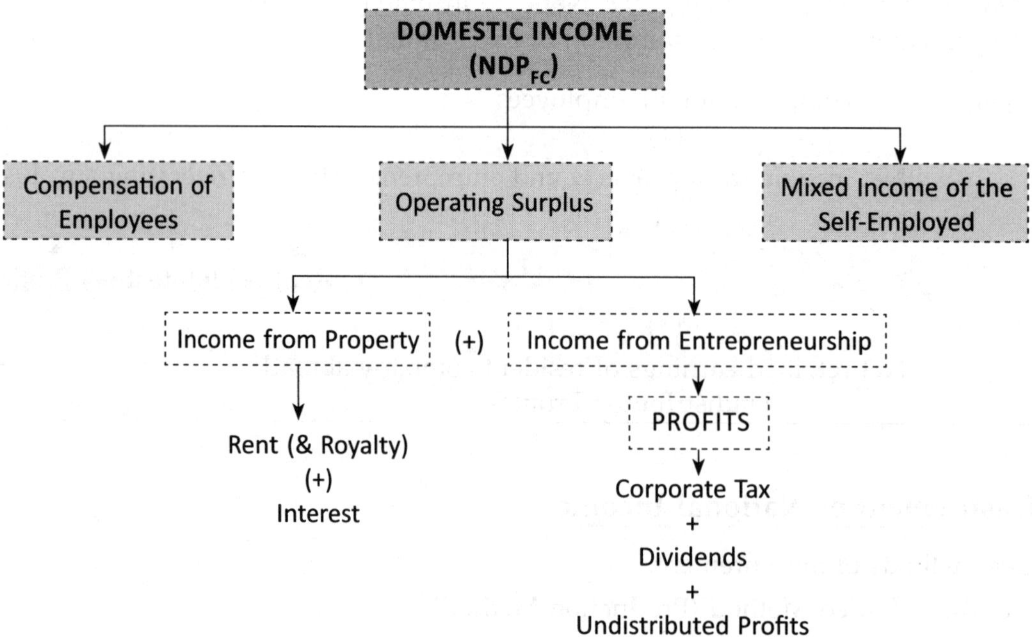

Steps involved:

1.	Calculate **Factor Income**	=	Compensation of Employees (wages, salaries in cash, allowances/non-cash or free services + employer's contribution towards social security schemes like insurance, PF, pension (**except Old Age Pension**) (+) Rent (imputed rent also), Royalty (rent from the use of patents, copyrights, etc.), Interest and Profits (Corporate {profit} Tax, Dividends and Undistributed Profits {reserve funds/corporate savings/savings of private sector}) (+) Mixed income of the self-employed
2.	Take the **sum total** of all factor income from the three sectors (*i.e.* Primary, Secondary and Tertiary) and we get NDP_{FC} (*i.e.* Domestic Income).		
3.	Finally, NNP_{FC} (*i.e.* National Income)	=	NDP_{FC} + NFIA

3. **Expenditure method** is the method which measures the final expenditure on GDP_{MP} during an accounting year.

Steps involved:

1.	GDP_{MP}	=	Private (Personal) Final Consumption Expenditure (+) Government Final Consumption Expenditure (+) Gross Domestic Capital Formation** (+) Net Exports (Exports{X} – Imports{M})
2.	Finally, NNP_{FC} (*i.e.* National Income)	=	GDP_{MP} (–) Depreciation (–) Net Indirect Taxes + NFIA

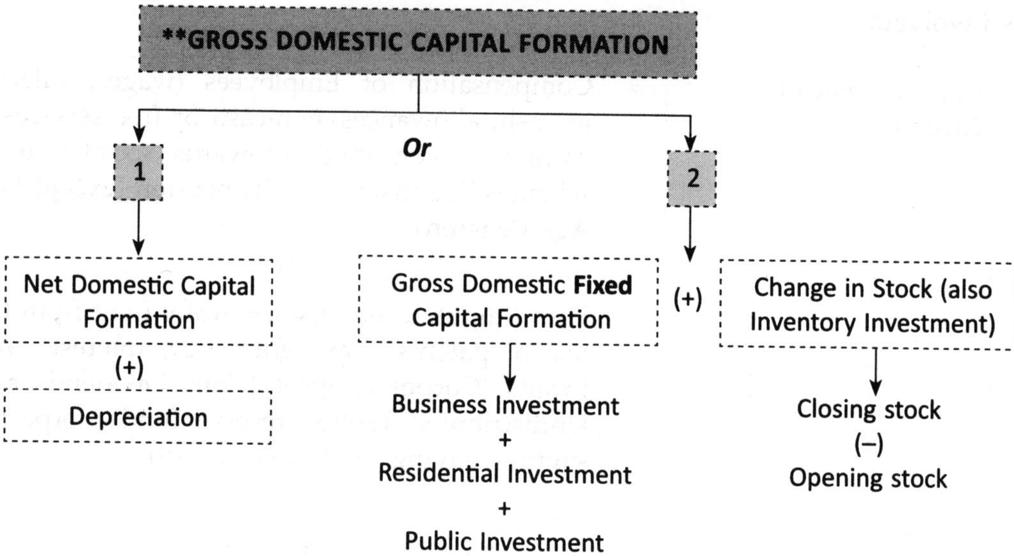

UNIT 2: MONEY AND BANKING

1. **Barter system**	• Barter system implies the direct exchange of goods for goods without the use of money. It is also known as C-C economy.
2. **Limitations of the barter system**	• Lack of double coincidence of wants • Lack of common measure of value • Lack of standard of deferred payments • Lack of store of value • Lack of system for transfer of funds
3. **Money**	• Anything that is generally accepted as medium of exchange and acts as measure and store of value.
4. **Evolution of money**	• agricultural crops ⟶ metallic coins ⟶ silver & gold coins ⟶ paper money ⟶ plastic money
5. **Primary functions of money**	• **Medium of exchange:** Money facilitates the acts of sale and purchase. • **Measure of value (Unit of account):** Money acts as a yardstick of value to which all goods and services can be attached to.
6. **Secondary functions of money**	• **Standard of deferred payments:** Money facilitates borrowing and lending. • **Store of value:** Wealth can be easily stored in terms of money.

7. **Money supply**	• The total stock of money held by people of a country at a point of time is called money supply. Money held by the government and banks are not included in money supply since they are the suppliers of money. – M_1 (Narrow money): Currency notes + Demand Deposits + Other Deposits with RBI – M_2: M_1 + Savings deposits with post office savings bank – M_3 (Broad money): M_1 + Time deposits of commercial banks – M_4: M_3 + Total deposits with post office savings organisation
8. **Bank**	• Bank is a financial institution whose primary function is lending and borrowing money.
9. **Commercial Banks**	• These are the financial institutions which accept deposits and give loans with the aim of **earning profits** (known as spread).
10. **Central Bank**	• It is the apex institution of monetary and banking system of a country. Eg.: the RBI in India.
11. **Legal Reserve Ratio (LRR)**	• It is the minimum ratio of demand deposits which every commercial bank has to keep as cash reserves. It can be of two types: – **Cash Reserve Ratio (CRR):** It is the minimum proportion of cash reserves which is kept by commercial banks with the central bank against its total deposits. – **Statutory Liquidity Ratio (SLR):** It is that proportion of total deposits which a commercial bank has to keep with itself in the form of liquid assets (*i.e.* cash, gold and unencumbered approved securities).
12. **Money creation**	• Initial deposit $\times \frac{1}{\text{LRR}}$ Here, $\frac{1}{\text{LRR}}$ is known as the money multiplier.
13. **Functions of the Central Bank**	• Bank of issue • Banker to the government • Banker's bank and supervisor • Custodian of the national reserves of international currency • Lender of last resort • Clearing house function • Credit control

14. **Quantitative methods of credit control (General control measures)**	• Bank rate • Repo rate & reverse repo rate policy • Open market operations • CRR and SLR
15. **Qualitative methods of credit control (Specific control measures)**	• Moral suasion • Margin requirement • Credit rationing

UNIT 3: DETERMINATION OF INCOME AND EMPLOYMENT

1. **Aggregate demand (AD)**	• It represents the **total expenditure** on goods and services in an economy. Its components are: – Household (private) consumption expenditure (C) – Investment expenditure (I) – Government consumption expenditure (G) – Net exports (X – M)
2. **Consumption expenditure (C)**	• Consumption is the function of income *i.e.* $C = f(Y)$ or mathematically, $C = \overline{C} + bY$ Here, $\overline{C}$ = Autonomous consumption *i.e.* consumption at zero level of income b = Marginal propensity to consume (MPC) or **slope** of a consumption curve Y = Income level
3. **Investment expenditure (I)**	• Investment is a function of rate of interest *i.e.* I = f(i) and it has an inverse relation with the rate of interest. Here, *i* = rate of interest *i.e.* rate at which banks grant loans to the firms.
4. **Types of investment**	• **Induced investment:** It refers to an investment made by the private sector with a motive of earning profits. It increases with an increase in income *i.e.* it has a direct relation with the level of income.

	• **Autonomous investment:** It refers to an investment made by the government with an objective of social welfare. It remains **constant** irrespective of the level of income. For the purpose of AD, only autonomous investment is considered.
5. **Aggregate supply (AS)**	• It is the money value of total output available in the economy for purchase during a given period. AS curve is represented by a 45° line or a guide line. Its components are: (a) Consumption (C) (b) Savings (S)
6. **Savings (S)**	• Savings is the function of disposable income *i.e.* $S = f(Y)$ or mathematically, $S = (-)\overline{C} + (1 - b)Y$ Here, $(-)\overline{C}$ = Dissavings which are equal to consumption at zero level of income $(1 - b)$ = Marginal propensity to save (MPS) or **slope** of savings curve Y = Income level
7. **Average propensity to consume (APC)**	• It is the ratio of consumption expenditure (C) to income (Y) *i.e.* $APC = \frac{C}{Y}$
8. **Marginal propensity to consume (MPC or b)**	• It is the ratio of change in consumption expenditure (ΔC) to change in income (ΔY) *i.e.* $MPC = \frac{\Delta C}{\Delta Y}$
9. **Average propensity to save (APS)**	• It is the ratio of savings (S) to income (Y) *i.e.* $APS = \frac{S}{Y}$
10. **Marginal propensity to save (MPS)**	• It is the ratio of change in savings (ΔS) to change in income (ΔY) *i.e.* $MPS = \frac{\Delta S}{\Delta Y}$
11. **APC + APS = 1** and **MPC + MPS = 1**	
12. **Break-even point**	• It is that point where consumption is exactly equal to the income or savings are nil.

13. **Equilibrium level of income or output:**	• **AD – AS approach:** The equilibrium level is where AD = AS *i.e.* Y = C + I. • **Savings – investment approach:** The equilibrium level of income or output is ex-ante (Planned) Savings = ex-ante (Planned) Investment.
14. **Investment (output) multiplier**	• It is the ratio of change in income (ΔY) to change in investment (ΔI), *i.e.,* $K = \frac{\Delta Y}{\Delta I}$ or $K = \frac{1}{1 - MPC}$ or $K = \frac{1}{MPS}$
15. **Relationship of "K" with MPC & MPS**	• Investment multiplier (K) has a **direct relation with MPC and an inverse relation with MPS.** The value of investment multiplier also lies between 1 to ∞ *i.e* – Minimum value of K = 1 – Maximum value of K = ∞ (Infinity)
16. **Ex-ante saving**	• The saving which the households desire to make in the economy during a period is called ex-ante (planned savings).
17. **Ex-ante investment**	• The investment which the firms or entrepreneurs desire to make during a period is called ex-ante investment.
18. Ex-post saving	• Savings which are actually undertaken by the savers measured at the end of the period.
19. **Ex-post investment**	• Investment actually undertaken by the investors at the end of the period.
20. **Voluntary unemployment**	• When people are **not willing to work** although suitable work is available to them, it is known as voluntary unemployment. These people are not included in the labour force of the country.
21. **Involuntary unemployment**	• When people are ready to work at the existing wage rate but do not find any work, it is known as involuntary unemployment.
22. **Full employment**	• It represents zero involuntary unemployment.

23. **Types of equilibrium**	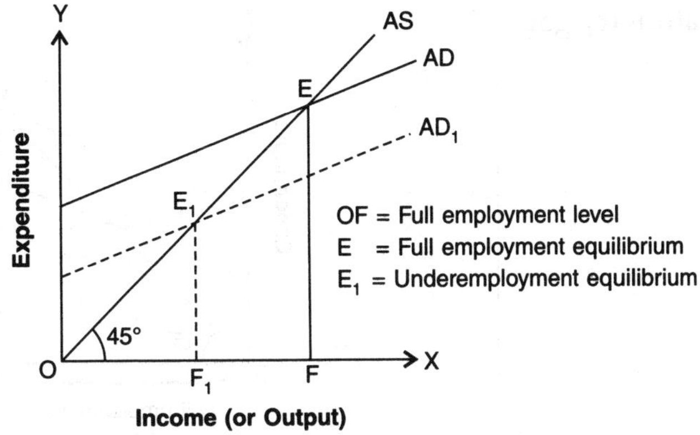 **Fig. 1** • **Full employment equilibrium:** It refers to the case when equilibrium between AD and AS takes place at the full employment level. • **Underemployment equilibrium:** It refers to the case when equilibrium between AD and AS takes place at less than the full employment level.
24. **Excess demand**	• It refers to a situation when AD > AS at the full employment level.
25. **Inflationary gap**	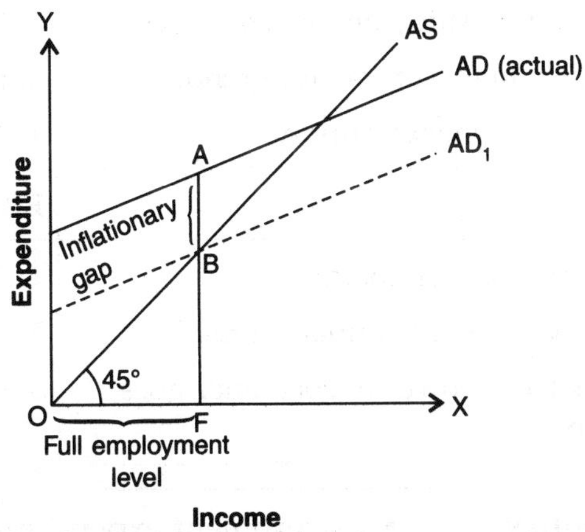 **Fig. 2** • It is the gap denoting the difference between actual AD and the AD required to establish equilibrium at the full employment level.
26. **Deficient demand**	• It refers to a situation when AD < AS at the full employment level.

27. Deflationary gap

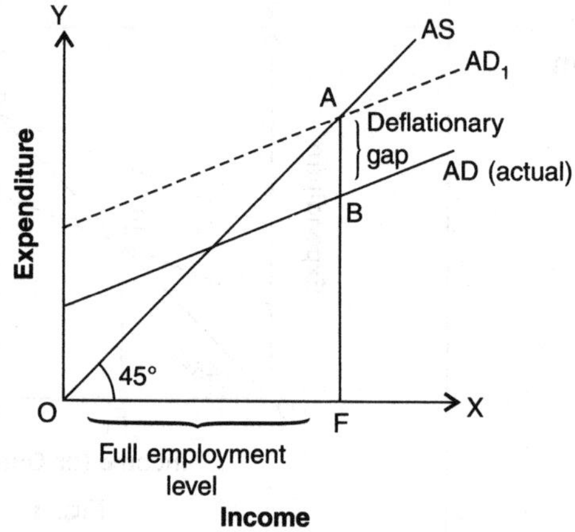

Fig. 3

- It is the gap denoting the difference between the AD required to establish full employment equilibrium and the actual AD.

28.	Excess Demand	Deficient Demand
	Reasons	**Reasons**
	1. Increase in consumption 2. Increase in Autonomous investment 3. Increase in Government expenditure 4. Increase in money supply	1. Decrease in consumption 2. Decrease in Autonomous investment 3. Decreasse in Government expenditure 4. Decrease in money supply
	Effects	**Effects**
	1. Rise in prices of goods 2. Producers get abnormal profits 3. Purchasing power of consumer goes down	1. Fall in price and income 2. Producer incurs losses 3. Purchasing power of consumer increases

29. **Fiscal policy (by the central government) to correct excess or deficient demand**	• Government expenditure (Eg.: subsidies) • Government revenue (Eg.: taxes) • Public borrowings • Deficit financing

30. **Monetary policy (by the RBI) to correct excess or deficient demand**	• **Quantitative instruments:** (a) Bank rate policy (b) Repo and reverse repo rate policy (c) Open market operations (d) CRR and SLR • **Qualitative instruments:** (a) Moral suasion (b) Margin requirement (c) Credit rationing

Measures to control Excess Demand and Deficient Demand

Measures	Excess Demand	Deficient Demand
I. Fiscal Policy (by the central government)		
(a) Government Expenditure	(↓)	(↑)
(b) Government Revenue (Taxes)	(↑)	(↓)
(c) Public Borrowings	(↑)	(↓)
(d) Deficit Financing	(↓)	(↑)
II. Monetary Policy (by the RBI)		
1. **Quantitative**		
(a) Bank Rate	(↑)	(↓)
(b) (Repo Rate and Reverse Repo Rate	(↑)	(↓)
(c) Open Market Operations	Sale of government securities	Purchase of government securities
(d) CRR/SLR	(↑)	(↓)
2. **Qualitative**		
(a) Moral Suasion	RBI advises to restrict credit	RBI advises to expand credit
(b) Margin requirement	(↑)	(↓)

UNIT 4: GOVERNMENT BUDGET

1. **Government budget**	• It is a statement showing item-wise estimated receipts and anticipated expenditure under various heads during a fiscal year (*i.e.* 1st April - 31st March).

2. **Objectives of government budget**	• Redistribution of income and wealth • Reallocation of resources • Economic stability • Generation of employment and economic growth • Management of public enterprises
3. **Public goods**	• Those goods which are provided by the government to the public like roads, parks, etc. are known as public goods.
4. **Private goods**	• Those goods which are bought and sold between buyers and sellers like food, clothes, etc. are called private goods.

5. **Components/Structure of Budget:**

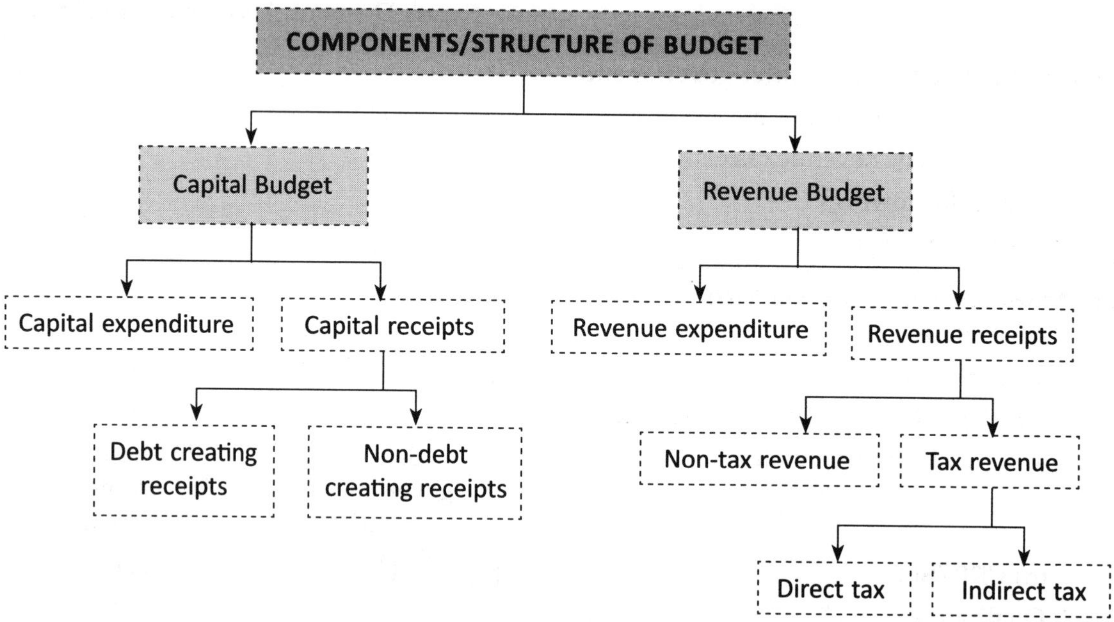

6. **Capital receipts**	• They are those receipts which either create liabilities or reduce assets like borrowings, disinvestment, recovery of loans, etc.
7. **Capital expenditure**	• These refer to those expenditure which either create assets or reduce liabilities like construction of bridges, purchase of land, repayment of loans, etc.
8. **Revenue receipts**	• Those receipts which neither create liabilities nor reduce assets like taxes, interest received, escheat, fees and fines, etc. are called revenue receipts.

9. **Revenue expenditure**	• Those expenditure which neither create assets nor reduce liabilities like payment of interest, grants given, subsidies given, etc. are called revenue expenditure.
10. **Budget receipts**	• It refers to estimated receipts of the government from various sources during a fiscal year.
11. **Fees**	• A payment to defray the cost of each recurring service undertaken by the government primarily in the public interest but conferring a measurable special advantage on the fee payer.
12. **Fine**	• Fines are amounts levied for an infringement of a law.
13. **Forfeitures**	• Penalties imposed by courts for non-compliance with orders for non-fulfilment of contract etc.
14. **Non-tax revenue**	• Income from sources other than taxes is called non-tax revenue. It arises on account of administrative function of the government, e.g. fees, fines, escheat, etc.
15. **Direct tax (progressive tax)**	• It is paid by the person on whom it is imposed *i.e.* shifting of burden is not possible like income tax, wealth tax (now abolished), corporate tax, etc. It puts the burden on rich people.
16. **Indirect tax (regressive tax)**	• It is paid by the consumer *i.e.* shifting of burden is possible like sales tax, service tax, excise duty, etc. It puts the burden on poor people.
17. **Balanced budget**	• When estimated total receipts = estimated total expenditure, it is known as balanced budget.
18. **Surplus budget**	• When estimated total receipts > estimated total expenditure, it is known as surplus budget.
19. **Deficit budget**	• When estimated total receipts < estimated total expenditure, it is known as deficit budget. (a) Revenue deficit = Revenue expenditure (–) Revenue receipts (b) Fiscal deficit = Total expenditure (–) Total receipts (excluding borrowings) *Or* Fiscal deficit = Budget deficit (+) Borrowings

	Or Fiscal deficit = Revenue deficit (+) Capital expenditure (–) Capital receipts (excluding borrowings) (c) Primary deficit = Fiscal deficit (–) Interest payments
20. **Revenue deficit**	• It refers to the excess of total revenue expenditure over its total revenue receipts during a fiscal year.
21. **Fiscal deficit**	• It is defined as excess of total expenditure over total receipts excluding borrowings during a fiscal year.
22. **Primary deficit**	• It is defined as fiscal deficit less interest payment on borrowings.
23. **Deficit financing**	• Borrowing of money by the government to meet its budget deficit by selling treasury bills or government securities to RBI is called deficit financing. It is the mode of financing budgetary deficit in the form of printing new currency.
24. **Measures to correct revenue deficit**	• Reduce public expenditure • Increase government revenue by imposing taxes.
25. **Sources of financing fiscal deficit**	• Deficit financing *i.e.* printing of extra currency notes by the RBI • Borrowings from domestic sources • Borrowings from external sources.
26. **Implications of revenue deficit**	• It indicates the dissavings of the government. • It implies higher repayment burden in future. • It leads to an inflationary situation in the economy.
27. **Implications of fiscal deficit**	• Increase in borrowings leads to an inflationary situation in the economy. • It leads to foreign dependence. • It leads to a **debt trap** situation. • It leads to wasteful and unnecessary expenditure by the government.

UNIT 5: FOREIGN EXCHANGE RATE AND BALANCE OF PAYMENTS

1. **Foreign exchange**	• It is the name given to all currencies other than the domestic currency. For example, US dollars, British Pounds, etc.

2. **Foreign exchange rate**	• It is the rate at which currency of one country is exchanged with the currency of another country. It is also known as **external value of currency.**
3. **Types of foreign exchange rate**	• **Fixed exchange rate**: It is the exchange rate which is officially fixed by the government or monetary authority and not determined by market forces. • **Flexible system of exchange rate**: That exchange rate which is determined by market forces. • **Managed floating system**: It is a system under which the central bank allows the exchange rate to be determined by market forces but intervenes at times to influence the rate.

CONCEPT OF CURRENCY DEPRECIATION AND CURRENCY APPRECIATION

Currency Depreciation	Currency Appreciation
Suppose yesterday 1 \$ = ₹ 60 And today 1 \$ = ₹ 65 This is known as **increase** in exchange rate which is also termed as Currency Depreciation. Hence, **currency depreciation** is the decrease in the value of domestic currency in terms of foreign currency.	Suppose yesterday 1 \$ = ₹ 60 And today 1 \$ = ₹ 55 This is known as **decrease** in exchange rate which is also termed as Currency Appreciation. Hence, **currency appreciation** is the increase in the value of domestic currency in terms of foreign currency.
This implies that for purchasing the same amount of dollars, we have to pay more rupees now. Also, Domestic currency depreciation = Foreign currency appreciation **Effect of currency depreciation** It will lead to an **increase in exports** because domestic goods are now cheaper. It will lead to a **decrease in imports** because foreign goods are now costlier. **How does the RBI bring down this high foreign exchange rate?** The RBI **increases the supply** of foreign exchange by **selling** foreign exchange from its reserves to bring down its value.	This implies that for purchasing the same amount of dollars, we have to pay less rupees now. Also, Domestic currency appreciation = Foreign currency depreciation **Effect of currency appreciation** It will lead to a **decrease in exports** because domestic goods are now costlier. It will lead to an **increase in imports** because foreign goods are now cheaper. **How does the RBI increase this low foreign exchange rate?** The RBI **increases the demand** of foreign exchange by **purchasing** foreign exchange from the market to increase its value.

4. **Foreign Exchange Market**	• It refers to a market where the sale and purchase of foreign exchange takes place. It is of two types: (a) **Spot market:** Market in which sale or purchase of foreign exchange is made immediately is called spot market. (b) **Forward (Futures) market:** Market in which sale and purchase of foreign exchange is made at some specified future date at the rate agreed upon in the present time is called futures/forward market.
5. **Functions of foreign exchange market**	• **Transfer function:** It involves transferring funds from one country to another country. • **Hedging function:** It involves reducing the risk of loss of foreign exchange. • **Credit function:** It involves providing credit for foreign trades.
6. **Demand (or outflow) of foreign exchange**	• There is an **inverse relation** between the rate of exchange and the quantity demanded of foreign exchange. The sources of demand for foreign exchange are: (a) To import goods and services (b) To send gifts to foreign countries (c) For investing in foreign countries (d) To undertake foreign tours
7. **Supply (or inflow) of foreign exchange**	• There is a **direct relation** between the rate of exchange and the quantity supplied of foreign exchange. The sources of supply for foreign exchange are: (a) Exports of goods and services (b) Receipt of gifts from foreign countries (c) Foreigners investing in domestic country (d) When foreign tourists come to home country
8. **Determination of foreign exchange rate (or equilibrium)**	• Foreign exchange rate is determined by the intersection of the demand and supply of foreign exchange.

9. **Change in demand or change in supply of foreign exchange:**

Change	Effect on home currency	Effect on foreign currency
Increase in demand	Currency depreciation	Currency appreciation
Decrease in demand	Currency appreciation	Currency depreciation
Increase in supply	Currency appreciation	Currency depreciation
Decrease in supply	Currency depreciation	Currency appreciation

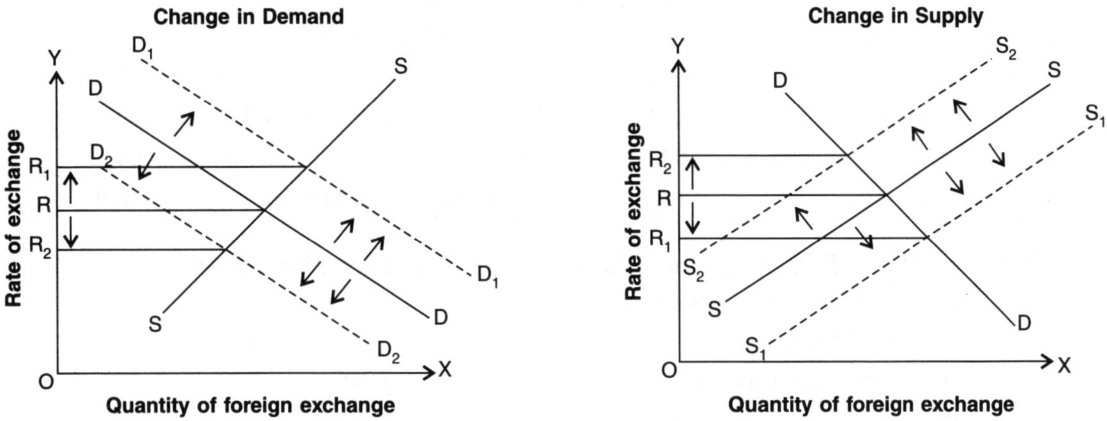

Fig. 4

10. **Balance of payments (BOP)**	• It refers to the summary statement in which all economic transactions that take place between one country and the rest of the world during a given period of time (generally one year) are recorded.
11. **Items included in BOP:**	• Visible items, *i.e.* goods and merchandise • Invisible items, *i.e.* services which cannot be seen • Investment income like interest, profit, dividend, royalty, etc. • Unilateral transfers, *i.e.* one way transfers such as gifts, donations, etc. • Capital transactions: Those transactions which cause a change in assets or liabilities of residents of a country. Eg.: borrowings or purchase of an asset.

12. **Structure of BOP**

BOP A/C

Credit Items (Inflows/Receipts)		**Debit Items (Outflows/Payments)**	
(1) CURRENT ACCOUNT			
Goods exported	100	Goods imported	200
Services exported	150	Services imported	100
Investment income received by residents	200	Investment income paid to non-residents	300
Unilateral transfer receipts	**400**	Unilateral transfer payments	350
Total (a)	**850**	**Total (a)**	**950**
(2) CAPITAL ACCOUNT			
Borrowings (by private firms and the government)	200	Lending (by private firms and the government)	300
Sale of asset(or gold)	**400**	Purchase of asset(or gold)	200
Total (b)	**600**	**Total (b)**	**500**
Total receipts (a + b)	**1,450**	**Total payments (a + b)**	**1,450**

From the above BOP A/C, the following conclusions can be drawn:

- Balance of Trade (Visible) = 100 (unfavourable)
- Balance of Invisibles = 50 (favourable)
- Net investment income = (–) 100
- Net unilateral transfers = (+) 50
- BOP (Current A/C) = 100 (unfavourable)
- BOP (Capital A/C) = 100 (favourable)
- Overall BOP = Balanced BOP

These are assumed figures for illustration purpose only.

BOP account has two sides:

(a) Credit side: All the inflows or receipts of foreign exchange are recorded on this side.

(b) Debit side: All the outflows or payments of foreign exchange are recorded on this side.

13. **Balance of trade**	• It is the difference between the value of goods exported and the goods imported. It can be favourable (where X > M) or unfavourable (where X < M) or in equilibrium (where X = M).
14. **Balance of invisibles**	• It is the difference between the value of services exported and services imported.
15. **Current A/c of BOP**	• It is that account which records imports and exports of goods, services and unilateral transfers.

16. **Capital A/c of BOP**	• It records all transactions between residents of a country which cause a change in assets or liability status of residents of a country or its government.
17. **Components of capital account of BOP**	• Private transactions • Official transactions • Direct investment • Portfolio investment
18. **Autonomous items in BOP (above the line items)**	• All transactions in capital or current account that are undertaken for profit motive are called autonomous items in BOP.
19. **Accommodating items in BOP (below the line items)**	• Transactions that are undertaken to cover the deficit in autonomous transactions and which are not undertaken for profit motives like government borrowings are called accommodating items in BOP.
20. **Disequilibrium in BOP**	• Autonomous receipts < Autonomous payments — Deficit in BOP • Autonomous receipts > Autonomous payments — Surplus in BOP
21. **Causes of disequilibrium in BOP**	• Economic factors • Political factors • Social factors
22. **Measures for correction in disequilibrium**	• Promotion of exports • Imposing import restrictions • Devaluation of domestic currency (It makes domestic goods cheaper.) • Other control measures by the government
23. **Devaluation**	• Deliberate fall in external value of a currency by government under fixed exchange rate system.
24. **Revaluation**	• When a country raises the value of its currency in terms of foreign currency under a fixed rate regime, it is called revaluation.
25. **Trade balance**	• It occurs when total value of exports equals total value of imports.
26. **Trade deficit**	• It occurs when total value of exports falls short of the value of imports.
27. **Trade surplus**	• It occurs when total value of exports exceeds value of imports.

INDIAN ECONOMIC DEVELOPMENT

CHAPTER 1: INDIAN ECONOMY ON THE EVE OF THE INDEPENDENCE

Prior to British advent:	**India was:** • Rich in resources and minerals • Was performing sustainable activities like subsistence agriculture, handicrafts, handlooms, pottery etc. • Worldwide known for spices, precious gems and textile printing
During the British rule:	**India:** • Became a stagnant economy – GDP growth rate was very low • Commercialisation of agriculture • Imposition of feudal relations – Zamindari system • Systematic destruction of Indian industry
Low level of Economic Development:	• No sincere efforts made by British Government to estimate Indian per capita income. • Individual efforts were made by renowned personalities e.g. Dada Bhai Naoroji, V.K.R.B. Rao, R.C. Desai etc. • Countries growth rate was less than 2% for much of twentieth century
Agriculture:	• Around 75% of the population was engaged in agriculture and derived their livelihood from it • The pattern of agriculture underwent a change from subsistence to commercial which was particularly seen in cash crops like Indigo cultivation • The British Raj introduced Zamindars who collected lagan from the peasants. This became an extremely exploitative system as the Zamindars collected more money to be kept as their share of profit. • There was little or no investment by the British government as India was only used as a feeder of raw materials
Industry:	• Two-fold policy was followed. India was reduced to a mere exporter of raw material and was used as a market for the British finished goods • No indigenous development was done to build an infrastructural base or carry out the production of heavy goods

	• The Britishers wanted the Indians to remain dependent on imports from Britain which led to massive unemployment in India
Infrastructure:	• A major landmark was the development of Railways. However, it was done for the ease of the law and order and to connect the interiors to the hinterlands. • Roads, water transport and communications were also developed
Foreign Trade:	• Major direction of the trade to Britain • Other few countries like Sri Lanka, China and Iran were allowed to trade with India. • Drain of Indian wealth which became even easier after the opening of Suez Canal
Demographic Indicators:	• High level of death and birth rate • Extremely low literacy rate ~ 16% • Widespread poverty • Hunger and poor health facility
On the eve of the independence:	• India witnessed the horrors of the partition • Divide and Rule policy was successful in creating communal divide • Economically too India lost large parts of fertile jute growing areas to East Pakistan • A great challenge before India: To restructure its depleted economy and to restore the social balance

CHAPTER 2: INDIAN ECONOMY (1950-1990)

Economic Planning:	• India adopted the Mixed Economy as Pandit Jawahar Lal Nehru was inclined towards the Soviet Model and it was felt that the country needed welfare policies. • 5-year plans were developed to restructure India's Economy.
Goals of the five-year plans:	• **Growth:** Refers to the increase in the efficiency of the production of goods and capital • **Modernisation:** Change in Social Outlook and adaptation of new technology • **Self-Reliance:** Inward looking policy and the reduction in the dependence on other countries • **Equity:** Refers to the capacity where every person is able to make his basic needs meet

The economic planning was done on the following fronts: 1. Agriculture:	• Agriculture was unproductive due to outdated technology, disguised unemployment, inefficient production • Land Reforms initiated to change the ownership of land holdings - abolition of intermediaries • Land ceiling was done to fix the unit of land which could be owned by an individual • Green revolution pursued in the 1960s brought a boom in the agriculture and wheat and rice production shot up benefits of green revolution included self-sufficiency in food grains but it also had some problems, e.g.- not being able to tackle the target group and risk of pest attack. • Subsidies in agriculture were provided so that the farmers could easily purchase inputs and encouraged to cultivate
2. Industry:	• The private sector was unwilling to invest in the country because it did not have sufficient resources. • Industrial Policy Resolution, 1956 was introduced according to which: (a) category A industries - owned by State (b) category B Industries to be a share of public and private (c) category C Industries to be under the control of private sector • Sufficient efforts were taken to develop the small-scale industry which had perished during the British era. • A licensing Policy was put in place - prior permission had to be sought in order to expand or to set up a new firm.
3. Import-export:	• The first few plans focus on import substitution - placing tariffs and quotas on the imports from abroad so that the domestic industries can flourish. • Tariff is a tax levied on good and quotas are the maximum limit on the imports of a commodity.
Aftermath of the Planning:	• GDP rose to almost double its figure • Import substitution gave a foundation to the domestic Industries to grow • Private sector was encouraged to take part in the infrastructural development of the country • Agriculture and industry both saw significant progress • However green revolution was a gestational strategy and it started showing the results after a decade.

	• The Licensing Policy was felt very restrictive • The plans laid sufficient importance on the industry thinking that the effects will trickle down to each of the areas in the primary division but the results were not commensurate.

CHAPTER 3: LIBERALISATION, PRIVATISATION AND GLOBALISATION: AN APPRAISAL

Reasons for economic reforms of 1991:	• Slow rate of growth • Deficient in balance of payment • Huge debt crisis • Poor performance of the public enterprises • Condition of the IMF and the World bank to open the economy in exchange for the loan which India asked for to meet the dismal condition of India during 1991
Liberalisation:	• Removal of entry barriers both in areas of export-import and licensing
1. Foreign exchange reforms:	• Devaluation of rupee
2. Trade reforms:	• Removal of export duties and reduction in import duties • Removal of quantitative barriers
3. Tax reforms:	• Reduction in taxes • Simplifying the process of paying them
4. Industrial reforms:	• Bringing leniency in the licensing policy for private sectors to freely enter now • Decrease in the sole ownership of the government on industries
5. Financial sector reforms:	• The role of the RBI was modified from a controller to facilitator • Increase in foreign investment by change in policies in India
Privatisation:	• Transfer of ownership to private enterprises • Performed in two ways: (a) Transfer of entire ownership to public sector companies (b) Privatisation of the public sector undertakings (PSUs) by selling off part of their share to the public. This is known as disinvestment

Globalisation:	• Integrating domestic economy with the rest of the world
Advantages of globalisation for India:	• Transfer of technology from developed countries to India • Reach of Indian commodities to foreign markets • Better connectivity with the world
Disadvantages of globalisation:	• Disproportionate benefits to developed countries • Increasing the rich-poor divide
Outsourcing:	• Contracting out activities to a third party which were earlier performed by the parent organisation. After the adoption of the new economic policy, India became a favourable destination of outsourcing because of: – Cheap labour – Abundant resources – Political policies in favour – Lax tax laws
World Trade Organisation:	• International organisation which looks after the trade relations between countries. It is the successor organisation of GATT
Critical appraisal of LPG policies:	**Pros** • Economic prosperity • Inflow of foreign investment • Rise in exports • Increase in consumption • Reduction in dependence on external commercial borrowing • Encouraging new innovation **Cons** • Neglect of agriculture • Insignificant employment potential • Interference with state sovereignty • Unhealthy MNC strategy to enter the emerging country economy • Concentration of growth in only select few areas

CHAPTER 4: POVERTY

Poverty:	• A state in which an individual is unable to fulfil even the basic necessities of life • Two ways of looking at poverty are - poor in rural areas and poor in urban areas
Characteristics of poor:	• Poor levels of food, clothing and shelter • Deteriorating health and sanitation • Low levels of employment and education • More children
Measures to estimate poverty:	• **Relative poverty:** Expressed in comparison to other people • **Absolute poverty:** Exact magnitude of people living below the poverty line
Determination of poverty line:	• Expressed in minimum calorie intake and minimum wages required • 2400 calories per person per day for rural areas and 2100 calories per person per day in urban areas • Rupees 816 per person in rural areas and rupees 1000 in urban areas
Types of poor:	• Chronic poor – persistent, extremely high level of poverty • Transient poor - moving in and out of poverty
Trends of poverty:	• The poor people in villages are still high, although the weight has begun shifting to urban areas due to the lookout for jobs • States like Uttar Pradesh, Bihar, Madhya Pradesh, West Bengal, Odisha are extremely poor. States of Southern India fare relatively better
Britishers in pushing India towards poverty:	• Indian industries were destroyed by the British government • About 75% of the Indian population was engaged in agriculture. This was commercial agriculture, the raw materials of which were used to produce finished commodities in England and sent back to India. • The situation today is also not very good as measures like land ceiling, redistribution of land has not fared very well. • Debt trap, suicide rates are very high in farmers which make up the largest share of poor in India

Causes of poverty:	• Low levels of education • Inadequate employment opportunities • Large size of the families • Poor state of agriculture • Unawareness about the various schemes run by the government • Hopelessness and distraught attitude of poor towards life
Government measures to reduce poverty:	• **Growth oriented approach:** The benefits of economic development should trickle down to the lowest of the lower sections. • **Poverty alleviation programmes:** Various schemes like Mahatma Gandhi National Rural Employment Guarantee Act, Swarna Jayanti Shahari/Gramin Rojgar Yojana, National food for work programme etc. • **Minimum needs programme:** Aim towards providing basic necessities to people
Performance of government programmes	Unsatisfactory outcomes due to: • Lack of funds • Accumulation of the funds at higher levels and existence of intermediaries in the process of transfer of funds • Lack of infrastructural facilities • Corruption • Ineffective implementation • Lack of active participation by the poor people themselves

CHAPTER 5: HUMAN CAPITAL FORMATION

Capital:	• **Physical capital:** Assets required for further production like machinery, raw materials, etc. • **Human capital:** Expertise, knowledge, skills in the people
Human capital formation:	Enhancement of the human capital using certain processes like: • Provision of education • Healthcare facilities • On the job training • Expenditure on information • Expenditure on migration

Advantages of human capital formation:	• **Promotes economic growth:** Innovations lead to cost effectiveness, thereby increasing country GDP • **Social development:** Education leads to change in attitude of people • Effective check on population growth • Increases life expectancy • Improves overall quality of life
Disadvantages of human capital formation:	• Brain drain whereby educated and healthy people leave the country for better job opportunities
Reasons for slow growth in human capital formation:	• Inadequate infrastructure to train people and enhance their abilities • Insufficient resources to direct towards this • Lack of awareness and motivation within people • Lack of training in people who in turn train others • Unsatisfactory development in Science and technology in a country like India which would support human capital formation
Human development:	• While human capital is concerned with enhancement in people's abilities to increase the labour productivity, Human Development is a process which enables people to make better decisions in life. Human Development treats people as ends in themselves
Human capital formation in India:	• Basic education and health are fundamental rights of every citizen of India • To improve education and make it accessible for all, many schemes like Sarva Shiksha Abhiyan and Right to Education were introduced • To aid these schemes, other schemes like 'Mid-day meal' were also introduced to attract students to attend schools • This has led to an increase in enrollment rates in attendance within students • In the health sector, many public health care services have been introduced • Asha workers function all across India to make health accessible for all • In Delhi itself, Primary Health Care units called Mohalla clinics have shown successful results. These are clinics established at every 5 kilometers of range

CHAPTER 6: RURAL DEVELOPMENT

Rural development:	• Socio economic processes which lead to an improvement in all aspects of rural life
Process of rural development:	• Development of infrastructure like roads, irrigation facilities, electricity provision etc. • Land reform measures like consolidation of land holdings, redistribution of land, abolition of intermediaries etc. • Eradication of poverty • Human capital formation by providing better health care and education facilities
Rural credit:	Due to the limited assets and technical know-how to the rural people, they often face problems in obtaining loans: • Sources of rural credit (a) **Traditional sources:** Money lenders, relatives, landowners, traders (b) **Institutional sources:** These are government bodies which have been formulated in order to reduce the exploitation faced by the farmers. NABARD is the apex bank which coordinates and controls the functioning of all these Financial Institutions of rural credit – Land Development Banks, Self-help groups, Government commercial banks- Their branches have extended their functioning to rural areas, Regional rural banks, Cooperative credit Even after such measures Rural banking remains insufficient due to • Political nexus leading to corruption • Intermediaries reducing the transparency of the process • Debt trap
Agricultural marketing:	• Assembling storage processing distribution
Critical appraisal:	• Insufficient knowledge of the market- thereby giving into the demands of the traders and selling the produce at a low price • Inaccessibility to the markets at farther distances and cities • Lack of storage facilities for the surplus produce to tackle such issues, various government interventions are required: – Minimum support price and other subsidies

	– Public Distribution system by a mechanism of ration shops – Regulation of markets – Government provision of infrastructure like roads and railways to transport effectively and quickly
Diversification of agricultural activities:	• Diversification of crop production – Multi cropping, leaving land fallow for rejuvenation, growing different crops which make use of different nutrients from the soil so that the entire fiscal year can produce three crops as against one • Diversification of production activities – Includes non-farm activities like: animal husbandry, dairying, horticulture, fisheries, information technology
Sustainable development of rural areas:	75% of the Indian population and majority of the rural fork is dependent on agriculture. Organic farming is the way forward **benefits** • Healthy • Economic • Generates income through exports • Non-hazardous to environment **Challenges** • Lack of popularity • Shorter shelf-life • Limited choice of crops

CHAPTER 7: EMPLOYMENT: GROWTH, INFORMALISATION AND OTHER ISSUES

Worker:	• Person involved is some economic activity to earn a living. Includes both people paid by employers and self-employed people
Labour force:	• Sum of all the people who are working and the people who might not be working but are looking for jobs
Labour force participation rate:	• The ratio of labour force to total population

Workforce:	• The people who are actually employed at a particular time
Employment:	• An activity which makes a person able to earn a living for himself or herself
Self-employment:	• A worker uses his own resources, knowledge, skills and expertise to earn a livelihood. For example- shopkeepers, entrepreneurs
Wage employment:	• The type of employment in which a worker sells his labour in return for wages. Wage employment is of two types: – Casual workers – Regular salaried workers
Trends in employment:	• Higher proportion of rural people in overall employment estimates • Higher proportion of male workers as compared to female workers • More women workers in rural areas as compared to the employed women in urban areas • Primary sector is the main source of employment for majority of people in India • Although service sector encompasses the minimum amount of labour force, it contributes the highest to the GDP • Self-employment is a major source of livelihood for both men and women • In case of regular salaried employees, there is a greater proportion of men in comparison to women as women find work at home, cottage industries etc.
Casualisation of workforce:	• Moving from regular salaried employment and self-employment to casual work
Formal/Organised sector:	• Establishments which employed 10 or more hired workers and are registered with the government • Give benefits like social security schemes, pension, medical benefits etc.
Informal/ Unorganised sector:	• Establishments which hire less than 10 workers • No regularity of wages or salary. No social security benefits
Unemployment:	• People who are willing and able to work at the existing wage rate and are not able to get work is called the situation of unemployment

Types of Unemployment:	• **Disguised unemployment:** More people engaged in work than are required • **Seasonal employment:** Employed only during certain specific periods of time in a year • **Open unemployment:** Phenomenon in which people are able and willing to work at existing wage rate but do not get work
Causes of unemployment:	• Low levels of education • Inadequate infrastructure to support employment opportunities population explosion • Insufficient creation of jobs in the secondary sector which is thought to absorb the highest amount of labour • Faulty planning • Sluggish agriculture
Government approach:	• **Direct employment:** Employing people in various departments and activities • **Indirect employment:** Creation of infrastructure which would in turn increase employment opportunities
Measures taken for unemployment reduction:	• Acceleration in GDP growth • Special emphasis on small scale industries • Efforts for education accessibility to majority of people • Check on population • Creation of infrastructure like industries • Employment generation schemes like National Food for Work Programme • Special incentives to entrepreneurs to take up startup activities • 'Make in India' and 'skill India' initiatives

CHAPTER 8: INFRASTRUCTURE

Infrastructure:	• Facilities which are required to provide services in an economy
Types of infrastructure:	• Economic – communication, energy • Social – health, education etc.

Importance of infrastructure:	• GDP growth • Socio-Political development • Improvement of quality of life • Accessibility to resources • Employment generation • Attract foreign companies to invest
State of infrastructure in India:	• From sole responsibility of the government to provide public services there has come a time of public private partnership • There is lack of infrastructure, particularly in rural areas in terms of electricity, roads, schools, hospitals • Due to excess of population in India, there is a scarcity of housing facilities which leads to a lot of slums. These are the breeding grounds for many diseases and unhygienic conditions
Energy:	• An important infrastructure for any nation
Commercial energy:	• Sources which command price in the market and purchased by the users in exchange for a monetary value
Non-commercial energy:	• Do not command any price in the market and are locally produced within homes. Agricultural waste and dried dung are some examples
Conventional energy:	• Sources of energy which have been traditionally used and have been in use since a long period of time coal and petroleum
Non-conventional energy:	• Newer methods of energy production which have recently come into use as alternatives to coal, petroleum and natural gas • These are renewable in nature
Power (electricity):	• **Thermal Power:** Generated by coal, oil and natural gas • **Hydroelectricity:** Generated by the action of water on the turbines • **Wind energy:** Generated by windmills • **Atomic energy:** Generated by nuclear fission or fusion
Challenges to power sector:	• Transmission and distribution loss • Shortage of inputs • Public indiscipline and non-cooperation • Underutilisation of the already installed units • Individual action such as switching off lights when not in use, use of CFL bulbs, LEDs

Measures to meet electricity crisis:	• Encourage using of renewable resources • Control of the distribution and transmission losses • Increase in investment in the electricity sector • Technological innovation and newer methods
Health:	• A state of mental, physical and emotional well-being
Three tier system of health infrastructure in India:	• Primary health care • Secondary health care • Tertiary health care
Rural-urban divide:	• The poor people living in villages do not have access to adequate medical facilities. The doctor patient ratio is skewed and patients have to travel large distances to see a doctor.
Women health:	• They suffer more disadvantages as compared to men and little measures were traditionally taken during their Maternity and post maternity child care. Female infanticide and foeticide were also very prevalent. However, the times are changing and success in securing women health has been seen.
Indian system of medicine:	• AYUSH—Ayurveda, Yoga, Unani, Siddha, Naturopathy and homeopathy
Critical appraisal of health infrastructure:	• India's health infrastructure suffers from the following problems: – Lack of manpower – Lack of infrastructure – Corruption – Poor sanitation facilities
Measures taken:	• Ayushman Bharat • Institution of Mohalla clinics • Provision of Maternity benefits in jobs • Asha workers and Anganwadi workers • Spread of yoga • Awareness towards better living styles, dietary habits and diseases

CHAPTER 9: ENVIRONMENT AND SUSTAINABLE DEVELOPMENT

Meaning:	• Refers to the sum total of our surroundings • Composed of two components-biotic and abiotic – Biotic is the living element like birds' animals – Abiotic elements are non-living like air, water, etc.
Functions of environment:	• Provider of natural resources • Habitat for a lot of species • Balancing force of the ecosystem • Provides aesthetical beauty and spiritual pleasure
Environmental crisis:	• The degradation of the environment is caused due to many factors like: – Increase in the population – Burning of fossil fuels – Increase in the consumption patterns – Meddling with the environment by creating more and more infrastructure on fragile surfaces – Inconsiderate human activities which lead to pollution
Two most alarming concerns:	• Global warming: refers to the general heating of the Earth due to increase in the greenhouse gases, especially carbon dioxide • Global warming has led to melting of the glaciers and submergence of a lot of areas. • Kyoto Protocol has been signed to rectify the damage done • Ozone depletion refers to the thinning of the Ozone Layer due to the emission of chlorofluorocarbons and bromine products • Results in skin cancer and cataract • A Treaty called Montreal protocol has been signed to curb the production of chlorofluorocarbons
India and the environmental concerns:	• Pollution of land, air and water • Loss of biodiversity • Deforestation

Pollution of land, air and water:	• **Land Degradation is caused by soil erosion:** By the action of wind and water. Factors like improper farming techniques, encroachment into forest land, loss of vegetation is some of the major reasons. • **Air pollution:** Adding of unwanted contaminants into the air • Emissions by the factories and vehicles are the major cause. • Promotion of public transport, carpool and using cleaner fuels are a way to curb air pollution. • **Water pollution:** Adding of unwanted contaminants into the water bodies. • Discharge of effluents by the factories and human activities are the major cause • Treating of sewage waste before discharging it into the water, finding alternative to bathing and washing clothes in water bodies and throwing garbage into the water can help to reduce water pollution.
Biodiversity loss:	• The variety of living flora and fauna in India is getting compromised due to loss of their habitats, poaching, etc.
Deforestation:	• Permanent destruction of forests. This leads to desertification of the land
Sustainable development:	• Judicial using of the resources so that they are left for the future generation. Can be achieved by: – Switching to alternate sources of energy – Reduce, reuse, recycle – Education and awareness – Sensitisation towards environment

CHAPTER 10: COMPARATIVE DEVELOPMENT EXPERIENCES OF INDIA AND ITS NEIGHBOURS

Similarities in the growth pattern of India, Pakistan and China:	• All began the developmental strategy at the same time • Planning played a very important role in the initial growth of economy in all these countries • Public sector was given a great importance in the initial years

	• All the three countries realised the importance of private players and foreign companies in the development of any country, thereby integrating the domestic economy with the world
China:	• **Great Leap Forward campaign:** Transform agrarian economy into highly modernised economy initiated by Mao but met with several problems eventually • **Great cultural revolution:** Using the potential of students and professionals in the development of the country • **1970s and beyond:** China opened up its economy to the world – Establishment of special economic zones to attract foreign investors – Reforms in agriculture and industry
Pakistan:	• Imposition of tariff barriers and restrictions on the foreign goods to encourage domestic industries till the 1960 • Green Revolution • Nationalisation of capital goods industries in the 1970s • In the late 1970s, the role of private sector was realized • Reforms were brought in the country during 1988 • Pakistan now follows the mixed economic model
India:	• Heavy dependence on the government for control of all the major industries • Five year plans which focused on agriculture, industry and other related areas • Agricultural sluggishness led to the adoption of Green revolution which showed impressive results • In 1991, the new economic policy was adopted which meant liberalisation, privatisation and globalisation
Comparative study:	**Growth indicators:** • In the 1980s, China registered the highest growth rate of 10.3%, followed by Pakistan and then India • In the 2011-15 period, the growth rate percentage of China and Pakistan fell, however in the case of India it increased slightly

	Demographic indicators: • China is the most populous country, followed by India and then China. However, the annual growth rate of population in China is the lowest and that of Pakistan is the highest • Sex ratio is the most skewed in India. China and Pakistan almost fare equally on the sex ratio which is better than India
	Human Development indicators: • The Human Development Index for China is the best followed by India and then Pakistan • Life expectancy at birth, mean years of schooling, access to improved water resources, sanitation, GDP per capita- all these indicators perform the best in China with India following at the second number • Pakistan records the highest number of people below the poverty line followed by India and then China
	Sectoral share of GDP and employment indicators: • In all the three countries, the industry and services sector have less proportion of workers but they contribute more in terms of output
Critical appraisal:	**China** • In China, every reform measure was not directly implemented in the entire country and was first experimented at a smaller level • Education and health facilities were given immediate attention • The combination of Communist government at a political level and that of a market system at an economic level has worked very well for China **Pakistan** • The development strategy of Pakistan was majorly based on agriculture. • Although it produced some great results in times of boon, it also led to severe deficits when the produce was not abundant • Political instability has led to the deterioration of the potential of the country to rise

	India • Although India has made some great strides in economic development, it still wrestles with problems like poverty, health, sanitation and literacy • The major push in India was the 1991 economic reforms which led to many economists terming India as one of the fastest growing economies of the world

SAMPLE PAPER 1
CBSE SAMPLE QUESTION PAPER 2019–20 (WITH SOLUTIONS) (FOR 2020 EXAMINATIONS)

Time allowed: 3 hours | *Maximum marks: 80*

General Instructions:

1. ***All** the questions in **both** the sections are **compulsory**. Marks for questions are indicated against each question.*
2. *Question number **1-10** and **18-27** are very short-answer questions carrying **1 mark** each. They are required to be answered in one word or one sentence each.*
3. *Question number **11-12** and **28-29** are short-answer questions caring **3 marks** each. Answers to them should not normally exceed **60-80 words** each.*
4. *Question number **13-15** and **30-32** are also short-answer questions carrying **4 marks** each. Answers to them should not normally exceed **80-100 words** each.*
5. *Question number **16-17** and **33-34** are long answer questions carrying **6 marks** each. Answers to them should not normally exceed **100-150 words** each.*
6. *Answer **should be brief** and **to the point** and the above **word limit be adhered** to as far as possible.*

SECTION A (MACROECONOMICS)

1. Value of Money Multiplier __________ (increases/decreases/remains unchanged) with an increase in Cash Reserve Ratio. **(1)**

2. Define an intermediate good. **(1)**

3. Average Propensity to Consume can never be __________. **(1)**

(a) positive (b) zero (c) more than one (d) less than one

4. Name any two quantitative tools to control credit creation in an economy. **(1)**

Or

What are demand deposits?

5. The monetary policy generally targets to ensure __________. **(1)**

(a) price stability in the economy

(b) employment generation in the country

(c) stable foreign relations.

(d) greater tax collections for the government

6. In an economy, break-even point and equilibrium point may lie at the same level of income, if ex-ante investments are __________. **(1)**

7. State whether the given statement is true or false:

'Managed Floating Exchange Rate is decided by market forces but remains within a specific range as decided by central bank.' **(1)**

8. The formula to calculate Primary deficit is __________. **(1)**

9. From the set of statements given in Column I and Column II, choose the correct pair of statements: **(1)**

Column I	Column II
a. Export of software to France	(i) Debit side of current account
b. Import of Machinery from China	(ii) Capital Account of Balance of Payments
c. Remittances to relative staying abroad	(iii) Debit side of Current Account of Balance of Payments
d. Investment by Apple phones firm in India	(iv) Credit side of Current Account of Balance of Payments

10. Government expenditure on Mid-Day Meal scheme running in government (state run) schools is a type of __________ expenditure in government budget. **(1)**

11. "India's GDP is expected to expand 7.5% in 2019-20: World Bank" - The Economic Times.

Does the given statement mean that welfare of people of India increase at the same rate? Comment with reason. **(3)**

12. Calculate the value of Marginal Propensity to Consume (MPC), if in an economy, autonomous consumption is ₹ 500 crores, ex-ante investments are ₹ 4000 crores and equilibrium level of Income of the economy is ₹ 18,000 crores. **(3)**

Or

Suppose in a hypothetical economy, the savings increase by ₹ 20 crores when national income increases by ₹ 100 crores. Compute the additional investments needed to attain an increase in national income by ₹ 6,000 crores?

13. Discuss any one of the following functions of a central bank:

(a) As government's bank (b) Open market operations **(4)**

14. "Foreign Institutional Investors (FIIs) remained net seller in the Indian capital markets over the last few weeks". - The Economic Times.

State and discuss the likely effects of the given statement on foreign exchange rate with reference to the Indian Economy. **(4)**

Or

'Many large Multinational Corporations (MNCs) have recently shifted their investments from China and have started their production in India, thereby boosting the Make in India plans of the Government'.

Presuming other factors being constant, discuss the effects of the given statement on Foreign Exchange rates with reference to the Indian Economy.

15. Elaborate the objective of 'reallocation of resources' in the government budget. **(4)**

16. (a) 'Real Gross Domestic Product is a better indicator of economic growth than Nominal Gross Domestic Product'.

Do you agree with the given statement? Support your answer with a suitable numerical example.

(b) Calculate 'Depreciation on Capital Asset' from the following data **(6)**

S.No.	Particulars	Amount (in ₹ crores)
i.	Capital value of the asset	1,000
ii.	Estimated life of the asset	20 years
iii.	Scrap Value	Nil

Or

(a) 'Circular flow of income in a two sector economy is based on the axiom that one's expenditure is other's income'.

Do you agree with the given statement? Support your answer with valid reasons.

(b) Calculate compensation of employees from the following data:

S.No.	Particulars	Amount (in ₹ crores)
i.	Profits after tax	20
ii.	Interest	45
iii.	Gross Domestic Product at Market Price	200
iv.	Goods and Services Tax	10
v.	Consumption of Fixed Capital	50
vi.	Rent	25
vii.	Corporate Tax	5

17. 'An economy is operating at under-employment level of income'. What is meant by the given statement? Discuss one fiscal measure and one monetary measure to tackle the situation. **(6)**

SECTION B (INDIAN ECONOMIC DEVELOPMENT)

18. Name any two taxes which were subsumed in Goods and Services Tax (GST). **(1)**

19. State weather the following statement is true or false:

'The latest demonetization of currency was undertaken by the Government of India on November 8, 2016.' **(1)**

20. Identify the correct sequence of alternatives given in **Column II** by matching them with respective terms in **Column I:** **(1)**

Column I	Column II
a. Land Ceiling	(i) Increase in production of food grain using high yielding variety seeds
b. Land reforms	(ii) Portion of agricultural produce sold in the market
c. Green Revolution	(iii) Fixing the maximum limit of land holding for an individual.
d. Marketed Surplus	(iv) Change in the ownership of land (land to tillers)

21. Agriculture marketing does not comprise of ________. **(1)**

(a) Transportation of the produce to the market place for sale.

(b) Grading of the produce according to the quality.

(c) Storage of the produce for sale in future.

(d) Credit taken to meet expenditure on agriculture.

22. Under ________ type of unemployment, marginal product gained by employing one additional unit of labour is zero. **(1)**

Or

________ an indicator which is used for analyzing the employment situation of a country.

23. In 1955, Karve committee was constituted for aiming the ________. **(1)**

24. Identify the correct sequence of alternatives given in **Column II** by matching them with respective terms in **Column I** **(1)**

Column I	Column II
a. Study Group formed by Planning Commission for Poverty	(i) 2005
b. 'Task Force on Projections of the Minimum Needs and Effective Consumption Demand'	(ii) 1962
c. Mahatma Gandhi National Rural Employment Guarantee Act	(iii) 2014
d. Jan DhanYojana	(iv) 1979

Choose the correct alternative:

(a) ii, iii, iv, i
(b) iii, ii, i, iv
(c) i, ii, iii, iv
(d) ii, iv, i, iii

25. Solar energy can be converted into electricity with the help of ________ (Photovoltaic cell/Lithium cells). **(1)**

26. Arrange the following events of China in chronological order and choose the correct alternative: **(1)**

(i) Great Proletarian Cultural Revolution

(ii) Great Leap Forward campaign

(iii) Introduction of Economic Reforms

(iv) First five year plan

Choose the correct alternative:

(a) ii, iv, iii, i (b) iv, ii, i, iii (c) ii, iv, i, iii (d) iv, i, ii, iii

27. Introduction of Economic Reform in Pakistan took place in ________. **(1)**

(a) 1978 (b) 1980 (c) 1988 (d) 1991

28. "Recently Indians have drifted away from the traditional knowledge and practices and caused large scale damage to environment".

Explain how, adopting the traditional practices can be helpful in achieving the objective of sustainable development? **(3)**

Or

'Power sector in India has major issues with its installed capacity'. Discuss the given statement.

29. 'Education Commission 1964-66 had recommended that at least 6 per cent of GDP must be spent on education'. How far India has been able to achieve the said goal? **(3)**

30. 'The opening up of the Indian Economy has led to a rapid increase in Foreign Direct Investments and Foreign Exchange Reserves of the country'. Defend or refute the given statement. **(4)**

31. Define the following terms **(4)**

(a) Disinvestment (b) Import Substitution

Or

Define the following terms

(a) Outsourcing (b) Quota

32. Answer the following questions on the basis of the following data: **(4)**

(a) Comment upon the population growth rates among the three countries.

(b) Which country has most skewed in sex ratio?

Country	Estimated Population (in million)	Annual Growth of Population (in %)	Sex Ratio
India	1311	1.2	929
China	1371	0.5	941
Pakistan	188	2.1	947

Source: World Development Indicators, 2015, www.worldbank.org

33. "Rural Economic development is essential for Indian Economic development". Do you agree with the given statement? Support your answer with valid reasons. **(6)**

34. 'In spite of the increase in public health expenditure Indian Health System is an ailing system in itself'. Defend the statement citing any three major problems of Health sector in India. **(6)**

Or

Study the following chart showing the Growth of Employment and Gross Domestic Product and analyse the trend of the two variables from 1990-2012.

Growth of Employment and Gross Domestic Product, 1951-2012 (%)

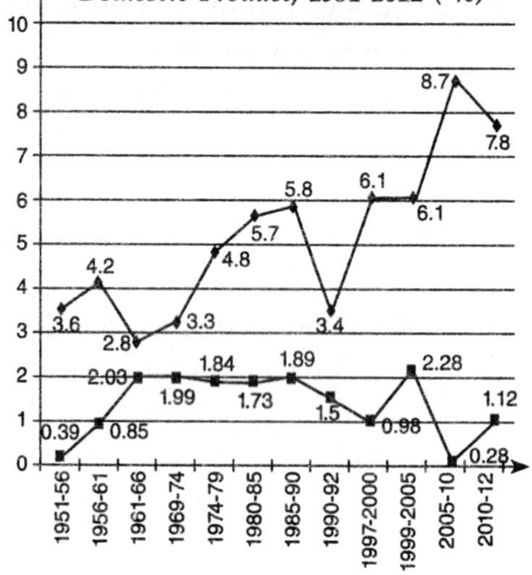

GDP ✦ *Employment* ▪

SOLUTIONS TO SAMPLE PAPER 1
CBSE SAMPLE QUESTION PAPER 2019–20

SECTION A (MACROECONOMICS)

1. Decreases

2. An intermediate good refers to that good which is purchased during the year by a firm for the purpose of further production/resale.

3. (b) Zero

4. (i) CRR, (ii) Bank Rate

Or

Demand deposits are the deposits which can be withdrawn on demand by the depositors from banks.

5. (a) price stability in the economy.

6. Zero

7. True

8. Primary Deficit = Fiscal Deficit – Interest Payments

9. c. (iii) is correct pair [a. (i), b. (ii), and d. (iv) are incorrect pairs]

10. Revenue

11. An increase in the Gross Domestic Product (GDP) of any economy ensure increase in welfare of the people of the country. Some of the main reasons for the same are:

(a) unequal distribution and composition of GDP,

(b) non-monetary transactions in the economy which are not accounted for in GDP, and

(c) occurrence of externalities in the economy (both positive and negative).

12. We know that consumption function is:

$$C = \bar{c} + MPC.\ Y$$

At equilibrium level of Income in the economy $Y = C + I$

Given, Autonomous Consumption $(\bar{C})$ = ₹ 500 crores and

Ex-ante Investments (I) = ₹ 4000 crores

$$18{,}000 = 500 + \text{MPC}\ (18{,}000) + 4{,}000$$

$$\text{MPC}\ (18{,}000) = 18000 - 4500$$

$$\text{MPC} = 13{,}500/18{,}000$$

$$\text{MPC} = 0.75$$

Or

$$\text{MPS} = \left(\frac{\text{Change in Savings}}{\text{Change in Income}}\right) = \left(\frac{\Delta S}{\Delta Y}\right) = \frac{20}{100} = 0.20$$

$$\text{Investment Multiplier (K)} = \frac{1}{\text{MPS}} = \frac{1}{0.20} = 5$$

$$\text{Investment Multiplier (K)} = \frac{\text{Change in Income}}{\text{Change in Investments}} = \left(\frac{\Delta Y}{\Delta I}\right)$$

$$5 = \frac{₹\ 6{,}000}{\text{Change in Investments }(\Delta I)}$$

Change in Investment (ΔI) = ₹ 1200 crores

Increase in investment by ₹ 1200 crores is required to attain additional income of ₹ 6000 crores.

13. Central Bank as government's bank:

(a) The Central Bank acts as a banker to the government.

(b) The Central Bank accepts receipts and makes payments for the government and carries out other banking operations on their behalf.

(c) It advances loan to the government to meet its requirements in case of crisis.

(d) It also acts as an agent to buy and sell government securities & advises the government on various financial matters.

Or

Open Market Operations by Central Bank:

(a) Open Market Operations refers to buying and selling of government securities (bonds) by the Central Bank from/to the general public.

(b) It is an important step which may be undertaken to control money supply in the economy.

(c) The Central Bank may sell government securities to reduce the money supply in the hands of general public and vice-versa.

14. Selling of securities by Foreign Institutional Investors (FII's) in Indian capital market will lead to fall in the supply of foreign currency in the economy. This situation might lead to excess demand of foreign currency at the prevailing foreign exchange rate.

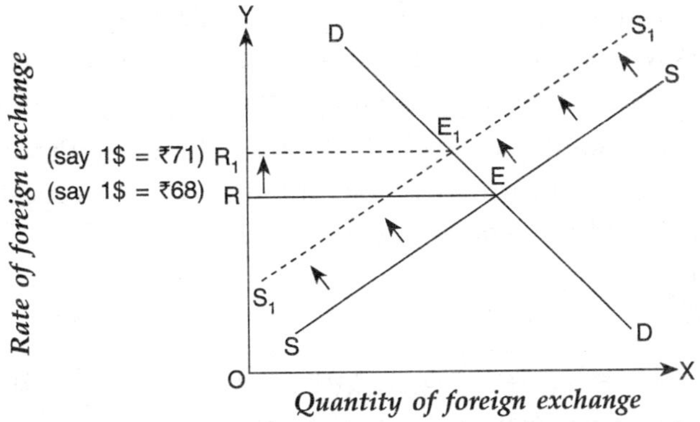

As a result, a new equilibrium rate of foreign exchange will be determined which will be higher than the prevailing foreign exchange rate, leading to depreciation of domestic currency.

Or

Investments by large multinational corporations (MNCs) in India will ensure greater inflow of foreign exchange, leading to an increase in the supply of foreign currency. This situation may result into excess supply of foreign currency in the economy at the prevailing foreign exchange rate.

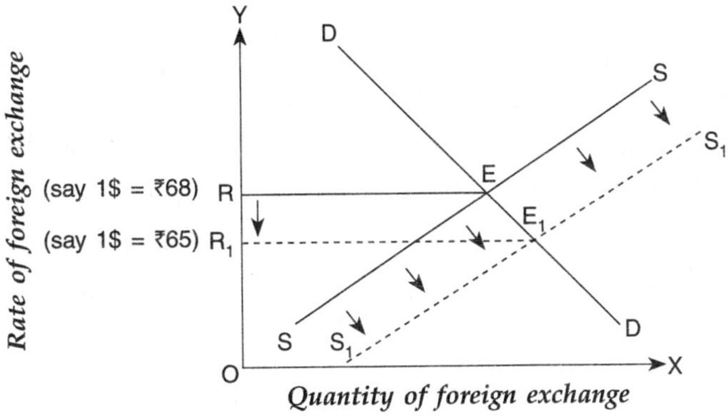

As a result, a new equilibrium rate of foreign exchange will be determined which will be lower than the prevailing foreign exchange rate, leading to appreciation of domestic currency.

15. **Reallocation of resources:** Government through its budgetary policies tries to reallocate resources to ensure the balance between goals of profit maximisation and social welfare. The government may influence the allocation of resources through:

    (a) Taxation policy: Heavy taxes may be imposed on harmful products to discourage their production and subsidies may be provided on the production of socially useful products to encourage their production.

(b) Government may directly undertake production of certain goods and services in the areas where private sector may not be willing to participate in production activities to discourage regional disparities.

16. (a) The given statement is correct. Real Gross Domestic Product (GDP) is a better indicator of economic growth than Nominal Gross Domestic Product (GDP) as it is not affected by changes in price level.

Numerical Example:

Goods	Price of Current Year (P_1) (in ₹)	Price of Base Year (P_0) (in ₹)	Quantity of Current Year (Q_1) (in units)	Nominal GDP (P_1Q_1)	Real GDP (P_0Q_1)
A	200	100	1000	2,00,000	1,00,000
B	100	50	2000	2,00,000	1,00,000
C	300	200	500	1,50,000	1,00,000
				ΣP_1Q_1 = 5,50,000	ΣP_0Q_1 = 3,00,000

In the above example the difference between Nominal GDP and Real GDP is 550000–300000 = ₹ 250000.

This is only the monetary difference as the quantity sold in the market remains unchanged and the variation in the value of GDP is merely due to the change in the prices in the economy. Hence, we can say that nominal GDP is not a good indicator of economic growth.

(b)

$$\text{Depreciation on capital asset} = \frac{\text{Cost of the capital asset} - \text{Scrap value}}{\text{Estimated life of the capital asset}}$$

$$\text{Depreciation} = \frac{1000 - 0}{20}$$

$$\text{Depreciation} = ₹\ 50 \text{ crores}$$

Or

(a) Yes, the given statement is correct. In a two sector economy, the firms produce goods and services and make factors payments to the households. The factor income earned by the households will be used to buy those goods and services only, which becomes income of firms. The consumption expenditure by the households in the economy is equal to the expenditure on goods and services produced by the firms in the economy. Circular flow of income is shown as below:

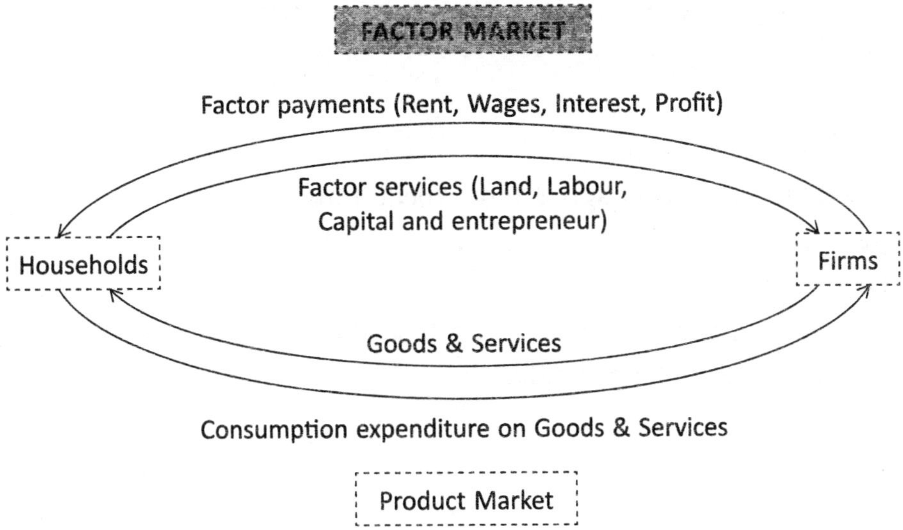

(b) Compensation of Employees = (iii) – (v) – (iv) – (vi+ii+i+vii)

= 200 – 50 –10 – (25+45+20+5)

= ₹ 45 crores.

17. Underemployment equilibrium situation occurs when equilibrium between AO and AS comes before the full employment level of output, i.e. planned aggregate expenditure falls short of available output in the economy, corresponding to the full employment level. It results in deficient demand (or deflationary gap) situation in the economy.

To tackle such a situation the aggregate demand has to be increased up to the level that the stocks can be cleared.

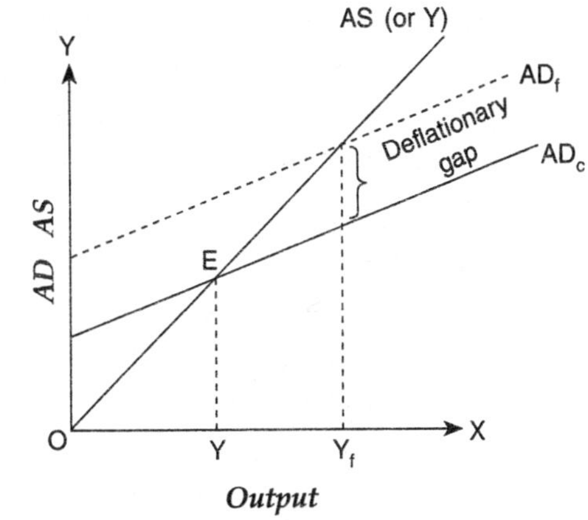

AD_c = Current aggregate demand curve
OY_f = Full employment level of output
AD_f = Aggregate demand required to achieve full employment equilibrium

Following measures may be taken for the same:

(i) **Decrease in taxes:** The government under its fiscal policy may decrease the rate of taxes (both direct and indirect taxes). This will increase the purchasing power of general public and will help to increase aggregate demand and remove the deflationary gap.

(ii) **Increase in money supply:** Central bank through its monetary policy can increase the money supply in the economy. Central bank can use tools like decrease in bank rate, cash reserve ratio, repo and reverse repo rates etc. to ensure greater money in the hands of general public which would in turn increase the aggregate demand in the economy and be helpful in reducing the deflationary gap.

SECTION B (INDIAN ECONOMIC DEVELOPMENT)

18. Service tax and sales tax.

19. True

20. a. (iii), b. (iv), c. (i), d. (ii)

21. (d) Credit taken to meet agriculture expenditure.

22. Disguised

Or

Work force participation rate

23. Development of small scale industries

24. (d) ii, iv, i, iii

25. Photovoltaic cell

26. (b) iv, ii, i, iii

27. (c) 1988

28. The given statement is correct. Indian traditional practices were environment friendly and worked as complementary to the system and not its controller. The traditional agriculture system, healthcare system, housing, transport etc. were environment friendly. The traditional practices used natural products and processes which were free from side effects. For example by adopting medicinal plants/ products we can conserve the resources and achieve the objective of sustainable development.

Or

The given statement states about the insufficiency of the installed capacity of production of power in India. If the Indian economy wants to touch the GDP growth rate between 7-8% it must target to produce electricity with a growth rate of 7% which is not possible with the present production capacity in the power sector. Thus, we need to work in two directions to improve installed capacity:

(i) increased investments (by both public and private players) in the power generation sector.

(ii) better utilisation of the present infrastructure.

29. Investment in education system in India has been a failure. The fact of the matter is that, in 1952 we were spending 0.6% of our GDP on education that rose to only 4% in 2014. This has fallen well short of 6% target as proposed by the Education Commission, 1964. Moreover, throughout this period the increase in education expenditure has not been uniform and there has been irregular rise and fall.

This shows the apathy of the government towards investment in the education system. One can imagine, if the recommended 6% p.a. of the GDP would have been spent properly the present education system would have reached unforeseen heights.

30. I, defend the given statement. The foreign investments, both Foreign Direct Investment (FDI) and Foreign Institutional Investment (FII), have increased from about US $100 million in 1990-91 to US $ 74 billion recently. This has changed the status of India from a 'begging bowl' in 1990's to a 'selfdependent' economy in the present ages.

Due to the opening up of the Indian Economy, we have become one of the largest foreign exchange reserve holders in the world. India been able to register an increase in the foreign exchange reserves from about US $ 6 billion in 1990-91 to about US $ 321 billion in 2014-15.

31. (a) **Disinvestment:** Privatisation of the public sector enterprises (PSEs) by selling off a part/whole of the equity to the general public or any private sector player is known as disinvestment.

(b) **Import Substitution:** The policy aimed at replacing or substituting imports with domestic production by protecting the domestic industries from foreign competition is known as Import Substitution.

Or

(a) **Outsourcing:** Hiring of regular service from external sources, mostly from foreign countries, which was previously provided internally or from within the country is known as outsourcing.

(b) **Quota:** Quantitative restrictions on imports for the protection of the domestic firms from foreign competition. Under this quantity of goods which can be imported is specified by the state.

32. (a) The given data shows that the annual growth rate of population is maximum in Pakistan standing at 2.1%, whereas; the same stands at 0.5% in case of China (might be a direct result of the One Child Policy adopted). The annual population growth rate of India is in the danger zone of more than 1% p.a. India will be overtaking China as the most populous country in the world in near future.

(b) Amongst the three countries stated above, India has most skewed sex ratio (929 female per 1000 male).

33. The given statement is correct. Mahatma Gandhi had always maintained that the real growth of India lies in the growth of villages. The importance of rural development in India lies in the fact that 2/3rd of the population still (directly or indirectly) depends on agriculture and around 1/3rd of the rural population still lives in abject poverty.

Some of the prime areas for the development of the rural India may be quoted as follows:

- **Infrastructure development:** Is the key to any development process. Basic infrastructure requirement like electricity, irrigation, credit availability, transport facilities, construction of village roads and feeder roads to nearby highways, etc. are the area which still need attention of the government so as to gain commanding heights.

- **Alleviation of poverty:** Poverty in rural India is an area that should be taken up as a mission for improvement in the living conditions of particularly those living at the bottom of pyramid. This problem may be tackled by emphasizing on greater access to productive employment opportunities.
- **Development of Human Capital:** Rural human capital must be developed by taking sincere steps in the direction of education and health.

34. The health system in India has undoubtedly improved over the years but the pace of improvement has been unreasonably slow and truly we carry an unhealthy health system.

Following may be the most important concerns ailing Indian health system:

- **Low Public Expenditure:** In India the health expenditure as a percentage of GDP is low as compared to some of the major developing countries. It stood at around 4.7% of the total GDP in the year 2014-15.
- **Urban Rural Divide:** People living in rural India do not have sufficient medical infrastructure. Nearly 70% of the population lives in rural areas which have only 20% of the total hospitals of the country.
- **Women and child health issues:** More than 50 per cent of married women in the age group of 15–49 years have iron deficiency, which has contributed to maternal deaths. Infant Mortality Rate per 1,000 live births in India is 34. Malnutrition and inadequate supply of vaccines lead to the death of millions of children every year.

Or

The period between 1990 to 2012 had been a significant one. Introduction of Economic Reforms in India has changed everything in India. Variables shown in the given graph show that GDP growth rate has taken an upwards tread over the years whereas the situation of Employment growth rate has seen major fluctuations while going down in overall trend.

GDP growth rate has increased from 3.4% in 1991 to 7.8% in 2012. However the employment growth rate has shown declining trends from 1.5% in 1991 to 1.12% in 2012. Between the period 1999-2005 the employment generation rate was at peak since independence i.e. 2.28% p.a. with the corresponding GDP growth rate standing at a decent 6.1% p.a.

The gap between the two variables is maximum between the period 2005-10 when the employment growth rate hit the lowest in history of Independent India i.e. 0.28%. In the same period the GDP growth rate had hit the highest level since independence to the tune of 8.7% p.a. Indian economy has witnessed the peculiar phenomena of 'jobless growth' over all these years. Learning from the situation government had put in serious efforts on employment front and brought it to a level of 1.12% p.a. between the period 2010-12.

In all the period between 1990-2012 has been a real roller coaster ride for the India economy on the two front of GDP and Employment Growth rate.

SAMPLE PAPER 2
(WITH SOLUTIONS)

Time allowed: 3 hours *Maximum marks: 80*

General Instructions:

1. ***All** the questions in **both** the sections are **compulsory**. Marks for questions are indicated against each question.*
2. *Question number **1-10** and **18-27** are very short-answer questions carrying **1 mark** each. They are required to be answered in one word or one sentence each.*
3. *Question number **11-12** and **28-29** are short-answer questions caring **3 marks** each. Answers to them should not normally exceed **60-80 words** each.*
4. *Question number **13-15** and **30-32** are also short-answer questions carrying **4 marks** each. Answers to them should not normally exceed **80-100 words** each.*
5. *Question number **16-17** and **33-34** are long answer questions carrying **6 marks** each. Answers to them should not normally exceed **100-150 words** each.*
6. *Answer **should be brief** and **to the point** and the above **word limit be adhered** to as far as possible.*

SECTION A (MACROECONOMICS)

1. Currency notes, coins and __________ are the components of M_1 measure of money supply? **(1)**

2. Define Disinvestment. **(1)**

3. If MPC is 0.25 then MPS will be **(1)**

(a) 0.75 (b) 0.25 (c) 1.25 (d) 0

4. State one limitation of using GDP at constant prices as an index in the measurement of social welfare? **(1)**

Or

Define capital goods.

5. Accommodating items are those items of BOP which: **(1)**

(a) are not determined by profit motive
(b) are conditioned by the positive or negative BOP status
(c) deal with capital transfers only
(d) both (a) and (b)

6. If an investment of ₹ 10 crores results in an increase in income by ₹ 50 crores, then the value of multiplier will be ________ crores. **(1)**

7. State whether the statement is True or False

"If ₹ 150 are required to buy \$2, instead of ₹ 100 earlier", then rupee value of import bill will increase. **(1)**

8. Primary deficit is ________ minus Net interest payments. **(1)**

9. From the set of statements given in column I and Column II, choose the correct match: **(1)**

Column I	Column II
a. MPS = 0.8	(i) Consumption expenditure is Zero
b. Break even point	(ii) Rate at which RBI takes loan from commercial bank
c. Repo Rate	(iii) Investment multiplier = 5 times
d. MPC = 0.8	(iv) Investment expenditure is Zero

10. ________ regulates the monetary policy in India. **(1)**

11. Estimate the value of ex-ante AD, when autonomous investment and consumption expenditure (A) is ₹ 50 crores, MPS is 0.2 and level of income is ₹ 300 crores. **(3)**

Or

Calculate Multiplier when MPC is $\frac{4}{5}$ and $\frac{1}{2}$. From the calculations establish the relation between size of Multiplier and size of MPC?

12. Use following information of an imaginary country: **(3)**

Year	2014 – 2015	2015 – 2016	2016 – 2017
Nominal GDP	6.5	8.4	9
GDP deflator	100	140	125

(a) For which year is real GDP and nominal GDP same and why?

(b) Calculate Real GDP for the given years. Is there any year for which Real GDP falls?

13. Illustrate with the help of an hypothetical numerical example the process of credit creation. **(4)**

14. Elaborate 'economic growth' as an objective of government budget. **(4)**

15. 'Devaluation and Depreciation of currency are one and the same thing'. Do you agree? How do they affect the exports of a country? **(4)**

Or

What is meant by 'official reserve transactions'? Discuss their importance in Balance of Payments.

16. State whether the following statement are true or false. Give valid reasons for your answers. (6)

(a) Unplanned inventories accumulate when planned investment is less than planned saving.

(b) Deflationary gap exists when aggregate demand is greater than aggregate supply in full employment level.

(c) Average propensity to save can never be negative.

17. (a) Define Externality.

(b) Find National Income from the following using expenditure method. (6)

S.No.	Items	(₹) in Crores
1.	Current transfers from rest of the world	50
2.	Net Indirect taxes	100
3.	Net Exports	–25
4.	Rent	90
5.	Private Final Consumption Expenditure	900
6.	Net Domestic Capital Formation	200
7.	Compensation of Employees	500
8.	Net Factor Income from Abroad	–10
9.	Government Final Consumption Expenditure	400
10.	Profit	220
11.	Mixed Income of Self Employed	400
12.	Interest	230

Or

Will the following factor income be included in domestic factor income of India? Give reasons for your answer:

(a) Compensation of employees to the resident of Japan working in India embassy in Japan.

(b) Payment of fees to a Chartered Accountant by a firm

(c) Rent received by an Indian resident from Russian embassy in India.

(d) Compensation given by insurance company to an injured worker.

SECTION B (INDIAN ECONOMIC DEVELOPMENT)

18. WTO stands for World __________ Organisation. (1)

19. State whether the statement is true or false

"An arrangement in which a worker uses his own resources to make a living is known as wage employment. (1)

20. From the set of statements given in column I and Column II, match the following: **(1)**

Column I	Column II
a. Swaranjayanti Gram Swarojgar Yojna	(i) Launched in 2012
b. Sampoorna Gramin Rojgar Yojna	(ii) Launched in 1999
c. Sawarnjayanti Shahri Rojgar Yojna	(iii) Launched in 1997
d. National Rural Livelihood Mission	(iv) Lunched in 2001

21. In which year, did the Indian government make education free and compulsory for children of 6-14 years of age? **(1)**

(a) 2001 (b) 2005 (c) 2007 (d) 2009

Or

Five year plan recognised the importance of human capital

(a) seventh (b) eighth (c) third (d) sixth

22. To protect goods produced in India from imports, government made use of tariffs and _________. **(1)**

23. Among India, China and Pakistan, _________ has the highest life expectancy at birth? **(1)**

24. State whether the following statement is true or false

"Subsistence farming reduces market risk." **(1)**

25. Quality of life is influenced by Income, _________ and Health. **(1)**

26. Which of the following is not a non institutional source of credit? **(1)**

(a) Money lenders (b) Relatives

(c) Traders and Agents (d) Land Development Bank

27. Who introduced the concept of 'Jail cost of Living'? **(1)**

(a) Mahatma Gandhi (b) Dadabhai Naroji

(c) Pt. Nehru (d) None of these

28. The two fold policy of the British rule was enforced to ensure the maximum advantage of their home country. Comment. **(3)**

29. How is human development a broader concept as compared to human capital? **(3)**

Or

Write a short note on operation flood.

30. What is unemployment? What are its types? **(4)**

31. What are some of the reasons behind the successful performance of China as a leading economy of the world? **(4)**

32. Mention some of the challenges to the mechanism of agricultural marketing **(4)**

Or

What are some of the criticisms of the concept of Poverty Line with respect to the Monthly per capita expenditure method?

33. **(6)**

Item	1960-61	1980-81	2008-09
Rice	35	54	99.2
Wheat	11	36	80.6
(a) Total cereals	69	119	219.2
(b) Total Pulses	13	11	14.7
(c) Total food grains (a+b)	82	130	233.9

Shows increase in the production of food crops since 1960-61 in million tonnes

Study the table given above carefully and identify the phenomenon being talked about in the figures. Give its features with respect to India.

Or

Import substitution was a major element of India's trade and Industrial Policy. Elucidate.

34. What is organic farming. How does it promote sustainable development? **(6)**

SOLUTIONS TO SAMPLE PAPER 2

SECTION A (MACROECONOMICS)

1. Demand deposits
2. Disinvestment refers to selling of shares of public enterprise held by the government.
3. (a) 0.75
4. Real GDP or GDP at constant prices does not consider the composition of GDP.

Or

Goods which directly satisfy human wants are called consumer goods.

5. (d) both (a) and (b)
6. 5 crores
7. True
8. Fiscal deficit
9. (d) MPC = 0.8 – (iii) Investment multiplier = 5 times
10. RBI
11. $\overline{C}$ = ₹ 50 crores   I = ₹ 50 crores

MPS = 0.2   MPS = 1 –MPC = 0.8

Y = ₹ 300 crores

We know,

$$AD = C + I$$

$$AD = [50 + 0.8 \times 300] \quad (\because C = \overline{C} + by)$$

$$= 290$$

Or

We know,

$$MPC = \frac{4}{5} \text{ and } MPC = \frac{1}{2}$$

$$K = \frac{1}{1 - MPC}$$

(i) Taking MPC as $\frac{4}{5}$,

$$K = \frac{1}{1-\frac{4}{5}} = \frac{1}{\frac{1}{5}} = 5$$

(ii) Taking MPC as $\frac{1}{2}$,

$$K = \frac{1}{1-\frac{1}{2}} = \frac{1}{\frac{1}{2}} = 2.$$

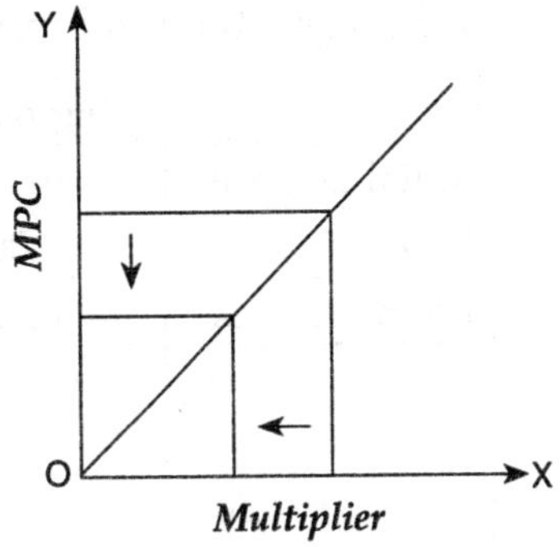

∴ There is direct relationship between value of multiplier and MPC.

12. (a) For the base year the nominal and real GDP would be the same.

(b) $\text{Real GDP} = \frac{\text{Nominal GDP}}{\text{GDP deflator}} \times 100$

$$2014\text{–}15 = \frac{6.5}{100} \times 100 = 6.5$$

$$2015\text{–}16 = \frac{8.4}{140} \times 100 = 6$$

$$2016\text{–}17 = \frac{9}{125} \times 100 = 7.2$$

Therefore, we can observe that the Real GDP declined in the year 2015–16.

13. The deposits accepted by the commercial banks are used for giving loans. However, the entire amount of deposits cannot be used for lending. They are required to keep a minimum percent of these deposits as reserves. This percentage is known as Liquidity Reserve Ratio or Cash-Reserve Ratio and is fixed by the central Bank.

The process of credit creation is as follows:

(a) Suppose LRR is equal to 20% and there is a fresh or primary deposit of ₹ 10,000. This implies that the bank is required to keep 20%, i.e., ₹ 2000 as cash reserve. The remaining ₹ 8,000 can be lent by the bank to the borrowers. This amount is not paid to them in cash rather, a new deposit account is opened by the bank in the names of the borrowers.

(b) Suppose the borrowers withdraw and spend the entire amount of ₹ 8,000 for making payments. Since all the transactions are routed through bank, the money spent by borrowers comes back into the bank in the form of deposit account of those who recieve this payment.

(c) Now with new deposits of ₹ 8000, banks again keep 20%, i.e., ₹ 1,600 as cash reserve and lend ₹ 6,400 to other borrowers. This money again comes back into the account of those who receive payments from the borrowers. Thus, the cash reserves and deposits keep on increasing with every round. This process will keep on repeating till secondary deposits become zero, i.e., total of cash resources is equal to initial fresh deposit.

(d) In this case, the total money creation is ₹ 50,000 as shown in the table below:

	Deposit (₹)	Loan (₹)	Minimum Reserve CRR (20%)
Initial Deposit	10,000	8,000	2,000
Round I	8,000	6,400	1,600
Round II	6,400	5,120	1,280
	⋮	⋮	⋮
	50,000	40,000	10,000

14. Economic growth means the increase in real GDP, that is, increase in value of goods and services produced in an economy. Budget helps in allocation of resources as follows:

- Government can provide subsidies to small scale manufacturers and encourage them to produce goods and services.
- Government expenditure plays at major role in creating demand and government can spend for welfare of the poor and enhance the resources of the economy.
- Government can use tax for collection of revenue so that it can be used for the welfare of the society.

15. • I don't agree with the above statement. Devaluation and depreciation of currency are different concepts, though both imply a fall in the value of external value of currency.

- Depreciation is fall in the value of currency due to market forces of demand and supply. This implies that the domestic currency becomes less valuable and loses its value in relation to a foreign currency. An individual needs more rupees to buy a dollar. For example, If US $ exchanges for ₹ 68 instead of ₹ 65 as earlier, the domestic currency or the Indian rupee has depreciated.
- Devaluation is a deliberate fall in the value of currency done by government in order to promote exports. It is a deliberate attempt by the monetary authority of the country to decline the value of domestic currency in relation to a foreign currency.
- Thus, depreciation and devaluation promote exports in the country as the domestic goods become cheaper.

Or

- The transaction which causes a change in the official reserves of foreign exchange maintained by RBI are known as official reserve transactions.
- They are important as they help in compensaticy for the deficit and surplus of balance of payment.

16. (a) True, when planned savings are more then inventory will accumulate in the factory and producers will cut down production which leads to fall in income till the time AD = AS.

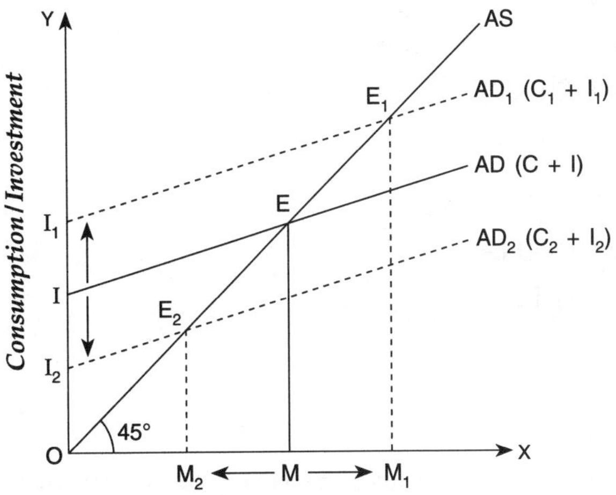

Output (or Income) (a)

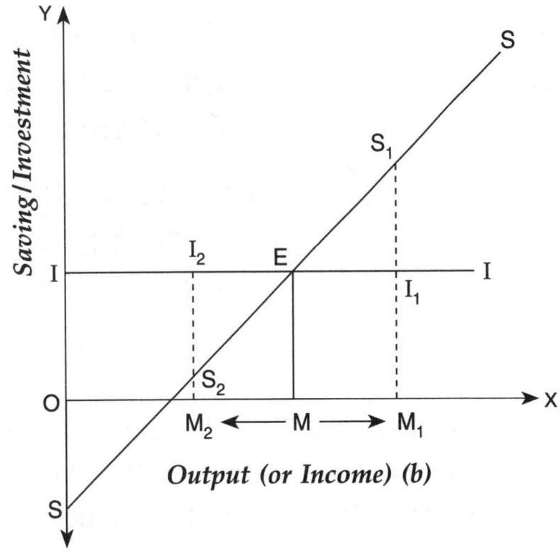

Output (or Income) (b)

In the above figures, we suppose that level of output is greater than equilibrium level of output. Therefore, saving function lies above the investment function curve. This implies that planned savings (S_1M_1) is greater than planned investment (I_1M_1). As a result, there is more saving in the economy and less spending. This leads to accumulation of unplanned inventories.

(b) False, when AD > AS at full employment equilibrium then it is known as inflationary gap.

From the figure we can say that, to achieve full employment level of output we require only EQ_f level of aggregate demand. However, the current aggregate demand is FQ_f. Thus, there is excess demand to the extent of FE. This surplus demand gives rise to price inflation and is known as the inflationary gap.

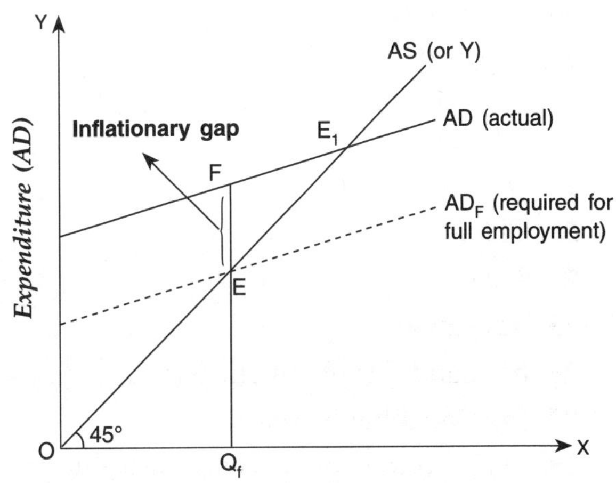

Income/Output

(c) False, the value APS can be negative. Average propensity to save means the ratio of total saving to total income. It is negative when at a particular level of income the saving is negative, i.e., in a situation of dissaving.

17. (a) When the economic activity provides with positive and negative side effects then it is known as externality. For e.g. production in factory causes pollution, production is backward region leads to civilised society which means construction of schools, hospitals etc.

(b)
$$
\begin{aligned}
GDP_{MP} &= \text{PFCE} + \text{GFCE} + \text{GDCF} + \text{Net exports} \\
&= 900 + 400 + (-)25 + (200 - 0) \\
&= 1{,}300 + 200 - 25 \\
&= ₹\ 1{,}475 \text{ crores}
\end{aligned}
$$

$$
\begin{aligned}
NNP_{FC} &= GDP_{MP} - \text{NIT} - \text{Dep} + \text{NFIA} \\
&= 1{,}475\ (-)\ 100\ (-)\ 0 + (-)\ 10 \\
&= 1{,}475\ (-)110 \\
&= ₹\ 1{,}365 \text{ crores}
\end{aligned}
$$

Or

(a) Yes, it will be included as they work in the domestic territory of our country.
(b) Payments of fees will not be included as it is intermediate consumption.
(c) No, it will not be included as the income does not occur in the domestic territory.
(d) No, as compensation is given by insurance company and not the employer.

SECTION B (INDIAN ECONOMIC DEVELOPMENT)

18. World Trade Organization
19. False, it is known as self employment
20. a. (ii), b. (iv), c. (iii), d. (i)
21. (d) 2009

Or

(a) seventh

22. Quotas
23. China
24. True
25. Education
26. (d) Land Development Bank
27. (d) Dadabhai Naroji
28. The two-fold policy was basically premised on discouraging industrialisation in India. Contrary to the popular belief, many small and medium sized industries were functional in India before the advent of the British which were systematically destroyed. The purpose was two-fold:
    - To procure raw materials from India at cheap rates and use them for the manufacture of goods in Britain.

- To sell the finished goods back in India at higher prices. This could be done easily after uprooting domestic industries that may have posed competition.

29. Human capital assumes that investment in human beings should be translated into efficiency and output. On the other hand, human development asserts that any investment in health or education definitely increases the well-being of the individual, beyond which labour productivity is immaterial.

- According to human capital, human beings are means to achieve ends, i.e. greater productivity and output, however according to human development; human beings are the ultimate end.
- Therefore, human development is a broader and a more human centric concept.

Or

- Operation flood, also known as the **white revolution** was started by National Dairy Development Board (NDDB) by **Dr. Verghese Kurien** in 1970.
- Under the operation, all farmers pooled in the milk produce and then disturbed it to the markets. This helped in bringing together many fragmented areas into a chain of systematic production.
- The farmers were ensured regular income and the operation became one of the largest and most successful cooperatives of the country—Anand Milk Union Limited (AMUL). The small practice of pooling that began in Gujarat can be seen almost everywhere in the country today.

30. Unemployment is a situation in which people, who are willing and able to work, do not get work. This means all those who voluntarily choose not to work due to any possible reason are not considered a part of the Unemployed.

From the point of view of economy, unemployment means inefficient utilisation of human resources, lower production and standard of living.

Types of unemployment:

- **Disguised unemployment:** A state in which more people are employed than are needed. It literally means hidden unemployment. It is most prevalent in agricultural sector, where all seem engaged on the fields, but the marginal productivity from any surplus labour is zero.
- **Seasonal unemployment:** This means not getting employment on round the year basis as many works are seasonal in nature. For example—agriculture, which only prevails from sowing to harvest. So, when there isn't much work, rural labour force usually move to cities to hunt for jobs.
- **Open unemployment:** A phenomenon in which people sit idle because they are not able to find work, despite being able and willing to work at the prevailing rates. It is called open because it is visible unlike disguised, where people appear to be working.

31. After the great leap forward and the proletarian revolution did not bear fruits as were expected, reforms were introduced in China in 1978.

- In the initial phase, reforms were introduced in agriculture by allocating small plots of lands to individual households from which all income could be keep after paying taxes.
- The later phase saw reforms in the industrial sector. Private sector firms were allowed to produce goods. The State-Owned Enterprises (SOEs) were made to compete in the market.
- Dual pricing was adopted. This meant that some commodities will be sold at the prices determined by the forces of demand and supply, whereas others will be fixed, particularly in the agricultural sector.
- Special Economic Zones (SEZs) were set up to attract investors.

Moreover, China fared very well as compared to its other Asian counterparts on the parameters of sex ratio, literacy and health. This meant it could extract much more from the human capital at a time when others were struggling.

32. Agricultural marketing refers to processing, assembling, storage, transportation and distribution of agricultural produce and products to different parts of the country. It faces the following problems at hand:

- **Lack of storage facilities:** A lot of harvest is compromised due to lack of improper storage facilities. To store grains or vegetables, refrigerated silos and granaries are required; however, a lot of farmers still store the produce in the traditional ways.
- **Untimely procurement:** One often hears the news of grains rotting in the godowns while people are dying of hinder. A major loophole in the marketing system is the inability to reach the target population.
- **Manipulation by big traders:** Faulty weighing and manipulation by middlemen is frequently witnessed.

Or

Poverty line is a cut off point on the distribution line which indicates the minimum level of income required to meet the basic living conditions.

- The method classifies all the poor together and does not make any distinction between the degrees of poverty.
- The method is only representative in nature. It does not help in identifying the very poor who should be the target group for all the schemes that are constituted.
- Poverty here, is only measured in economical terms (assets and liquid money). However, poverty is a much broader problem that constitutes access to education, basic health facilities, respect and dignity - which are neglected.

As a result, many alternate ways are also made use of. For example—Sen index developed by Amartya Sen.

33. The phenomenon being discussed here is Green Revolution as it shows the spurt in the production of food grains from 1960s onwards. Green revolution refers to the large increase in the production of food grains by the adoption of new techniques and high yielding variety (HYV) of seeds. The major crops that received a boost were wheat and rice. The man behind the miracle was Mr. M.S. Swaminathan.

It was the need of the hour because India was an agrarian country and $3/4^{th}$ of our population derived their livelihood from it. At such a large rate, it was important that agriculture be made more productive and the dependence on rains be reduced by construction of irrigation facilities. Application of chemical fertilizers and pesticides was also brought in.

Following were its benefits:

- On the same area under cultivation, the HYV seeds gave a much larger harvest.
- India increased its self-sufficiency on food production. Infact, we moved from subsistence to marketable surplus.
- States like Punjab, Haryana and Andhra Pradesh became the major beneficiaries of the green revolution.
- The government could now procure sufficient grains and keep it under storage for emergency situations.
- As the supply of these grains increased, their prices came down. The poor could now purchase it at affordable rates.

That is how from a grain deficient nation, we moved to achieving food security for all!

Or

In order to be self-reliant in vital sectors, India has followed the strategy of replacing many imports by domestic substitution. The policy, also called Inward Looking Policy had 2 major aims: one was of course self-reliance and the other was to preserve the foreign exchange reserves. This protection was realised by the imposition of Tariffs and Quotas.

- Tariffs refer to levying of taxes on imported goods to discourage people from bringing foreign goods in India.
- Quotas refer to fixing the maximum quantity of goods that can be imported.

India was in its initial stages of conception and it was difficult for the infant industries to compete with the global market. The government knew that had import substitution not been done, these industries were most likely to perish.

Import substitution was a major part of India's Trade and Industrial policy in the 1950s.

34. Organic farming is the form of agriculture that relies on eco-friendly techniques like crop rotation, green manure, natural composting and biological pesticides and fertilizers. The method is averse to any form of chemicals or synthetic elements.

It has following benefits:

- Healthy and non-toxic food by using purely natural ways of production. It does not even make use of any genetic engineering to increase the harvest or make the crop pest resistant.
- It is a substitute to many costlier inputs like HYV seeds, chemical fertilizers and pesticides.
- It generates more employment opportunities as more hands are needed at work in organic farming than conventional farming.
- Organic farming practices also reduce pollution, conserve water, reduce soil erosion, increase soil fertility and use less energy.

In doing all these things, it promotes sustainable development which means producing in such a way that not only harms the environment of today but also protects it for the posterity to indulge in.

SAMPLE PAPER 3
(WITH SOLUTIONS)

Time allowed: 3 hours *Maximum marks: 80*

General Instructions:

1. ***All*** *the questions in* ***both*** *the sections are* ***compulsory****. Marks for questions are indicated against each question.*
2. *Question number* ***1-10*** *and* ***18-27*** *are very short-answer questions carrying* ***1 mark*** *each. They are required to be answered in one word or one sentence each.*
3. *Question number* ***11-12*** *and* ***28-29*** *are short-answer questions caring* ***3 marks*** *each. Answers to them should not normally exceed* ***60-80 words*** *each.*
4. *Question number* ***13-15*** *and* ***30-32*** *are also short-answer questions carrying* ***4 marks*** *each. Answers to them should not normally exceed* ***80-100 words*** *each.*
5. *Question number* ***16-17*** *and* ***33-34*** *are long answer questions carrying* ***6 marks*** *each. Answers to them should not normally exceed* ***100-150 words*** *each.*
6. *Answer* ***should be brief*** *and* ***to the point*** *and the above* ***word limit be adhered*** *to as far as possible.*

SECTION A (MACROECONOMICS)

1. To increase money supply in the economy, RBI will _________ the government securities. **(1)**

2. Define fiscal deficit. **(1)**

3. State the difference between depreciation and capital loss on basis of "Provision". **(1)**

4. What is not true about the term National Income? **(1)**

(a) National Income excludes NFIA.
(b) National Income excludes transfer income.
(c) National Income excludes depreciation.
(d) National income excludes indirect taxes.

Or

Two–sector economy consists of

(a) household and government
(b) household and firm
(c) firm and government
(d) household and external sector

5. In which of the following categories are economic transactions of balance of trade recorded? **(1)**

(a) Visible items (b) Invisible items

(c) Capital transfers (d) All of the above

6. APC + APS = __________ **(1)**

7. State whether he following statement is true or false **(1)**

'Flexible exchange rate is also known as pegged exchange rate.'

8. Capital Receipt are those receipts which either __________ or __________ . **(1)**

9. From the set of statements given in column I and Column II, match the following: **(1)**

Column I	Column II
a. GDP at current prices	(i) Revenue Receipts
b. GST collection of government	(ii) Real GDP
c. Disinvestment by government	(iii) Nominal GDP
d. GDP at constant prices	(iv) Capital Receipts

10. If MPS is 0.6, ΔS will be __________ when income increases by ₹ 100. **(1)**

11. Explain with the help of an example, the basic of classifying goods into final goods and intermediate goods. **(3)**

12. An economy is in equilibrium. From the following data about an economy calculate autonomous consumption. **(3)**

(a) Income = ₹ 5000

(b) Marginal propensity to save = 0.2

(c) Investment expenditure = ₹ 800

Or

An economy is in equilibrium. From the following data, calculate the marginal propensity to save:

(a) Income = 10,000

(b) Autonomous consumption = 500

(c) Consumption expenditure = 8,000

13. Explain the "banker's bank" function of the central bank. **(4)**

Or

Explain the process of credit creation by commercial bank.

14. Explain how government budget can be used to influence distribution of income. **(4)**

15. Distinguish (a) between current account and capital account, and (b) between autonomous transactions and accommodating transactions of balance of payments account. **(4)**

16. Assuming that increase in investment is ₹ 1000 crores and marginal propensity to consume is 0.9, explain the working of multiplier. **(6)**

17. Explain 'non-monetary exchanges' as a limitation of using gross domestic product as an index of welfare of a country **(6)**

Or

How will you treat the following while estimating domestic product of a country? Give reasons for your answer:

(a) Profits earned by branches of country's bank in other countries
(b) Gifts given by an employer to his employees on Independence Day
(c) Purchase of goods by foreign tourists

SECTION B (INDIAN ECONOMIC DEVELOPMENT)

18. WTO was the successor organisation of which of the following? **(1)**

(a) Generic Agreement on Trade and Tariff
(b) General Agreement on Trade and Tariff
(c) General Association of Trade and Tariff
(d) Gestational Agreement on Trade and Tariff

Or

When was the New Economic Policy announced?

(a) June 1991 (b) May 1991 (c) July 1991 (d) January 1991

19. In India, __________ regulate the health sector **(1)**

20. State whether the following statement is true or false **(1)**

'The first passenger train in India ran between Bombay and Pune'.

21. Mention two causes of inflation. **(1)**

22. The Planning Commission set up in the year __________ . **(1)**

23. Which one of the following is not a regional grouping? **(1)**

(a) SAARC (b) BRICS (c) ASIAN (d) European Union

24. From the set of statements given in column I and Column II, match the following: **(1)**

Column I	Column II
a. Open unemployment	(i) More people are engaged in work than required
b. Self Employment	(ii) Able people fail to get work
c. Disguised unemployment	(iii) Zero involuntary unemployment
d. Full employment	(iv) Worker uses his own skills for living

25. Infant mortality rate includes: **(1)**

(a) Number of infants dying (b) The base taken is 1000 live births
(c) The criteria are children before 1 years of age
(d) All of the above

26. Seasonal unemployment occurs mainly in ________ sector. **(1)**

27. The scheme of Micro finance is extended through- **(1)**

(a) Self Help Groups (b) Land Development Banks

(c) NABARD (d) Regional Rural Banks

28. The introduction of railways in India by the Britishers was a noble step. Do you agree or disagree? **(3)**

29. Bring out the importance of Animal Husbandry. **(3)**

Or

Discuss the two main types of wage employment.

30. What are the differences between the poor in urban and the poor in rural areas?

Or **(4)**

What is global warming? What are its effects?

31. What are the landmark developments that took place in Indian economy post-independence? Answer with respect to highlighting India's policies in relation to its neighbours. **(4)**

32. What is economic and social infrastructure. Highlight their relation with each other. **(3)**

33. List down some of the goals of the five-year plans that were a key pillar of tour Economic Planning. **(6)**

34. What are some of the challenges faced by the health infrastructure in India? **(6)**

Or

IN THE RACE

The 2017 Sustainable Development Goals Index

Rank	Country	Score
1	Sweden	85.6
2	Denmark	84.2
3	Finland	84
4	Norway	83.9
5	Czech Republic	81.9
6	Germany	81.7
7	Austria	81.4
8	Switzerland	81.2
9	Slovenia	80.5
116	**India**	**58.1**

Source: SDG Index and Dashboards Report

The above data shows India's dismal performance on the parameters of sustainable development. Suggest some ways to improve the situation.

SOLUTIONS TO SAMPLE PAPER 3

SECTION A (MACROECONOMICS)

1. Purchase
2. Fiscal deficit is excess of total expenditure over total receipts excluding borrowings.
3. Provision for depreciation is maintained by the firms but no such provision is maintain for capital loss.
4. (a) National Income excludes NFIA.

   Or

   (b) household and firm
5. (a) Visible items
6. 1
7. False
8. Increase liability or decreases asset
9. a. (iii), b. (i), c. (iv), d. (ii)
10. (b) ₹ 60
11. Final goods are those goods which are used for final consumption or for production of other goods. For e.g. machines, computers etc.

    Intermediate goods are those which are purchased for the purpose of resale in same period or form a part or component of the final good.

    For e.g. if rice is purchased by the household for consumption then it will be termed as final good. But if the same rice is purchased by a hotel for making their food then it will be considered as intermediate good.
12. At equilibrium,

$$Y = C + I$$
$$Y = \overline{C} + by + I$$
$$5000 = \overline{C} + (0.8 \times 5000) + 800$$
$$4200 = \overline{C} + 4000$$
$$\therefore \quad \overline{C} = 200$$

Or

$$Y = 10{,}000$$
$$\overline{C} = 500$$
$$C = 8{,}000$$

$$C = \overline{C} + by$$
$$8{,}000 = 500 + b(10{,}000)$$
$$(MPC) \text{ or } b = 0.75$$
$$MPS = 1 - MPC$$
$$= 1 - 0.75 = \boxed{0.25}$$

13. Banker of the Government

(a) **Banking business:** As the government's bank, the central bank accepts deposits, makes payments, and carries out exchange and remittances on behalf of the government.

(b) **Extends loans:** It provides short-term credit to the government by printing money against its security and bills to finance government deficit.

(c) **Agent:** A central bank also provides various services as an agent of the government. It manages public debts. It undertakes payment of interest on this debt and all sorts of other services relating to public debt.

(d) **Advisor:** The central bank gives advice to the government regarding taxation, interest rates, credit expansion, etc.

Or

Credit creation process depends upon two factors:

(a) Initial fresh deposits

(b) Legal Reserve Ratio (LRR)

Credit creation can be explained with the help of the following illustration:

	Deposits	Loans	Cash reserves
Initial	1,000	800	200
I Round	800	640	160
II Round	640	512	128
.	.	.	.
.	.	.	.
.	.	.	.
.	.	.	.
.	.	.	.
	₹ 5,000	**₹ 4,000**	**₹ 1,000**

Let us assume that there is a fresh deposit of ₹ 1,000 and LRR is 20%. As required, the banks keep 20% *i.e.* ₹ 200 as cash and lend the remaining ₹ 800. Those who borrow, use this money for making payments. As assumed, those who receive payments put the money back into the banks. In this way, banks receive fresh deposits of ₹ 800. The banks again keep 20% *i.e.* ₹ 160 as cash and lend ₹ 640, which is also 80% of the last deposits. The money again comes back to the banks leading to a fresh deposit of ₹ 640. The money goes on multiplying in this way and ultimately, total money creation is:

$$\text{Total money creation} = \text{Initial deposit} \times \frac{1}{\text{LRR}} \times 100$$

$$= 1000 \times \frac{1}{20\%} = ₹\ 5{,}000$$

14. The government through its budgetary policy attempts to promote fair and right distribution of income in a society. This is done through taxation and expenditure policy. On one hand, through its taxation policy, the government taxes the higher income group and on the other hand, through expenditure policy (subsidies, transfer payments, etc.), it transfers the purchasing power in the hands of the poor section of the society. With the help of these policies, the government aims at fair distribution of income in the society.

15. (a)

Basis	Current A/c	Capital account
Influence	1. Current account transactions affect the current income level of the country.	1. Capital account transaction affect the capital stock of the company.
Components	2. It records export/imports of goods and services, unilateral transfers and investment income received or paid.	2. It record transaction relating to sale/purchase of assets and borrowings/ lending.
Concept	3. It is a flow concept.	3. It is a stock concept.

(b)

Basis	Autonomous transaction	Accommodating transaction
Meaning	1. These items are those transaction which are undertaken for profit motive.	1 These items refer to those transaction which are undertaken to cover up disequilibrium in BOP.
Dependency of BOP	2. These transactions are independent of state of BOP.	2. These transactions are not independent of state of BOP.
Type of Account	3. These are both current a/c and capital a/c transactions.	3. These are only capital a/c transactions.
Other name	4. These are known as above the line item.	4. These are known as below the line item.

16. If there is an increase in investment by ₹ 1,000 goods and MPC is 0.9 then working of the multiplier can be explained as follows:

- Initially it will lead to increase in income by ₹ 1,000 crores and when MPC = 0.9, consumer will spend ₹ 900 crores on consumption, which become income for producers in round II.

- This process will continue till ΔI is equal to ΔS and it results in increase in income.
- The working of multiplier is illustrated with the help of given table.

	ΔI	ΔY	ΔC	ΔS
Round 1	1,000	1,000	90	10
Round 2	—	90	81	9
Round 3	⋮	81	72.9	8.1
	⋮	⋮	⋮	⋮
	⋮	⋮	⋮	⋮
	1,000	10,000	9,000	1,000

$$K = \frac{\Delta Y}{\Delta I} = \frac{10,000}{1,000} = 10 \text{ times}$$

17. Economic activities that are not marketed and are not evaluated in terms of money are called non market transactions or non monetary exchanges. These non monetary exchanges are not included in the estimation of GDP because no money is paid under these transactions. For instance, services rendered by the housewives to the family members greatly add to their welfare but they are not counted in GDP because no money is paid for them. All barter exchanges which takes place in the informal sector, without the help of money, are not registered as a part of economic activity and hence, GDP. Since these barter and informal exchanges are not included in the estimation of GDP there is underestimation of GDP, particularly in developing countries, like India. Hence, GDP which does not take into consideration the barter or informal exchanges, cannot be regarded as the true index of welfare of the nation.

Or

(a) Profit earned by branches of country's bank in other countires is **not included** in domestic product of the country because it does not fall within the domestic territory of India.

(b) Gifts given by employer to his employees on independence day **is included** in domestic product of the country because it is part of compensation of employees which fall within the domestic territory of India.

(c) Purchase of goods by foreign tourists is **included** in domestic product of the country because domestic goods are produced within the domestic territory of India.

SECTION B (INDIAN ECONOMIC DEVELOPMENT)

18. (b) General agreement on trade and tariff

Or

(c) July 1991

19. ICMR

20. False

21. (a) High growth rate of population

(b) Increase in public expenditure

22. 1950

23. (c) ASIAN

24. (a) (ii), (b) (iv), (c) (i), (d) (iii)

25. (d) All of the above

26. Agricultural

27. (a) Self helf groups

28. While it is true that the most important contribution of the British Rule was to introduce Railways in India which helped tremendously to integrate the country, it was a deed done on self-interest and not social service. The railways served the following purpose for the British:

- To exercise effective control and administration over the vast expanse of the Indian Territory.
- To transport goods and raw materials from the interiors of the country to the ports so that they could be easily shipped to Britain.
- Railways also served the purpose of mobilising British Army within India.

29. Animal Husbandry is the branch of agriculture which is concerned with breeding, rearing and caring for farm animals. It is also known as Livestock Farming.

- India owns one of the largest livestock populations in the world, consisting of cattle, goats, fowls, etc.
- This non farming activity provides alternate livelihood options to over 70 million people. A significant number of women also find employment.
- In terms of numbers, the numbers are quite impressive with poultry having the largest share of 58%. However, the productivity is quite low.
- Improved veterinary care and credit facilities have enhanced the plight of livestock rearing in the country.

Or

Wage employment refers to an arrangement whereby a worker/ employee sells his labour in return for requisite wages.

Wage employment is of two types:

- **Regular workers:** When a worker is paid remuneration on a regular basis, he is called a regular worker. He receives, what is called a salary, usually on a monthly basis.

When regular workers are hired on a permanent basis, they also get social security benefits like pension, PF, etc.

Example—teachers, doctors etc.

- **Casual workers:** Casual workers are not hired on a permanent basis and hence do not get a regular income, job security or social benefits. They are usually employed on an everyday basis and receive the day's remuneration, called wages (Dehaari).

  Casual workers outnumber the regular workers in India.

30. The poor in the urban areas is the overflow from the rural establishments who have migrated to cities in search of work.

They live in the out skirts of the cities, often in slum areas characterised with cramped spaces and makeshift houses. For example—Dharavi in Mumbai is the largest slum of India. Poverty does not work in isolation, it also leads to social exclusion like going to different schools than the rich kids, etc. Therefore, the urban rural divide becomes more evident with the intersection of poverty. The poor in rural areas usually includes the agricultural workforce: the landless labourers, tenants, farmers with small land holdings etc. Poverty in villages is characterised by insufficient farm produce, crop failure due to pests and rodents and similar such things. This forces the small farmers to take loans from local money lenders and get caught in the vicious cycle of debt. Therefore, when often hears the poor farmer committing suicide!

Or

Global warming is the gradual heating of earth's surface and atmosphere due to the increase in the emission of greenhouse gases. Green house gases include carbon dioxide, methane, water vapors. These gases trap the infra-red radiations of the sun and provide it a livable temperature, in the absence of which the temperatures would run in-150 or more. However, the increase in the emission of these gases through burning of fuels and deforestation has led to a crisis. Following are the effects:

- The increase in the levels of oceans and increased incidence of floods due to the melting of glaciers. Some low-lying parts of the world are already getting submerged.
- Increase in the prevalence of diseases like malaria, cholera etc.
- The weather and climate pattern all around the world are witnessing serious changes. Winters have become short. Even a 1 degree increase in the temperature of the earth is disastrous. Many species are becoming extinct as they cannot survive in the hot-humid kind of climate.

31. • 1951: This year saw the launch of the First five-year plan and from here on began the practice of five-year planning, keeping in mind the long-term and short-term goals.

- 1956: Industrial policy came in that assigned greater role of the public sector over the private sector as India was a fragile economy and needed government intervention.
- 1961: The seeds of green revolution were sown that bore fruits in the later decades.
- 1991: The new economic policy was launched on the motto of "Liberalisation, Privatisation and Globalisation." It integrated India with the economies of rest of the world.
- 2016: The railway budget was merged with the general budget.
- 2017: The Planning Commission was replaced with NITI Ayog, signifying a shift from 5-year planning to 15-year vision.

32.
- The infrastructure which fuels the economic activities of the country is called the economic infrastructure, whereas the infrastructure which directly influences the quality of life is called social infrastructure.
- Power, transportation, telecommunication come under economic infrastructure. Heath and education are examples of social infrastructure.
- Both kinds of infrastructure are interdependent. Roads and better means of transport increase the accessibility for all, thereby leading to social inclusion. On the other hand, better health facilities aid in human capital formation, which in turn leads to increase economic output.
- For a long time, infrastructure was only understood in economic terms. Amartya Sen gave the capabilities approach, which stressed the importance of social indicators in the development of any economy.
- India has made great strides in both forms of infrastructure, however true development cannot come unless the mindsets change and we become more accepting of each other's' differences – be it caste, class, race etc.

33. The basic goals of the Five-year plans were:
- Growth
- Equity
- Modernisation
- Self-reliance

Growth: This refers to the increase in the output of the country's economy. The growth can either be in terms of quantity, that means production or also in terms of the efficiency, which means producing more from the same inputs. This was the need of the hour post-independence as the economy plunged during the British era. The best measure of growth is Gross Domestic Product (GDP) which refers to the final value of all the goods and services produced in the country.

Equity: This means the equitable distribution of the resources so that the gap between the rich and poor is reduced. If GDP is a pie, then simply the size of the pie is not important, it is also crucial that each person gets a share of that pie.

Modernisation: Modernisation refers to two things. Firstly, it means an up gradation in the technology by using latest machines and programmes. Secondly, it also means the change of social outlook like gender parity of income, removing caste-based discrimination, etc.

Self-Reliance: This means not depending on other countries for assistance. It is necessary because external loans come with a lot of unjust terms and conditions. Using own resources will develop the local industries too. Moreover, external interference limits the freedom of the country to make decisions for its people's welfare.

34. From the time of independence until now, India has progressed a lot in terms of health indicators. The life expectancy has improved; infant mortality and deaths during pregnancy have reduced. However, there still remain some significant key areas of problem:

- **Shortage of hospitals and doctors:** There is just one doctor for every 921 people, as per 2017 data. There is dearth of hospitals in rural areas, where people have to travel great distances to seek treatment.
- **Spread of diseases:** The recent outbreak of Nipah virus in Kerala, or the deaths reported through malaria or dengue are alarming. The prime reasons for this are unsanitary conditions, which include open drains, impure drinking water, cluttered surroundings, etc.
- **Difficulty in access:** The government hospitals are usually crowded and hence it takes long waiting hours. The private hospitals are expensive and therefore remain ill affordable by the poor. The public and the private sector need to work hand in hand to improve the situation
- The level of technology is also catching up with the various new ailments that crop up.
- Unqualified doctors or ones who do not obtain their education through proper channels also pose a threat to medical treatment.

Or

Sustainable development means judiciously using the resources, in a way that they suffice the present needs and also remain for the future generations. Following are some strategies which can help to achieve it:

- **Use of non-conventional sources of energy:** Solar, wind, geothermal, tidal and similar forms of energy should be used to meet our power needs. They are available abundant in nature and are cleaner fuels. On the other hand, we should limit the usage of coal and petroleum, otherwise given the rate at which they are consumed presently, they will get exhausted in another fifty years.
- **Recycling:** One should not waste resources and recycle them. For example—the water that you use for washing clothes can be used to wash your car or the

water used to wash pulses can be used to water plants. This will conserve our very precious water by recycling it at individual level.

- **Afforestation:** Trees are the key to meeting half of the world problems. They are reservoirs of innumerable resources and having them in abundance would make the world meet its various needs. For example—the recent burning down of Amazon forests is a serious attack on the sustainability of the ecosystem and of mankind itself.
- **Population explosion:** If the population is kept under control, there wouldn't be burden on the resources and sustainability would be ensured. For example—the government has taken many steps to spread awareness in the direction like Hum Do Hamare Do campaign, etc.
- **Using eco-friendly methods and use of traditional knowledge:** The ancient practices of Ayurveda, Unani, Yoga or the home remedies by using natural ingredients limits commercialisation and the culture of consumerism.

Lastly, educating the masses and sensitising each other towards environment is the best way. Example—conducting competitions, drives and advertisements.

SAMPLE PAPER 4
(WITH SOLUTIONS)

Time allowed: 3 hours *Maximum marks: 80*

General Instructions:

1. ***All** the questions in **both** the sections are **compulsory**. Marks for questions are indicated against each question.*
2. *Question number **1-10** and **18-27** are very short-answer questions carrying **1 mark** each. They are required to be answered in one word or one sentence each.*
3. *Question number **11-12** and **28-29** are short-answer questions caring **3 marks** each. Answers to them should not normally exceed **60-80 words** each.*
4. *Question number **13-15** and **30-32** are also short-answer questions carrying **4 marks** each. Answers to them should not normally exceed **80-100 words** each.*
5. *Question number **16-17** and **33-34** are long answer questions carrying **6 marks** each. Answers to them should not normally exceed **100-150 words** each.*
6. *Answer **should be brief** and **to the point** and the above **word limit be adhered** to as far as possible.*

SECTION A (MACROECONOMICS)

1. A _________ bank is a bank that creates credit. **(1)**

2. Define Indirect Tax. **(1)**

3. State any three non tax revenue of the government. **(1)**

4. Real flow refers to the flow of factor services from **(1)**

(a) firm to household (b) household to firm
(c) firm to government (d) household to government

Or

Milk used by the confectioner to prepare sweets is

(a) intermediate goods (b) final goods
(c) consumption goods (d) capital goods

5. A country's BOT is ₹ 500 crores. Value of exports of goods is ₹ 650 crores, then the value of imports will be **(1)**

(a) ₹ 1150 crores (b) ₹ 500 crores
(c) ₹ 150 crores (d) none of these

6. MPC being equal to 0.5, ΔC will be _________, if income increases by ₹ 100? **(1)**

7. State whether the following statement is true or false **(1)**

'Depreciation in domestic currency leads to decrease in country's export.'

8. Surplus budget is that where _________ is greater than _________. **(1)**

9. From the set of statements given in column I and Column II, match the following: **(1)**

Column I	Column II
a. Increase in demand of foreign exchange	(i) Contraction of credit
b. Increase in bank rate	(ii) Currency depreciation
c. Increase in supply of foreign exchange	(iii) Expansion of credit
d. Decrease in reverse repo rate	(iv) Currency appreciation

10. MPS is expressed as **(1)**

(a) $\frac{S}{Y}$ (b) $\frac{Y}{S}$ (c) $\frac{\Delta Y}{\Delta S}$ (d) $\frac{\Delta S}{\Delta Y}$

11. Giving reason state how the following are treated in estimation of national income: **(3)**

(a) Payment of interest by banks to its depositors.

(b) Expenditure on old age pension by government.

(c) Expenditure on engine oil by car service station.

12. What is the difference between marginal propensity to consume and marginal propensity to save? What is the relation between the two? **(3)**

Or

What is meant by aggregate demand? State its components.

13. Explain the role of Reverse Repo Rate in increasing money supply. **(4)**

14. Government provides essential items of food grains almost free to the families below the poverty line. Which objective the government is trying to fulfil through the government budget and how? Explain. **(4)**

Or

Explain how the economic stabilisation objective can be fulfilled through the government budget.

15. Distinguish between the fixed exchange rate and the floating exchange rate. If exchange rate falls, explain its effects on exports and imports. **(4)**

16. Derive saving and investment approach from aggregate demand and aggregate supply approach for determination of equilibrium level of national income. Explain what happens if saving is greater than investment. **(6)**

Or

Given the consumption function C = 100 + 0.75Y and the autonomous expenditure as ₹ 1,100, calculate:

(a) Equilibrium level of income

(b) Consumption at the equilibrium level of income

(c) Investment multiplier

17. Calculate GNP_{MP} from the following information: **(6)**

	(₹ in crores)
(a) Compensation of employees	4,000
(b) Rent	800
(c) Profits	1,500
(d) Undistributed earnings	400
(e) Mixed income of the self-employed	1,800
(f) Net imports	30
(g) Net investment	900
(h) Gross domestic fixed capital formation	1,000
(i) Inventory investment	50
(j) Interest	900
(k) Net indirect taxes	500
(l) Net factor income to abroad	(–) 80

SECTION B (INDIAN ECONOMIC DEVELOPMENT)

18. What is the meaning of conventional sources of energy. **(1)**

19. The phenomenon of moving from one place to another in search of better job opportunities and remuneration, preferably abroad is known as __________. **(1)**

20. From the set of statements given in column I and Column II, match the following: **(1)**

Column I	**Column II**
a. Machinery, Factory, Building	(i) Monetary Policy
b. Central bank policy to control money supply	(ii) Human capital
c. Skill, ability, Knowledge of person	(iii) Physical capital
d. Central government policy to control money supply	(iv) Fiscal Policy

21. The ratio of labour force to total population is known as:

(a) work force participation rate (b) labour force participation rate

(c) employment ratio (d) none of these

Or

The "S" in AYUSH scheme stands for:

(a) sarvodaya (b) sampoorna (c) siddha (d) salva

22. State whether the following is true or false **(1)**

'Outsourcing is good for India because it provides employment on a large scale.'

23. __________ sector of the economy contributes the highest to India's GDP? **(1)**

24. The government set up the Central Pollution Control Board to control: **(1)**

(a) Water pollution (b) Noise pollution (c) Soil pollution (d) Air pollution

25. Which one of the following was not introduced in China? **(1)**

(a) Great leap forward (b) One child policy
(c) Proletarian cultural revolution (d) Look east policy

26. Electricity generated from radioactive elements is called __________. **(1)**

27. From the set of statements given in column I and Column II, match the following: **(1)**

Column I	Column II
a. Male workforce in primary sector	(i) 25%
b. Female workforce in primary sector	(ii) 45%
c. Male workforce in Tertiary sector	(iii) 19%
d. Female workforce in Tertiary sector	(iv) 57%

28. List down three major reasons behind the introduction of the new economic policy (1991). **(3)**

29. What do you understand by soil erosion as a challenge to India's environment? **(3)**

Or

Explain the concepts of Buffer Stock, Minimum Support Prices (MSP) and Public Distribution System (PDS).

30. Differentiate between human and physical capital. **(4)**

31. Compare and contrast the plight of the economies of India, Pakistan and China in the recent decades. **(4)**

32. List down the educational achievements of India. **(4)**

Or

What does the term rural development imply?

33. Write a short note on World Trade Organization. **(6)**

Or

What are the problems that agriculture in India faces?

34. The annual report (July 2017-June 2018) of the Periodic Labour Force Survey (PLFS) pegs the all India unemployment rate at 6.1 per cent in the given year. Unemployment was higher in the urban areas as compared to the rural. For the rural areas, the unemployment rate was 5.3 per cent, while in the urban areas it was 7.8 per cent.

Analyse the given data and give reasons for such trends which are observed in India despite massive GDP growth and employment generation schemes. **(6)**

SOLUTIONS TO SAMPLE PAPER 4

SECTION A (MACROECONOMICS)

1. Commercial

2. A tax, the burden of which can be shifted on to the others, is called indirect tax.

3. (a) Dividends + profits

(b) Fees and Fines

(c) Escheat

4. (b) household to firm

Or

(a) intermediate goods

5. (c) ₹ 150 crores

6. ₹ 50

7. False

8. government revenue > government expenditure

9. a. (ii), b. (i), c. (iv), d. (iii)

10. (d) $\frac{\Delta S}{\Delta Y}$

11. (a) Yes, it will be **included** in the national income as such interest is paid on loan taken for productive purpose. It is a factor payment by a producer.

(b) No, it will **not be included** in national income as old age pension is a transfer payment made by the government.

(c) No, it will **not be included** as it is a part of intermediate consumption expenditure.

12.

Basis	MPS	MPC
Meaning	It is the ratio of change in savings to change in income.	It is the ratio of change in consumption to change in income.
Formula	$MPS = \frac{\Delta S}{\Delta Y}$	$MPC = \frac{\Delta C}{\Delta Y}$

- The sum of MPC and MPS is equal to one. It can be proved as under:

  $\Delta Y = \Delta C + \Delta S$

  dividing both sides by ΔY

  $$\frac{\Delta Y}{\Delta Y} = \frac{\Delta C}{\Delta Y} + \frac{\Delta S}{\Delta Y}$$

  MPC + MPS = 1

This is because total incremental income is either used for consumption or for saving.

Or

Aggregate demand is the total demand of goods and services in the economy. Basically it represents **total expenditure** on goods and services in the economy. The components of aggregate demand are as follows:

(a) **Household (Private) consumption expenditure (C):** It refers to total amount of expenditure incurred by the household on the purchase of consumption goods to satisfy their wants.

(b) **Investment expenditure (I):** It refers to expenditure incurred by private firms or government on purchase of capital goods such as machinery, plant etc.

(c) **Government consumption expenditure (G):** It refers to expenditure incurred by government on purchase of goods and service.

(d) **Net exports:** It is the difference between exports and imports.

13. Reserve repo rate is the rate at which RBI borrows money from commercial banks and increase in reverse repo rate can prompt the commercial banks to park more funds with RBI to earn higher returns on idle cash. Thus an increase in reverse repo rate will ultimately lead to contraction of credit.

- So we can say that there is an **inverse relationship** between **reverse repo rate** and **money supply** in the economy.
- In order to **increase** the money supply we have to **reduce the reverse repo rate**. So a decline in reverse repo rate can pause the way towards increasing money supply.

14. Government by way of providing essential items of food grains almost free to the families below poverty line is trying to fulfil the objective of **reducing inequalities of income and wealth**.

- By providing essential food grains to poor people it will lead to **improvement of there health** and because of this they will become capable of doing work.
- This may provide them with **opportunities** to work and **contribute** in national income of the country.

- Government aims to influence distribution of income by **imposing taxes on rich** and **spending more on the welfare of poor people**.
- It **reduces** income of rich and raise standard of living of poor people.
- Such expenditure by government would help in development of the country.

Or

One of the objective of government budget is to ensure economic stability in the economy. The government budget prevents business fluctuations and maintains price stability.

- If AD > AS, then the government will have to take some measures to encourage savings and discourage investments. For this purpose government would decrease the public expenditure and increase the taxes.
- If AD < AS then the government would discourage savings and encourage investment. For this purpose the government will increase the public expenditure and decrease the taxes.

15.

Basis	Fixed exchange rate	Floating exchange rate
Determination of exchange rates	It is officially fixed in terms of gold or any other currency by government.	It is determined by forces of demand and supply of foreign exchange.
Government control	There is complete government control as only government has the power to change it.	There is no government intervention and it fluctuates freely according to market conditions.
Stability in exchange rate	The exchange rate generally remains stable and only a small variation is possible.	The exchange rate keeps on changing.

- To explain the effects of fall in exchange rate on imports and exports, let us take the following example:

  Earlier 1\$ = ₹ 70

  1\$ = ₹ 65

∴ Foreign exchange rate decreases and it is known as **currency appreciation**.

- Currency appreciation means increase in value of domestic currency in terms of foreign currency due to which:

  (i) Imports increases as foreign goods become cheaper.

  (ii) Exports decreases because domestic goods become costlier

16. • The equilibrium condition is as follows:

$$AD = AS$$
$$C + I = C + S$$
$$S = I$$

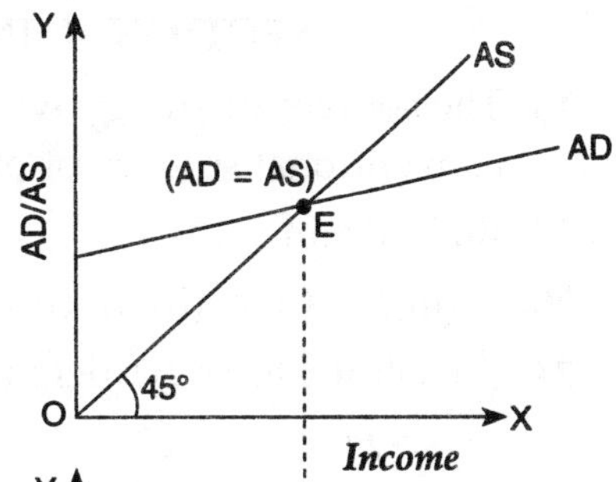

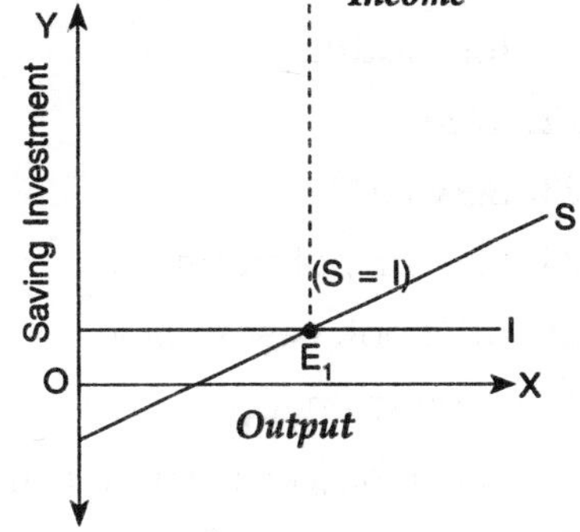

- The equilibrium level using saving and investment approach is determined by the point where **ex-ante savings are equal to ex-ante investments.**
- If S > I

  Then it means that households **save more** and not consuming as much as the firms expect them to.

  As a result inventory **rises** above the desired level and to clean the unwanted stock, firms **will reduce the production** i.e. till savings become equal to investment.

Or

(a)
$$C = 100 + 0.75\,Y \text{ (given)}$$
$$\bar{A} = 1100 \text{ (given)}$$
$$\bar{A} = \bar{C} + \bar{I}$$
$$1100 = 100 + \bar{I}$$
$$\Rightarrow \quad I = 1000$$
$$Y = C + I$$
$$Y = 100 + 0.75Y + 1000$$
$$Y(1 - 0.75) = 1100$$
$$Y = \frac{1100}{0.25} = \boxed{₹\ 4{,}400}$$

(b)
$$C = 100 + 0.75Y$$
$$= 100 + 0.75 \times 4{,}400$$
$$= 100 + 3{,}300 = \boxed{₹\ 3{,}400}$$

(c)
$$K = \frac{1}{1 - MPC}$$
$$= \frac{1}{1 - 0.75} = \frac{1}{0.25}$$
$$= \boxed{K = 4}$$

17. $GNP_{MP} = a + b + c + e + j - l + h + i - g + k$

$= 4{,}000 + 800 + 1{,}500 + 1{,}800 + 900 - \{-80\} + 1{,}000 + 50 - 900 + 500$

$=$ ₹ 9,730 crores

SECTION B (INDIAN ECONOMIC DEVELOPMENT)

18. The sources of energy which are in use since long and can be stored, are known as conventional sources of energy.

19. Brain drain

20. a. (iii), b. (i), c. (ii), d. (iv)

21. (b) labour force participation rate

Or

(c) siddha

22. True

23. Service

24. (d) Air pollution

25. (d) Look east policy

26. Atomic energy

27. a. (ii), b. (iv), c. (i), d. (iii)

28.
- **Insufficient Forex reserves:** The foreign exchange reserves with the government fell to levels that were not even sufficient to finance two week's imports.
- **Unfavourable Balance of Payments account:** The levels of imports still exceeded the exports, despite the quotas and tariffs, owing to the inferior quality of goods produced and the inability to compete with the cheap global prices.
- **Poor performance of government led initiatives:** The public-sector enterprises were neither being profitable, not contributing to welfare. The government expenditure was more than the revenue it could collect through taxes.

All these factors led to an emerging need to open up the economy to foreign players, so that a better efficiency and growth could be achieved.

29. Soil erosion refers to the weathering of the uppermost layer of the soil due to the agents of wind and water.

- The present rate of deforestation has exposed the soil to erosion. The roots of the trees bind the soil particles together, thereby preventing erosion. The sporadic pattern of rainfall and the occurrence of floods has also compromised the quality of the soil.
- Important minerals like potassium, nitrogen, phosphorus is lost in great quantities. The salinity and alkalinity of the soil is also greatly altered.
- India, which is the second most populous country of the world exerts a great deal of pressure on the limited land available for housing, mining, pastures, construction and so on. We might be blinded by the short-term advantages of such meddling with nature, but economic development can never be done on the ruins of nature.

Or

P[1] is the price at which the food grains are sold in the ration shops, which is lower than the market price.

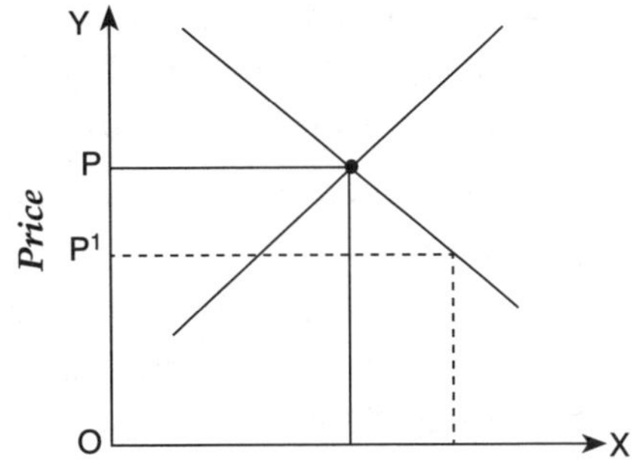

Public distribution system (PDS) is a network of fair price shops, also called ration shops which distribute grains to the poor at prices lower than the market price. For example— as per the data of 2016, rice was being supplied at ₹ 3/kg and wheat at ₹ 2/kg.

Buffer stock refers to the excess of food grains that are procured by the Food Corporation of India (FCI) to be stored in the godowns and used whenever there is a shortage due to natural calamity or otherwise.

Minimum Support Price is the price offered by the government to the farmers at which it will purchase all the produce—like wheat, rice, maize, etc. This is an assured price to the farmer, without having to deal with the negative fluctuations in the market price. The MSP is fixed before the sowing season.

30.

Physical capital	Human capital
(a) Physical capital refers to the tangible assets which can be used to produced other goods.	Human capital refers to the knowledge, creativity, intelligence and expertise of human beings to make use of the existing physical resource efficiently.
(b) Physical capital benefits primarily the owner.	Human capital benefits not just the one who owns it but also the society at large. Example—a teacher imparts knowledge to students.
(c) Physical capital can be separated from the owner.	Human capital cannot be separated from the owner.
(d) Example—any physical resource can be turned into physical capital. For example—land into industrial area.	Human resource can be turned into human capital by investing into it in terms of health and education.

31. India:

- Post 1991, India opened its doors to integrate its economy with the rest of the world. LPG brought a significant boost to the economy as licenses were abolished and private players gained greater autonomy.
- The GDP and per capita income increased and India became one of the fastest growing economies of the world.
- Many schemes were brought in to curb poverty and check money leaks. In 2016, India saw the historic demonetisation which was premised on the hope to reduce black money and the funds directed to terrorist organisations.

Pakistan:

- Pakistan has been under constant political turmoil with changing leadership and military takeovers. This has resulted in its neglect of the economy and seeking of aid from other nations.
- However, in the 2000s, many economic indicators showed positive GDP growth.
- As of now, Pakistan's economy is on a downward spiral. The country's under massive debts, rampant corruption, unemployment, inflation and widening fiscal deficit.

China:

- China became the fastest growing economy recently, overtaking USA.
- It is able to achieve this through selective capitalisation of the economy with retaining the communist pattern as the political setup. For example—the Special Economic Zones (SEZs).

  However, in the recent past, China is seeing protests in large numbers against being authoritarian, like in Hong Kong.

32.
- The literacy rate has improved from 18.33 % in 1951 to approximately 75% in 2015.
- Adult literacy, Youth literacy and Primary education completion rate—which are the indicators of educational progress of any nation have improved. The dropout rate has decreased and the enrollment rate has increased, courtesy schemes like midday meal
- The government launched the Right to Education Act in 2009 to provide elementary education to children from 6-14 years of age. Sarva Shiksha Abhiyan was a step in the similar direction, launched in 2011.
- As many as 304 universities are providing higher education in the country in 2005-06. Of these, there are 20 central universities. Besides, there are 40 deemed to be universities.
- The gender gap in accessibility to education has decreased.

Or

Rural development means the enhancement of the living conditions and the opportunities available to the people in the rural areas by undertaking socio-economic policies.

The process includes the following-

- **Development of infrastructure:** This includes building of roads, houses, power supply, drinking facilities, etc. to improve the quality of life of the village people.
- **Social provision:** This includes rectifying problems faced by the society at large that relate to mindsets. For example—encouraging parents to send their kids

to schools instead of working on the farms, allowing women to work in non-agricultural activities and so on.

- **Developmental projects:** Taking the bigger projects of development to rural backward areas will help in the overall growth of the area. For example—thermal power stations which are established in remote villages to create job opportunities for the people.
- In India, 75% of the population is in villages and dependent on agriculture. This means that methods of removing the disguised employment from agriculture and development of the non-farm activities is a top priority of rural development.

33.
- World Trade Organization (WTO) is a successor body of the General Agreement on Trade and Tariff. WTO came into being in 1995 and presently constitutes of 164 member nations.
- It regulates the trade between nations and lays down guidelines which have to be adhered to.
- It mainly prescribes for removal of trade barriers so that **free and fair trade** could take place between nations.
- It settles trade disputes arising out of malpractices like dumping of goods. (note: dumping refers to selling of goods at a lower price than it costs to produce it to capture market- like China does to India.)
- It fosters new trade agreements and negotiations. Example—the Doha conference, Bali package, etc.

India is a member nation of the WTO and has largely followed all rules. However, many developing countries feel that WTO guidelines favour the developed world and removing all custom duties on trade actually harms the growing economies.

Or

India is an agrarian nation, which means a large part of the country attains its livelihood from farming. It is not a hidden fact that the condition of agriculture is India has improved over the years but still faces some challenges:

- **High dependency on monsoon:** A lot of peasants still depend on rains and irrigation or artificial means of watering has still not reached remote villages
- **Middlemen:** The traders are often heard to exploit the farmers by forcing them to sell the produce at lower prices, quoting wrong market value.
- **Obsolete technology:** The means to predict weather or separate the husk from seeds is still done in the traditional way, which is both time consuming and inefficient.
- **Debt cycle:** The facility of loans is very difficult to avail for the farmers as they do not have anything to keep as mortgage or assure the banks. That is why, they borrow from money lenders who charge very high rates of interest and the farmer is trapped in the vicious cycle of debts.

- **Disguised unemployment:** More people are working on agricultural lands than are needed. This is partly due to the insufficient job creation in other non–farm activities and also because many a times, all the family members are engaged in farming on the same land, thinking it would be more productive.
- **Fragmented land holdings:** The land keeps on getting divided as the future generations become inheritors and this renders the land unviable and too small to farm. For example—Ram has 4 sons, after his death the land gets divided into 4 equal parts.

34. Although India is making progress in terms of GDP growth, the kind of growth observed is primarily jobless growth. This means there is huge unemployment in the country, which can be attributed to the following factors:

- The education in the country is not skill or vocational based and hence the educated youth is not recruited because although they do have knowledge but lack on the job training and experience.
- The enormous population makes it extremely difficult for the government to create proportional jobs as many areas have struck their saturation.
- The dropout rates are still high and this suggests that many sections of the population cannot afford education and take up any job which comes their way. These people, then are employed on a temporary basis because they do not have the bargaining power to ask for healthy working conditions and a decent pay. A lot of people, due to lack of higher education get removed from jobs like this.
- The traditional small-scale industries have declined significantly because the government was unable to maintain their value in the market. Lots of artisans, basket weavers, printing and dyeing cottage industries- which used to absorb labour have gradually perished.
- Agriculture could not generate enough employment opportunities like it did in the western countries and now there is a surplus of people in the cities, looking for jobs.

  The industrial sector, which absorbs the maximum labour in all other countries, failed to do so in India. In fact, it is believed that India made a jump from agricultural sector to the services. Also, production through labour intensive techniques were not retained and capital-intensive techniques were brought in, despite the abundance of labour force in India.

SAMPLE PAPER 5
(WITH SOLUTIONS)

Time allowed: 3 hours *Maximum marks: 80*

General Instructions:

1. ***All** the questions in **both** the sections are **compulsory**. Marks for questions are indicated against each question.*
2. *Question number **1-10** and **18-27** are very short-answer questions carrying **1 mark** each. They are required to be answered in one word or one sentence each.*
3. *Question number **11-12** and **28-29** are short-answer questions caring **3 marks** each. Answers to them should not normally exceed **60-80 words** each.*
4. *Question number **13-15** and **30-32** are also short-answer questions carrying **4 marks** each. Answers to them should not normally exceed **80-100 words** each.*
5. *Question number **16-17** and **33-34** are long answer questions carrying **6 marks** each. Answers to them should not normally exceed **100-150 words** each.*
6. *Answer **should be brief** and **to the point** and the above **word limit be adhered** to as far as possible.*

SECTION A (MACROECONOMICS)

1. Money supply is a __________ variable. **(1)**

2. In the context of government budget, which of the following statement is correct? **(1)**

(a) budget is a statement of expected annual receipts and expenditure of the government

(b) it is a detail of actual receipts and expenditure of the government in a financial year

(c) it offers a detailed description of achievement of the government during the 5-year plan

(d) it indicates BOP status of the domestic economy.

3. Define Statutory Liquidity Ratio. **(1)**

4. Which one includes depreciation? **(1)**
   (a) GNP at Market Price (b) NNP at Market Price
   (c) NNP at Factor Cost (d) None of these

Or

Which of the following is a semi-durable goods?
(a) Radio (b) Clothes (c) Milk (d) Petrol

5. What are accommodating transactions. **(1)**
6. The value of the multiplier is __________ related to the value of MPC. **(1)**
7. State whether the following statement is true or false **(1)**
   'Under employment equilibrium represents deficient demand in the economy.'
8. Deficit budget refers to the situation when __________ is more than __________. **(1)**
9. From the set of statements given in column I and Column II, match the following: **(1)**

Column I	Column II
a. Import of machine from Japan	(i) Credit side of Current A/c of BOP
b. Export of insurance service to Australia	(ii) Debit side of Capital A/c of BOP
c. Purchase of shares of Microsoft by Indian Resident	(iii) Debit side of Current A/c of BOP
d. Foreign Institutions directly invested in India	(iv) Credit side of Capital A/c of BOP

10. Fill in the blank : 1 (–) __________ = MPC **(1)**
11. In the city of Agra lies one of the seven wonders i.e., Taj Mahal. But, with the proceeding year, its marbles are turning yellow in colour. A lot of factories are set up in Agra. Explain the concept mentioned in the above lines. **(3)**

Or

Find net value added at factor cost:

	₹
(a) Sales	100 lakhs
(b) Closing stock	20 lakhs
(c) Excise duty	15 lakhs
(d) Opening stock	10 lakhs
(e) Depreciation	12 lakhs

12. Explain the relationship between income, consumption and APC using a schedule and diagram. **(3)**
13. If total deposits created by commercial banks is ₹ 12,000 and legal reserve requirement is twenty five percent, then calculate the amount of initial deposits. **(4)**

14. Find (a) Fiscal deficit, and (b) Primary deficit from the following information: **(4)**

	(₹ in crores)
(a) Revenue expenditure	70,000
(b) Borrowings	15,000
(c) Revenue receipts	50,000
(d) Interest payment	25% of revenue deficit

15. Recently, the rate of dollars has shot up and the Indian rupee has become very weak against dollars. What does this indicate? Use a numerical example. Also explain its effect on the economy and balance of trade of the country. **(4)**

Or

If inflation is higher in country A than in country B and the exchange rate between the two countries is fixed, what is likely to happen to the balance of trade between the two countries?

16. What is deflationary gap? Also explain the role of (a) Repo rate, and (b) Reserve repo rate in the above mentioned situation. **(6)**

Or

What is inflationary gap? Also explain the role of (a) Open market operations (b) CRR in the above mentioned situation.

17. Calculate GNP_{MP} by (a) Income Method (b) Expenditure Method. **(6)**

	(₹ in crores)
(a) Personal consumption expenditure	700
(b) Wages and salaries	680
(c) Contribution to the Social Security Scheme	400 (25% by employer)
(d) Gross business fixed investment	60
(e) Inventory investment	20
(f) Profits	100
(g) Government purchase of goods & services	200
(h) Rent	50
(i) Net imports	(–)20
(j) Gross residential construction investment	70
(k) Interest	40
(l) Mixed Income	100
(m) Net factor income to abroad	10
(n) Depreciation	30
(o) Gross public investment	40
(p) Net indirect taxes	10

SECTION B (INDIAN ECONOMIC DEVELOPMENT)

18. The New Economic Policy was started under the Prime Ministership of which Indian leader: **(1)**

(a) Manmohan Singh (b) P V Narsimha Rao

(c) Rajeev Gandhi (d) Atal Bihari Vajpayee

19. What does the term "Rural Development" means? **(1)**

20. From the set of statements given in column I and Column II, match the following: **(1)**

Column I	Column II
a. Year of first official census	(i) 1850
b. British rule introduced railways in the year	(ii) 1881
c. Year of great divide	(iii) 1966
d. India adopted HYV programme for first time	(iv) 1921

21. State whether the following statement is true or false **(1)**

'Natural gas is not a renewable source of energy.'

22. From the conception of NITI Ayog, the 5-year plans have been transformed into ________ year vision **(1)**

(a) 10 (b) 15 (c) 20 (d) 25

Or

A literate is a person who is 7 years of age and can:

(a) read and write in any language

(b) read, write and speak in any language

(c) read and speak any language

(d) speak and write any language

23. State whether the following statement is true or false **(1)**

'Liberalisation refers to transfer of ownership, management and control of public enterprises to the entrepreneurs in the private sector.'

24. When was the planning commission set up? **(1)**

25. The rank of India on human development index is ________. **(1)**

26. When we indicate poverty of a country, we mean **(1)**

(a) absolute poverty (b) relative poverty

(c) both (a) and (b) (d) neither (a) or (b)

27. ________ Protocol was signed to freeze the consumption and production of CFC; **(1)**

(a) Geneva (b) Copenhagen

(c) Bandung (d) Montreal

28. Briefly explain the following economic systems: (3)
(a) Capitalist pattern
(b) Socialist pattern
(c) Mixed pattern

29. Differentiate between the formal and informal sector of employment in India. (3)

Or

What is ozone depletion. What are its effects?

30. Investing in human capital is the key to development for any nation. What can be the problems in the quest of this achievement? (4)

Or

What do you mean by non-institutional sources of credit in rural India? What are they?

31. What is poverty? How can you categorise the poor? (4)

32. What are the various indicators of human development. (4)

33. Explain Privatisation as a part of the New Economic Policy. (6)

34. Write a note on the diversification of agricultural activities. (6)

Or

India aims to reduce high electricity transmission and distribution system losses

Electricity transmission and distribution (T & D) losses in India and other regions percent of total electricity generated

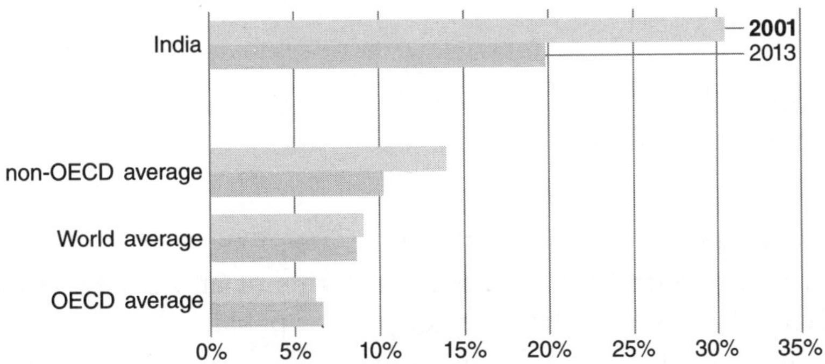

Source: U.S. Energy Information Administration, based on International Energy Agency

The graph shows challenges to the energy sector of India which occur due to distribution and transmission losses. Comprehend the data by giving adequate reasons for such patterns and also list down other problems which are faced by the energy sector.

SOLUTIONS TO SAMPLE PAPER 5

SECTION A (MACROECONOMICS)

1. Stock

2. (a) budget is a statement of expected annual receipts and expenditure of the government

3. It refers to liquid assets that the commercial banks must hold with itself as a certain percentage of their total deposits.

4. (a) GNP at market price

Or

(b) Clothes

5. The transactions which are taken to make equilibrium in BOP are called accommodating transactions.

6. directly

7. True

8. budget expenditure > budget receipt

9. a. (iii), b. (i), c. (ii), d. (iv)

10. MPS

11. The concept hidden in the above case is 'Negative Externalities'.

- Externalities refer to the benefits or harms of an activity caused by a firm or individual, for which they are not paid or penalised.
- Activities which result in harm to others are termed as **negative externalities**.
- Environmental pollution caused industrial places in Agra is degrading the Taj Mahal and affecting our country.

Or

$$NVA_{FC} = a + b - d - e - c$$
$$= 100 + 20 - 10 - 12 - 15$$
$$= ₹\ 83 \text{ lakhs}$$

12. APC is the ratio of total consumption to total income *i.e.*

$$APC = \frac{C}{Y}$$

The below mentioned schedule illustrates the relationship between income, consumption and APC:

Income (Y)	Consumption (C)	APC (C/Y)	
10 20	14 22	1.40 1.10	Y < C
30	30	1	Y = C
40 50	38 44	0.95 0.92	Y > C

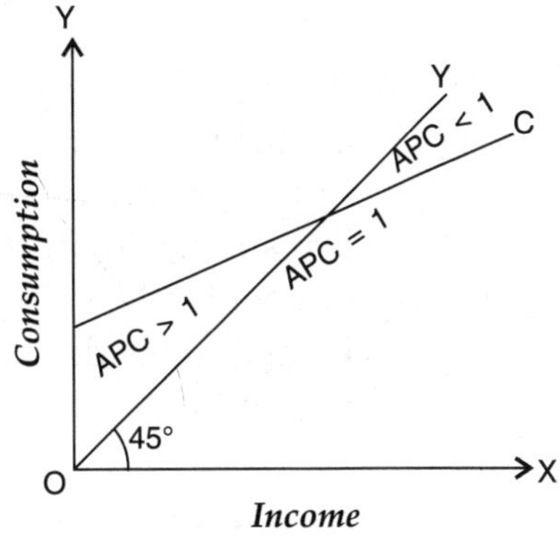

Here ,

1. When Y < C, APC > 1.
2. When Y = C, APC = 1.
3. When Y > C, APC < 1.

13. Total deposits = ₹ 12,000

LRR = 25%

We know, Total deposits = Initial deposit × $\frac{1}{LRR}$

12,000 = Initial deposit × $\frac{1}{0.25}$

∴ Initial deposit = ₹ 3,000

14. (a) Fiscal deficit = Borrowings

= ₹ 15,000 crores

Revenue deficit = a (–) c

= 70,000 (–) 50,000

= ₹ 20,000 crores

(b) Primary deficit = Fiscal deficit (–) Interest payments

= 15,000 (–) 25% of 20,000

= 15,000 (–) 5,000

= ₹ 10,000 crores

15. When Indian rupee becomes weaker against US dollars, then it is known as domestic currency depreciation. For example,

Earlier, 1$ = ₹ 60

Now, 1$ = ₹ 65

This shows domestic currency depreciation *i.e.* now an Indian has to pay more rupees in order to buy 1 $.

Currency depreciation has two major effects:

(a) It will lead to an increase in exports because domestic goods are now cheaper.

(b) It will also lead to a decrease in imports because foreign goods are now costlier.

So, the balance of trade will be on a surplus side since exports are increasing and imports are decreasing.

Or

(a) If inflation is higher in country A than in country B, it means that goods available in country A are costlier as compared to goods available in country B. In this situation, people in country A will start importing goods from country B resulting in an increase in imports of country A and an increase in exports of country B.

Balance of trade shows the net difference between exports of goods and import of goods

$$i.e.\ \text{BOT} = \text{X}\ (-)\ \text{M}$$

As a result of these transactions, the balance of trade for country A will be in deficit because of increasing imports and balance of trade for country B will be in surplus because of increasing exports.

16. Deflationary gap is the difference between the level of aggregate demand (AD) required to establish full employment equilibrium and the actual level of aggregate demand (AD). Deflationary gap measures the amount of deficient demand (as shown in the given diagram):

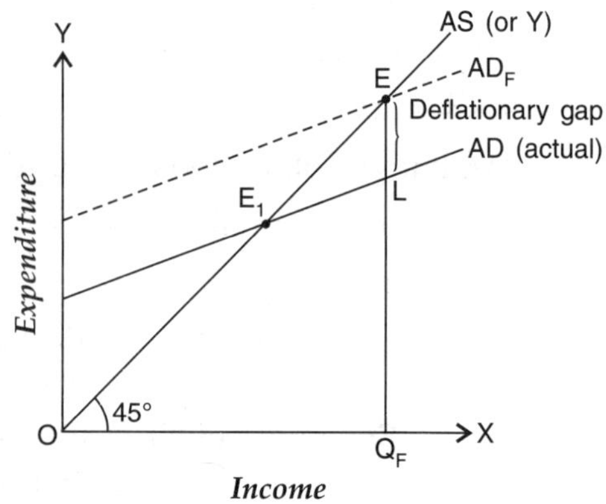

Here, AD_F = AD required for full employment level

Q_F = Full employment level of output/income

(a) **Role of repo rate in deflationary gap:** Repo rate is the rate at which the central bank advances loans to commercial banks. A decrease in the repo rate by the RBI lowers the interest rate of commercial banks as well and the business community tends to borrow more. This leads to expansion of credit in the market and the situation of deficient demand (or deflationary gap) will be corrected.

(b) **Role of reverse repo rate in deflationary gap:** Reverse repo rate is the rate at which the central bank borrows money from commercial banks. A decrease in the reverse repo rate by the RBI will discourage commercial banks to keep their funds with the central bank and as a result, they will be in a position to advance more credit in the market. This will lead to a correction in deficient demand (or deflationary gap).

Or

Inflationary gap is the difference between the actual level of aggregate demand (AD) and the level of aggregate demand (AD) required to establish full employment equilibrium. Inflationary gap measures the amount of excess demand (as shown in the given diagram):

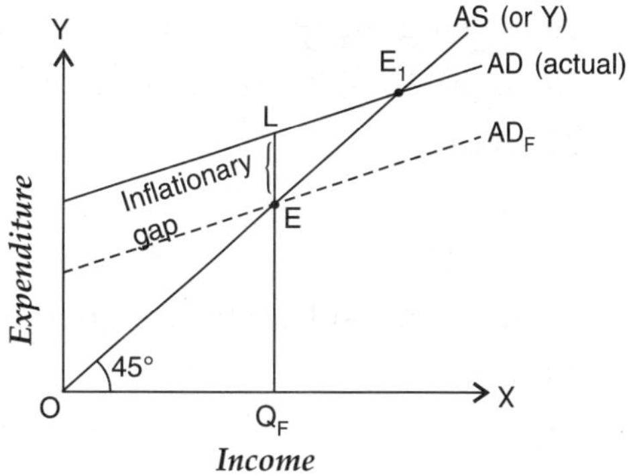

Here, AD_F = AD required for full employment level

Q_F = Full employment level of output/income

(a) **Role of open market operations in inflationary gap:** Open market operations mean buying and selling government securities in the market. In case of an inflationary situation, the central bank starts selling the government securities which reduce the cash reserves of commercial banks and finally result in the decline of credit in the market. In this way, open market operations help to correct the excess demand (or inflationary gap) in the market.

(b) **Role of CRR in inflationary gap:** Every commercial bank is required to keep a minimum percentage of its total deposits with the central bank. This is termed as cash reserve ratio (CRR). An increase in cash reserve ratio reduces the cash reserves of commercial banks which in turn reduces the credit creation capacity of the banks. Thus, the central bank increases the CRR to curb the situation of excess demand (or inflationary gap) in the market.

17. (a) Income Method

NDP_{FC} = (b) + (c)* + (f) + (h) + (k) + (l)

= 680 + 100 + 100 + 50 + 40 + 100 = 1070

*only employer's contribution to the Social Security Scheme should be considered

i.e. $400 \times \frac{25}{100} = 100$

GNP_{MP} = NDP_{FC} + Depreciation + NFIA + Net Indirect Tax

= 1070 + 30 + (–10) + 10

GNP_{MP} = ₹ 1,100 crores

(b) Expenditure Method

GNP_{MP} = (a) + (g) + (d) + (e) + (j) + (o) – (i) – (m)

= 700 + 200 + 60 + 20 + 70 + 40 – (–20) – 10

GNP_{MP} = ₹ 1,100 crores

SECTION B (INDIAN ECONOMIC DEVELOPMENT)

18. (b) PV Narsimha Rao

19. Raising the quality of life of rural people as a whole refers to rural development.

20. a. (ii), b. (i), c. (iv), d. (iii)

21. True

22. (b) 15

Or

(a) read and write and any language

23. False

24. 1950

25. 130

26. (a) absolute poverty

27. (d) Montreal

28. (a) **Capitalist Pattern:** A capitalist model rests on the principle of profit making. The prices are determined by the market forces of demand and supply and the government acts only as a facilitator. This system caters to the problem of "For whom to produce", i.e. goods are produced only for those who can afford it. Example—USA, Canada.

(b) **Socialist Pattern:** A socialist model emphasizes on collective ownership of resources and the government plays the central role. It is based on the idea of an equal society; hence the prices are fixed by the government and basic amenities are provided to all by the State. Example—Cuba, erstwhile Soviet Union.

(c) **Mixed Pattern:** A mixed economy is a combination of the above two mentioned. The government and the private players work hand in hand. It provides competitive prices to the consumers, giving social security to the producers at the same time. Example—India adopted the mixed economy post-independence.

29.

Organised	Unorganised
(a) The establishments listed with the government which employ 10 or more people are called organised sector.	The establishments which are not registered under the government.
(b) The workers are entitled to a lot of benefits like pension, paid leaves, medical facilities, etc.	The workers are not entitled to any such benefits and have low, irregular incomes. Since, they are not protected under the government, working conditions are usually below standard.
(c) In India, very few people are employed in the organised sector.	More than 2/3rd of the population works in the unorganised sector.

Or

Ozone depletion means the gradual thinning of the ozone layer due to the chlorofluoro and compounds present in the refrigerators, aerosol sprays and air conditioners. This had led to the formation of an Ozone hole above Antarctica.

Ozone protects us from the harmful ultra violet rays of the sun, in the absence of which—

- Skin cancer is caused
- The crops are destroyed
- Aquatic life is harmed

30. Human capital development requires investments in health, education and in the overall well-being of individuals.

Following are some of the problems it faces:

- **Brain drain:** A lot of educated people migrate to other countries in search of better work opportunities. This has become a trend and poses serious problems as the country's resources go in the development of these people and their services are utilized elsewhere.
- There isn't enough infrastructure to be sufficiently allocated to the human resource development with the high population pressure that we have.
- **Exclusivity:** Huge funds are required to provide avenues for Research and Development to individuals. This leads to channeling of resources to selected few, while the larger sectors of primary and secondary education are ignored.
- Many at times it is observed, even in the developed countries that the government has invested enough in the health sector but the results are not commensurate. This is because unless the lifestyle of individuals changes for the better, no amount of medical progress can cure them.

Or

Non-institutional sources of credit are informal bodies or agents, which neither have any prescribed rate of interest, nor do they offer assured credit at the time of need.

Following are the sources:

- **Friends and relatives:** This borrowing generally does not involve any rate of interest and is given to help the near and dear one.
- **Employers or landlords:** The landlords or the employers of the peasants are often the ones who people go to in times of need as they are more likely to lend money to their own workers. The landlords charge high rates of interest or keep any valuable thing as mortgage.
- **Money lenders:** These are rich people of the village who lend money on very high interest rate, more than the banks. They justify this by arguing that more risk is involved in lending to the people who have no means to return.
- **Traders:** Traders generally lend loans on the condition that farm produce would be sold to them at very low prices as a conditionality.

31. Poverty is a condition wherein the individual is not able to have the basic necessities of life-food, clothing and shelter. It is also defined in terms of the calorie intake and the minimum wage earned for a day.

Following are the categories of poor:

- **Chronic poor:** These people are poorest of the poor and barely survive. Also, they are always poor, their conditions varying seldom.
- **Transient poor:** These people move in and out of poverty due to various reasons like, inflation, seasonal employment etc. They are also called Churning poor.
- **Borderline poor:** These are the ones who are on the edge, probably because one or two persons have broken the cycle of poverty in their family and acquired a decent job. They pull their families out of poverty in due course of time.
- **Non-poor:** These people never experience poverty.

32. • **Mortality rate (infant and maternal):** Infant mortality rate (IMR) is the number of deaths per 1,000 live births of children under one year of age.

  Maternal mortality refers to deaths due to complications from pregnancy or childbirth.

- **GDP growth and per capita income:** GDP measures the economic output of a nation.

  Per capita income (PCI) or average income measures the average income earned per person in a given area (city, region, country, etc.) in a specified year.
- **Life expectancy at birth:** The average period that a person may expect to live.
- **Literacy rate:** Literacy rate is the total percent of population above 7 years of age who can read and write in any language
- **Mean years of schooling, dropout rate and Gross enrolment ratio:** Mean years of schooling is a calculation of the average number of years of education received by people ages 25 and older in their lifetime.

Dropout rate refers to the percentage of students that do not complete their high school education

Gross Enrolment Ratio (GER) Gross Enrolment Ratio determine the number of students enrolled in school at several different grades level.

There are some other indicators too, which are used sometimes like sanitation, drinking water, health facilities people above poverty line Employment opportunities.

33. The LPG that was enacted brought in various reforms. Privatisation, essentially means selling off the ownership or assets of the government enterprises to the private sector.

- Government chose the policy if 'disinvestment' to gradually sell off the shares of the public sector companies to private players. Disinvestment, as the name suggests is directing the investment to private sector or the withdrawal of investment from the government institutions.

- This had to be done because the public sector institutions were making heavy losses and the individuals were not able to function independently. Therefore, an urgent need to transform the ownership was realised.
- Many areas were handed over to the private companies, with keeping only few strategic ones with the government like—Railways, atomic energy, defense, etc.
- Indian Government started selling shares of PSU's to public and financial institution e.g. Government sold shares of Maruti Udyog Ltd.
- This proved to be fruitful for India as we made significant strides after the change in the policy

34. Agricultural diversification means adopting technology, inputs and means of production different from the ones presently being used. It also means searching for activities other than agriculture to depend on livelihood for.

Following are the reasons for diversification:

- To reduce the risk of depending exclusively on agriculture to earn a living.
- To provide sustainable options of employment opportunities to rural people.

Diversification can be done in the following ways:

- Pursuing different practices of agriculture like crop rotation and multi cropping. This removes the dependence of farmers of only one crop in a sowing season. Crop rotation is the practice of growing a series of different types of crops in the same area in sequential seasons and multicopying is the practice of growing two or more crops in the same piece of land in same growing seasons instead of one crop.
- Exploring other allied activities like dairy farming, horticulture, animal husbandry, etc.
- Exploring non-farm activities like pottery, handlooms etc.
- Shifting to commercial agriculture from subsistence agriculture by making use of better techniques like spray pesticides, nutrient replenshishers, etc.

Or

Following are the problems faced by energy sector:

- **Challenges to State Electricity Boards (SEBs):** The electricity is transmitted to all households through SEBs. However, there are transmission and distribution losses. This is partly due to insufficient infrastructure, partly due to theft of electricity and also because the laws are lax and do not penalise such stealing
- **Insufficient generation:** Although the energy generation has increased manifolds in India, it is still short of the consumption needs of the vast population. Hence, regular power cuts are often suffered by the people.
- **Lack of raw materials:** To produce such abundant magnitude of power, huge quantities of coal are required. Due to mining laws in India, it is not permissible to mine at densely populated places. This leads to imports of inputs.

- **Limited role of private sector:** So far only the government has been investing funds as generation of electricity requites setting up of large expensive power plants.
- **High tariffs:** The rate is which electricity is supplied is high, despite the provision of subsidies.
- Other sources of power generation like solar and wind energy, have gained importance but are still not as widely in use as thermal power due to the initial high cost of installation and dependence of sunlight and speedy wind.

SAMPLE PAPER 6
(WITH SOLUTIONS)

Time allowed: 3 hours *Maximum marks: 80*

General Instructions:

1. ***All** the questions in **both** the sections are **compulsory**. Marks for questions are indicated against each question.*
2. *Question number **1-10** and **18-27** are very short-answer questions carrying **1 mark** each. They are required to be answered in one word or one sentence each.*
3. *Question number **11-12** and **28-29** are short-answer questions caring **3 marks** each. Answers to them should not normally exceed **60-80 words** each.*
4. *Question number **13-15** and **30-32** are also short-answer questions carrying **4 marks** each. Answers to them should not normally exceed **80-100 words** each.*
5. *Question number **16-17** and **33-34** are long answer questions carrying **6 marks** each. Answers to them should not normally exceed **100-150 words** each.*
6. *Answer **should be brief** and **to the point** and the above **word limit be adhered** to as far as possible.*

SECTION A (MACROECONOMICS)

1. Sale of securities in the open market can be used by central bank to correct a situation of __________. **(1)**

2. The objective of government budget is **(1)**

(a) economic stability (b) redistribution of income and wealth
(c) both (a) and (b) (d) none of these

3. What is meant by deflationary gap? **(1)**

4. Which one of the following is not withdrawal in the circular flow of income? **(1)**

(a) savings (b) taxes (c) investments (d) imports

Or

While estimating national income, which of the following item is not included?

(a) Rent (b) Mixed income
(c) Fixed investment (d) Undistributed profits

5. What is the relation between price of foreign exchange and supply of foreign exchange. **(1)**

6. Which one is not the component of aggregate supply? **(1)**
   (a) rent (b) wages
   (c) interest and profit (d) investment

7. If BOT is (–) ₹ 800 crore and value of exports is ₹ 600 crore then the value of imports will be ________. **(1)**

8. State whether the following statement is true or false **(1)**

   'Revenue deficit is ₹ 20 crore when revenue expenditure is ₹ 80 crore and revenue receipts is ₹ 100 crore.'

9. From the set of statements given in column I and Column II, match the following: **(1)**

Column I	Column II
a. Consumption	(i) Remains constant
b. Savings	(ii) Can never be zero
c. Investment	(iii) Is 45® Line
d. Income	(iv) Can be negative

10. C/Y indicates ________. **(1)**

11. Distinguish between stock and flow. Between net investment and capital, which is stock and which is flow? Compare net investment and capital with the flow of water into a tank. **(3)**

Or

'Production of all products contribute equally to the economic welfare of an economy.' Defend or refute.

12. Find National income from the following information: **(3)**

	(₹ in crores)
(a) Average propensity to save	(–) 0.3
(b) Consumption level in the economy	260
(c) Transfer income	210
(d) Net factor income to abroad	20

13. Given consumption function C = 100 + 0.75 Y (where C = consumption expenditure and Y = National Income) and investment expenditure = 1,000, calculate; **(4)**
    (a) Equilibrium level of National Income
    (b) Consumption expenditure at equilibrium level of National Income.

14. "Government has recently issued BPL (Below Poverty Line) cards to the poor people in India so that they get minimum food from ration shops and avail subsidised

medical facilities at big hospitals." Which objective of budget is fulfilled here, explain its need through the budget. **(4)**

15. Recently, the Government of India launched the 'Incredible India' campaign to promote tourism in India. How will this affect the price of foreign exchange. **(4)**

Or

Are the following transactions entered on the credit side or debit side in BOP account? Give reasons.

(a) Exports

(b) Imports

(c) Borrowing from rest of the world

(d) Lending to rest of the world

16. What is fiscal policy? How does it affect the level of output and employment in the economy? **(6)**

Or

Distinguish between:

(a) Fixed and flexible exchange rates

(b) Direct tax and indirect tax

17. Calculate (a) GDP_{MP} by income method, and (b) national income by expenditure method: **(6)**

	(₹ in crores)
(a) Compensation of employees	240
(b) Exports	50
(c) Mixed income	280
(d) Imports	60
(e) Interest on national debt	10
(f) Private final consumption expenditure	510
(g) Gross fixed capital formation	130
(h) Consumption of fixed capital	80
(i) Subsidies	20
(j) Government final consumption expenditure	70
(k) Inventory investment	40
(l) Indirect tax	90
(m) Net factor income from ROW	(–)20
(n) Rent, interest & profits	100

SECTION B (INDIAN ECONOMIC DEVELOPMENT)

18. State any two non-commercial sources of energy? **(1)**

19. State whether the following statement is true or false. **(1)**

'Poverty line is used to measure absolute poverty in India.'

20. From the set of statements given in column I and Column II, match the following: **(1)**

Column I	Column II
a. Growth	(i) Overcoming the need of external assistance
b. Modernisation	(ii) Increase in country's capacity to produce more output
c. Self Reliance	(iii) Raise the standard of living of people.
d. Equity	(iv) Inequality in distribution of income should be reduced.

21. The importance of human capital was realised in which of the following five-year plans? **(1)**

(a) 5th (b) 6th (c) 7th (d) 8th

Or

Which of the following is not an example of the "Farmers Market"? (Farmers markets link the producers to the consumers directly, thereby eliminating middlemen)

(a) Apni Mandi in Punjab and Haryana
(b) Hadapsar market in Pune
(c) Rythu bazaar in Andhra Pradesh
(d) Chandni chowk in Delhi

22. The maximum contribution to GDP of China is due to __________ sector. **(1)**

23. Which organisation collects data on poverty in India ? **(1)**

24. Why do people work? **(1)**

(a) To earn a livelihood
(b) To kill boredom
(c) To realise self-worth and gain more control over one's life
(d) Both (a) and (c)

25. Explain the term "Golden Revolution". **(1)**

26. Carrying capacity implies: **(1)**

(a) Resource extraction < resource replenishment
(b) Generation of waste should remain with the absorption capacity
(c) Maximum population size of the species that the environment can sustain indefinitely
(d) All of the above

27. Power generated from water is called __________. **(1)**

28. Why did India opt for mixed economy? **(3)**

Or

Subsidies in agriculture have always been a contentious issue. What is your view on it?

29. Write a short note on horticulture. **(3)**

30. The Brundtland Commission published a report called "Our Common Future" to highlight the state of our ailing planet. What according to you are some of the reasons for environmental crisis? **(4)**

Or

Are there differences in accessibility to health in urban and rural areas? If yes, why?

31. Compare the sectoral share of GDP and employment among India, China and Pakistan. **(4)**

32. How does expenditure on migration lead to human capital formation. **(4)**

33. Describe the Indian economy on the eve of independence. **(6)**

34. Give an account of National Health Policy. **(6)**

Or

APH WEDNESDAY 4 OCTOBER 2000

Seeing through the illusion of progress

India has the fourth largest collective purchasing power in the world, but its economy is far from being in fine fettle, writes **Nilanjan Banik**

economies of the West. However, by virtue of these services being non-tradeable, this is not reflected in the exchange rate. For example, a barber will charge anything between $20-30; likewise, the service cost of a carpenter in Japan is eight to 10 times higher than that in India.

The true purchasing power of a country is the basket of goods and services the dollar equivalent of that country's currency can buy in the other country. For example, going by the current exchange one gets around Rs 45 by selling a dollar. In calculating PPP, one calculates the value of goods and services that Rs 45 (or one dollar) can buy in the US, or Rs 39 (or one euro) can buy in the UK.

Arguing on another plane, the fact that India has the fourth largest collective purchasing power in the world hardly implies that the economy, or at least its tradeable segment, is in fine fettle. Export growth dipped ominously in July, whereas rising global oil prices contributed to a sharp increase in imports.

"The value of currencies in developing countries like India is far more than the official exchange rate vis à vis the currencies of the developed world"

Latest trade data shows that India's export growth dipped to 16.46 per cent in July after a near 30 per cent growth in the first quarter of this fiscal. Oil imports nearly doubled to $ 5.46 billion during April-July. The trade deficit continued to be high at $3.71 billion dollars in April-July this year, against $ 3.02 billion in the corresponding period in 1999.

In the social sphere, India is faced with wide-ranging disparities. Regional, class and gender differences continue to widen. While the Indian middle class now has grown to an extraordinary 365 million, the enormous population of the poverty-stricken and the dispossessed has grown to 329 million.

Nearly one in three in this country

Cheaper to shop

worse than the average of the poorest countries of the world. Rural-urban disparities have widened as well.

With more than three-quarters of state funds going towards wages, healthcare and education have suffered. Ever since independence, there has been disproportionate investment

launched several poverty alleviation and income generation programmes for the disadvantaged that failed to reach the poorest.

The government has now conceded that only direct investment in health and education will significantly contribute to sustainable development.

The single biggest threat is the growing mismanagement of the soil. Over 50 per cent of the total land area is subject to serious environmental degradation. Nearly 60 per cent of cultivated land is in need of soil conservation measures.

In the next 20 years, an area equal to the entire cultivated land area of the country — about 140 million hectares — will be lost if soil erosion continues unabated. In one monsoon season six centimetres of top soil, representing nearly 2,400 years of local ecological history, disappears on the highly grazed Shivalik hills. In fact, in six months, more topsoil gets washed away than has been used to build all the brick houses in the country.

Over one million hectares of forests are cut every year and only 10 per cent of forest land has adequate tree cover. The consequences of this extensive deforestation are increasing floods, silting of dams and changes in the microclimate. The land area prone to floods has doubled in the past 10 years and stands at about 40 million hectares. The problem of overgrazing is acute in India as it has a very high cattle population.

"The high rate of population growth has slowed down progress on all fronts. Close to 330 million will be added in the next two decades"

Fuel scarcity is so acute that women have to walk upto 15 kilometres to get their wood to use as fuel. Tribal populations who live off forest produce have been marginalized because of the commercialization of forest products.

The high rate of population growth has slowed down progress on all fronts. Projections indicate that close to 330 million, which is equal to the total population of India at the time of independence, will be added in the next two decades.

The population of India is expected to stabilize at two billion in the second

The image given above is an article from a leading newspaper daily, titled "Seeing through the illusion of Progress." It takes a bitter stand on poverty which is so normalised that it is hardly seen as a social evil. In your opinion, what are some of the reasons for such an observation.

SOLUTIONS TO SAMPLE PAPER 6

SECTION A (MACROECONOMICS)

1. Excess demand

2. (c) both (a) and (b)

3. Deflationary gap measures the extent to which the current aggregate demand falls short of the aggregate demand that is required to achieve full employment level of output.

4. (c) Investments

Or

(c) Fixed investment

5. There is a direct relation between price of foreign exchange and supply of foreign exchange.

6. (d) Investment **7.** ₹ 1,400 crore **8.** False

9. a. (ii), b. (iv), c. (i), d. (iii)

10. APC

11. Difference between stock and flow is as follows:

Basis	Stock	Flow
1. Time	Stock is measured at a particular point of time.	Flow is measured over a particular period of time.
2. Dimension	It has no time dimension.	It has a time dimension.
3. Concept	It is a static concept.	It is a dynamic concept.
4. Example	Capital is a stock concept.	Net investment is a flow concept.

Comparison of net investment and capital with the flow of water into a tank: When water is flowing into a tank, then it can be considered as net investment but when the tank is filled and total water in the tank is measured at that of point of time, then it can be considered as capital.

Or

I refute the above statement that production of all products contribute equally to economic welfare because GDP includes various kinds of products like food items, military goods & services, etc. Thus, their contribution to the economic welfare depends upon their usage in the economy and not on their quantity of production. For example, increase in production of military goods may increase the GDP of the country but not necessarily depict the welfare of the economy.

12. APS = (–) 0.3

$\therefore$ APC = 1 + 0.3 = 1.3

Now, APC = $\frac{C}{Y}$ = 1.3

C = 260

$\therefore \frac{260}{Y} = 1.3$

$\Rightarrow Y = \frac{260}{1.3}$ = ₹ 200 crores = National Income

13. C = 100 + 0.75 Y, I = ₹ 1,000

(a) Y = C + I

Y = (100 + 0.75Y) + 1,000

Y = 1,100 + 0.75Y or Y – 0.75Y = 1,100

so, Y = 1100/0.25 = ₹ **4,400**

(b) C = 100 + 0.75 Y

= 100 + 0.75 × 4,400

= 100 + 3300 = ₹ **3,400**

14.
- With the introduction of BPL cards the government is trying to fulfil the objective of reducing inequalities in income and wealth.
- Economic inequality is an inherent part of every economic system. Government aims to reduce such inequalities of income and wealth, through its budgeting policy. Government aims to influence distribution of income by imposing taxes on the rich and spending more on the welfare of the poor. It will reduce income of the rich and raise the standard of living of poor, thus reducing inequalities in the distribution of income.

15.
- With the launch of the 'Incredible India' campaign, the foreign tourists will be encouraged to visit India. As more and more foreigners visit India, the supply of foreign exchange will also increase. Its effect on the price of foreign exchange is shown in the given diagram.
- With the launch of Incredible India campaign, the supply of foreign exchange in India will also rise resulting in decreasing the price of foreign exchange.

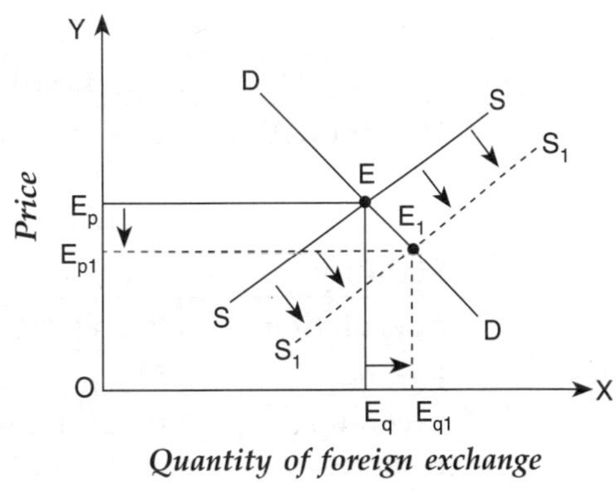

Quantity of foreign exchange

Or

(a) Export is a credit item because it brings in foreign exchange.
(b) Import is a debit item because it leads to outflow at foreign exchange.
(c) Borrowing from the rest of the world is a credit item because there is an outflow of foreign exchange.
(d) Lending to the rest of the world is a debit item because there is an outflow of foreign exchange.

16. The policies of the central government (related to its revenue, expenditure and borrowings) which help the economy to cope up with inflationary or deflationary situations in the economy is known as fiscal policy.

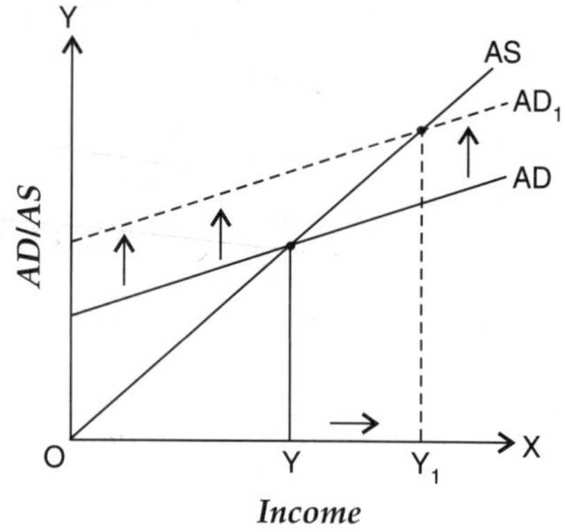

Income

Through the changes in expenditure and taxes, the central government attempts to increase output and income and seeks to stabilise the ups and downs in the economy. Since fiscal policies affect the aggregate demand in the economy, thus, it in turn affects the output and employment as well. Two major fiscal policies of the government are as follows:

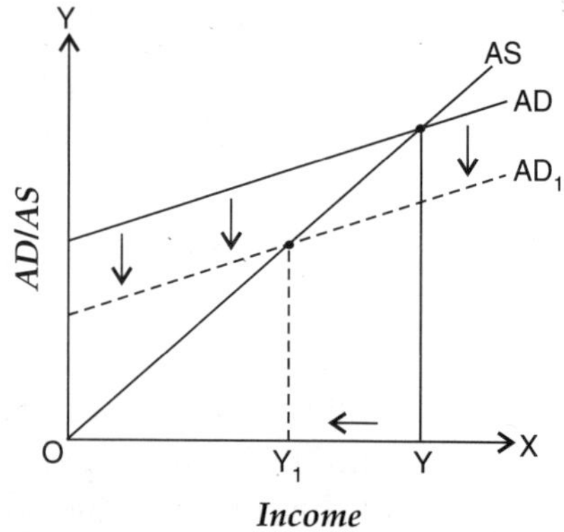

Income

(a) **Government Expenditure:** When government expenditure increases, the level of aggregate demand increases which results in an upwards shift in AD. With the increase in AD, the level of income also increases as shown in the diagram.
(b) **Government Revenue:** When government revenue (*i.e.* taxes) increases, the disposable income reduces which leads to a decrease in the level of aggregate demand. The AD curve shifts downwards and with the decrease in AD, the level of income decreases as shown in the diagram.

Or

(a)

Basis	Fixed Exchange Rate	Flexible Exchange Rate
Determination	It is the rate which is officially fixed in terms of gold or other currency by the government.	It is the rate determined by the forces of demand and supply of foreign exchange.
Stability	It ensures stability.	It does not ensure stability.
Speculation	It prevents speculation.	It does not prevent speculation.
Foreign exchange reserves	The government needs to hold minimum foreign exchange reserves.	There is no need for the government to hold foreign exchange reserves.

(b)

Basis	Direct tax	Indirect tax
Shifting of burden	It is paid by the person on whom it is imposed *i.e.* shifting of the burden is not possible.	It is paid by the consumers *i.e.* shifting of the burden is possible.
Nature	It is progressive in nature.	It is regressive in nature.
Imposed on	It is imposed on persons.	It is imposed on commodities.
Examples	Income tax, corporate tax	Sales tax, Service tax

17. (a) GDP_{MP} by income method = a + c + n + h + l – i

= 240 + 280 + 100 + 80 + 90 – 20

= ₹ 770 crores

(b) NNP_{FC} by expenditure method

= f + j + k + g + b – d – h + m – l + i

= 310 + 70 + 40 + 130 + 50 – 60 – 80 + (–20) – 70

= ₹ 570 crores

SECTION B (INDIAN ECONOMIC DEVELOPMENT)

18. Firewood and dried dung

19. True

20. a. (ii), b. (iii), c. (i), d. (iv)

21. (c) 7th

Or

(d) Chandni chowk in Delhi (you don't have to know about all markets, you simply have to reason which is not: Chandni chowk has shopkeepers and retailers, not the actual producers)

22. Manufacturing

23. National Sample Survey Organisation (NSSO)

24. (d) Both (a) and (c)

25. The period of 1991--2003 is known as "Golden Revolution" because during this period, the planned investment in horticulture became highly productive and the sector emerged as a sustainable livelihood option.

26. (d) All of the above

27. Hydro power.

28. India opted for a mixed economy because:

- We had seen the tyranny of the British rule and the horrors of the partition, and hence wanted to stand for a just, equal and welfare nation. This was not possible if all power was vested in private players.

- Complete dilution of private sector did not seem feasible as there was a heavy need of growth and industrialisation in the infant stages of independent India.
- Therefore, a mixed economic system was opted for whereby socialist and capitalist ideologies will thrive together and bring in the best of both words.

Or

Theoretically, subsidies in agriculture are provided to farmers for purchase of expensive inputs. More practically, they work as an incentive to farmers to cultivate and add as a shock absorber in times of crisis.

- They were essential at the time when India began with Green Revolution as the HYV seeds, chemical fertilisers, pesticides were expensive.
- However, it is a fact that a major chunk of subsidies does not go the target poor who are landless labourers and marginal farmers. Instead, they are availed by the rich land owners. Moreover, they are an added expense on the Indian exchequer and years after the success of green revolution, they can be reduced, if not completely revoked.
- Therefore, as much as I agree that the tiller of the country needs to be safeguarded against the uncertainties of nature, it is important that subsidies are channeled to the deserving poor.

29. Horticulture refers to the cultivation of fruits, vegetables, herbs, medicinal plants, flowers, spices and so on. India is one of the largest producers of both fruits and vegetables in the world.

- India, due to its varied soil type and climatic conditions produces a lot of produce through horticulture.
- It exports valuable fruits like mangoes, nuts, coconut and spices which contribute significantly to the GDP.
- Horticulture has opened up newer opportunities for employment in alternate agriculture.

30. Following are the reasons for environmental crisis:

- **Overuse of resources:** The consumption rate is increasing day by day which is faster than the rate at which the resources can be replenished.
- **Population explosion:** The addition of people on the earth puts a substantial pressure on the limited resources which leads to environmental degradation.
- **Use of fossil fuels:** Although fossil fuels are of extreme value, they also lead to carbon dioxide pollution. This has given rise to one of the most pressing problems of the world today-Global Warming.
- **Poverty:** It leads to dependence on forests to extract maximum needs like felling of trees to obtain wood, etc.
- Many other substances like use of CFCs, burning of crackers, discharging of untreated waste into the water bodies have also amounted to significant degrees of damage.

Or

The rural-urban divide reflects in the accessibility to healthcare as well.

- The rural areas have sparse incidence of hospitals. Sometimes, people have travel 25-50 kms to avail medical treatment.
- The doctor patient ratio in India is 924:1. in rural areas, it is worse. That is why, the government instituted Primary Healthcare Centers and Community healthcare workers. This has ensured the availability of first aid but the complex procedures and high-end services like gynecology, CT Scan are still not there.
- A considerable amount of income of poor people is spent on medical treatment.
- As far as the urban areas are concerned, the poor of cities often find it difficult to afford the services of the private hospitals and the government hospitals are overly crowded.
- States like Uttar Pradesh, Haryana, Rajasthan fare poorly on health indicators.

31.

India	Pakistan	China
(a) Maximum people are engaged in agriculture, then service, followed by service.	Maximum people are engaged in agriculture, then service, followed by service.	Maximum people are engaged in service, then industry, followed by agriculture.
(b) Highest contribution to GDP comes from service sector, then industry, followed by agriculture.	Highest contribution comes from service, then agriculture, followed by industry.	Highest contribution to GDP comes from service sector, then industry, followed by agriculture.
(c) The growth is mainly contributed by the service sector.	Service sector contributes the maximum to the GDP.	The growth is mainly contributed by the industry. China is also known as the factory of the world.
(d) India made a direct shift from the agricultural sector to the service sector. This is why the industry could not prosper and absorb the labour force.	Pakistan witnessed a similar fate.	China has very less cultivable land, and therefore it exploited the manufacturing sector very efficiently.

32. • Migration refers to the movement of people from one place to another in search of better living conditions. This may include education facilities, political stability, weather conditions but is majorly influenced by higher salary and job opportunities.

- The costs of migration include travelling expenses, housing expenses and so on. The villagers migrate to cities and the urban dwellers move abroad.

- The benefits which come from moving to another place are more than the costs incurred and hence investment in migration is a form of human capital formation.
- However, such practices have led to the crowding and congestion of cities and the brain drain of educated individuals from the country.

33. The plight of India at the time of independence was:
    - **Stagnant economy:** The growth rate of output was very low, about 2%. This happened because the British reduced the Indian economy to mere exporters of primary products.
    - The agriculture took the major hit due to the introduction of **Zamindari system** which was extremely exploitative. Commercialisation of agriculture also led to a shift from subsistence agriculture and thus to food grain insufficiency.
    - **Demographic indicators:** Literacy rate, poverty, per capita income, sectoral occupation – all fared poorly under the 200 years of colonisation and enslavement of India.
    - **Drain of wealth:** All the precious metals, handicraft, prints of textile and valuable minerals were used up by the British to fill up their coffers in Britain.
    - **The divide and rule:** This policy of the British divided India on communal lines which resulted in the horrors of partition and the ongoing tussle between Hindus and Muslims in the country.
    - The indigenous industries declined under the British rule and there was a complete absence of capital goods industries. There was some infrastructure that was developed like the railway and telegraph services, but that was only to ease the administration and control for the British.

34. - The National Health Policy, 2017 (NHP, 2017) seeks to provide an integrated way to move towards wellness.
    - The primary goal is to attain the highest possible level of health and well-being for all ages. This would be achieved through increasing access, improving quality and lowering the cost of healthcare delivery.
    - The plan of action includes -Increase Life Expectancy at birth from 67.5 to 70 by 2025, reduce Under Five Mortality to 23 by 2025 and ensure availability of paramedics and doctors in high priority districts by 2020.
    - Preventive and Promotive Health - The policy identifies coordinated action on seven priority areas for improving the environment for health:

      – The Swachh Bharat Abhiyan

      – Balanced, healthy diets and regular exercises.

      – Addressing tobacco, alcohol and substance abuse

      – Yatri Suraksha – preventing deaths due to rail and road traffic accidents

      – Nirbhaya Nari – action against gender violence

– Reduced stress and improved safety in the work place

– Reducing indoor and outdoor air pollution

- The development of public healthcare services in rural areas is also one of the top priorities.

Or

The causes of poverty are as follows:

- **Low levels of literacy:** More than 70 years after independence too, we have not been able to achieve full literacy. Low levels of education, leads to difficulty in finding jobs and thereby the puddle of poverty.
- **Over population:** The rate of reproduction, especially among the poor leads to "more mouths to feed", instead of "more hands at work".
- **Insufficient employment opportunities:** The industrial sector, which was meant to absorb the labour force failed in doing so. The agricultural sector has $2/3^{rd}$ people working on the field, which does not mean being efficiently employed, it is disguised employment.
- **Debt trap:** Falling in the vicious cycle of indebtedness takes away all the possessions of the poor. The seasonal nature of work forces the poor to borrow money, pushing them deeper into poverty.

  Lack of will and determination: a lot of times we can comfortable with whatever our situation is and grow averse to change. It is when we stop striving to get out of poverty, that it becomes a condition of life.

SAMPLE PAPER 7 (WITH SOLUTIONS)

Time allowed: 3 hours *Maximum marks: 80*

General Instructions:

1. ***All** the questions in **both** the sections are **compulsory**. Marks for questions are indicated against each question.*
2. *Question number **1-10** and **18-27** are very short-answer questions carrying **1 mark** each. They are required to be answered in one word or one sentence each.*
3. *Question number **11-12** and **28-29** are short-answer questions caring **3 marks** each. Answers to them should not normally exceed **60-80 words** each.*
4. *Question number **13-15** and **30-32** are also short-answer questions carrying **4 marks** each. Answers to them should not normally exceed **80-100 words** each.*
5. *Question number **16-17** and **33-34** are long answer questions carrying **6 marks** each. Answers to them should not normally exceed **100-150 words** each.*
6. *Answer **should be brief** and **to the point** and the above **word limit be adhered** to as far as possible.*

SECTION A (MACROECONOMICS)

1. M_1 is __________ definition of money. **(1)**

2. What does a government budget show? **(1)**

(a) Actual expenditure and actual revenues
(b) Estimated expenditure and actual revenues
(c) Estimated expenditure and estimated revenues
(d) Actual expenditure and estimated revenues

3. What is meant by Inflationary Gap ? **(1)**

4. GDP at constant prices is called **(1)**

(a) real GDP
(b) nominal GDP
(c) real national income
(d) nominal per capita income

Or

What will be deducted to get NDP_{MP} from GDP_{MP}?

(a) NFIA
(b) Indirect tax
(c) Depreciation
(d) Transfer of payment

5. Which type of transactions are recorded in the capital account of BOP? **(1)**

6. An economy attains equilibrium level of income only when ex–ante saving is equal to __________ . **(1)**

7. State whether the following statement is true or false **(1)**

   'Foreign exchange is demanded by domestic residents to purchase goods from other countries.'

8. In government budget primary deficit is ₹ 30,000 crore, interest payment is ₹ 5,000 crore, then fiscal deficit is ₹ __________ crore. **(1)**

9. From the set of statements given in column I and Column II, match the following: **(1)**

Column I	Column II
a. Excess demand	(i) Will lead to rise in imports
b. Currency appreciation	(ii) Prices are rising
c. Deficient Demand	(iii) Will lead to rise in exports
d. Currency depreciation	(iv) Prices are falling

10. At equilibrium level **(1)**

    (a) C = I (b) AD = S (c) S = I (d) C = S

11. Calculate intermediate consumption from the following information: **(3)**

	(₹ in lakhs)
(a) Value of output	4,000
(b) Depreciation	80
(c) Subsidy	20
(d) Excise duty	60
(e) Net value added at factor cost	3,200

12. What is the relation between MPC and multiplier? **(3)**

    Or

    What is the relation between MPS and multiplier?

13. How can government budget be helpful in altering the income distribution? Explain. **(4)**

14. "Balance of payments always balances". Discuss. **(4)**

    Or

    Explain 'revenue deficit' in a government budget? What does it indicate?

15. Distinguish between voluntary unemployment and involuntary unemployment. **(4)**

16. Explain the concept of inflationary gap. Explain the role of repo rate in reducing this gap. **(6)**

17. From the following data, calculate national income by (a) income method, and (b) expenditure method. **(6)**

	(₹ in crores)
(a) Private final consumption expenditure	2,000
(b) Net capital formation	400
(c) Change in stock	50
(d) Compensation of employees	1,900
(e) Rent	200
(f) Interest	150
(g) Operating surplus	720
(h) Net indirect taxes	400
(i) Employee's contribution to S.S. schemes	100
(j) Net exports	20
(k) Net factor income from abroad	(–)20
(l) Government final consumption expenditure	600
(m) Consumption of fixed capital	100

Or

Giving reasons, state whether the following statements are true or false.

(a) Real gross domestic product can be equal to nominal gross domestic product.

(b) Savings are a stock.

(c) Butter is only a final product.

SECTION B (INDIAN ECONOMIC DEVELOPMENT)

18. Land reforms were the most successful in: **(1)**

(a) Kerala (b) Tamil Nadu

(c) West Bengal (d) Both (a) and (c)

19. State whether the following statement is true or false **(1)**

'The prime reason for educated unemployment is lack of vocational training.'

20. From the set of statements given in column I and Column II, match the following: **(1)**

Column I	Column II
a. Reduction in Industrial Licencing	(i) Financial Sector reforms
b. Origin of Private Banks	(ii) Industrial Sector reform
c. Devaluation of Rupee	(iii) Trade policy reforms
d. Removal of export duties	(iv) Foreign Exchange reforms

21. Identify the two major environmental issues facing the world. **(1)**

22. Schedule A, B, C are classification of industries based on: **(1)**

(a) Ownership (b) Inputs used

(c) Size of the firm (d) Number of workers

Or

The partition of India after the Britishers left, made India lose its valuable ________ areas to Bangladesh:

(a) Cotton (b) Jute

(c) Sugarcane (d) Rice

23. Which of the following countries has the lowest expectancy at birth: **(1)**

(a) Pakistan (b) China

(c) India (d) None of the above

24. ________ city (is a part of the state), have the highest literacy rate in India. **(1)**

25. Great Leap forward Campaign was initiated by: **(1)**

(a) Xi Jinping (b) Mao Zedong

(c) Fa Xian (d) Liang Qichao

26. What is meant by casualisation of workforce? **(1)**

27. The effects of Ozone depletion do not include: **(1)**

(a) Skin cancer (b) Cataract

(c) Sunburn (d) Bleeding nose

28. What were some of the challenges and risks involved in Green Revolution: **(3)**

29. List down any 2 major environmental crises that the world is facing today. Name any one international treaty signed to cater to each. **(3)**

Or

The level of education of women in urban areas is higher than rural areas but employment rate is comparatively low? Why do you think such is the case?

30. Distinguish between conventional and non- conventional sources of energy. **(4)**

Or

What are the challenges to organic farming?

31. How do China, India and Pakistan stand on the education related indicators? **(4)**

32. Which of the following cannot be considered a worker and why? **(4)**

(a) A child of 10 years serving tea in a restaurant

(b) A mother cooking for her child

(c) A woman running a salon at her home

(d) An engineer working in Google

33. What was the Industrial Policy Resolution, 1956? **(6)**

34. Highlight some factors leading to land degradation. **(6)**

Or

The Indian Scenario Health Care Funding

Sector	Population	
	Urban	Rural
Public (75-90% state govt.)	23.5%	30.6%
Private	74.8%	66.2%

Public & Private Sector Shares in Service Delivery

Source: National Family Health Survey.

Analyse the given data and highlight the growing emergence of private sector in the provision of healthcare services.

SOLUTIONS TO SAMPLE PAPER 7

SECTION A (MACROECONOMICS)

1. Narrow

2. (c) Estimated expenditure and estimated revenues

3. Inflationary gap measures the extent to which the current aggregate demand is in excess of the aggregate demand required to achieve full employment level of ouptput.

4. (a) real GDP

Or

(c) Depreciation

5. It records the international transactions which affect the assets and liabilities of the domestic country with the rest of the world.

6. ex-ante investment **7.** True **8.** 35,000

9. a. (ii), b. (i), c. (iv), d. (iii)

10. (c) S = 1

11. Intermediate consumption = (a) – [(e) + (d) – (c) + (b)]

= 4,000 – [3,200 + 60 – 20 + 80]

= ₹ 680 lakhs

12. Multiplier (k) = $\frac{1}{1 - MPC}$

The relation between MPC and multiplier is direct *i.e.* higher the MPC, higher the multiplier. This can be shown in schedule below:

MPC	K
0	1
0.25	1.33
0.50	2
0.75	4

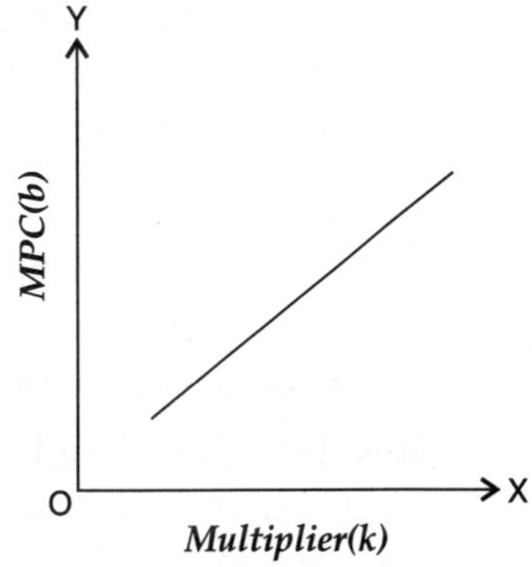

The above schedule illustrates the direct relation between MPC and multiplier.

Or

$$\text{Multiplier (k)} = \frac{1}{\text{MPS}}$$

The relation between MPS and multiplier is inverse *i.e.* higher the MPS, lower will be the multiplier. This can be shown in the following schedule:

MPS	Multiplier
0.25	4
0.50	2
0.75	1.33
1	1

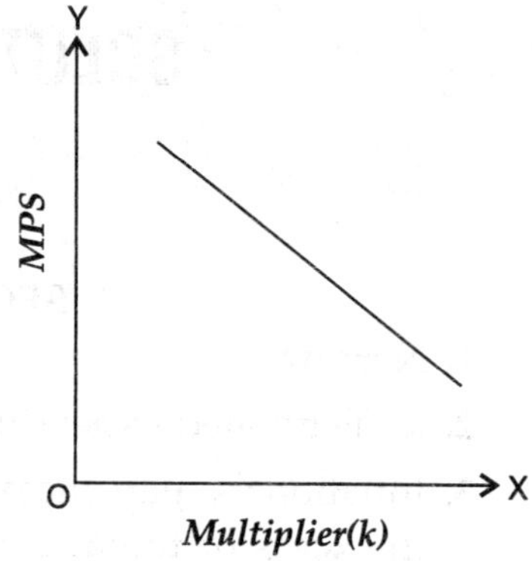

The above schedule illustrates the inverse relationship between MPS and multiplier.

13. Through the budget, the government may affect the pattern of redistribution of income. The government can change income distribution through fiscal measures such as taxation, subsidies, public expenditure etc. The government can levy more taxes on higher income group people thereby reducing their income and spending the same for the welfare activities relating to poor people. This will reduce income of the rich and rise the standard of living of the poor.

14. Generally, balance of payments of a country always remain in balance. This can be understood in the following two manners:

(a) **Balance of payment in accounting sense:** In the accounting sense, balance of a payments of a country always balance. Because balance of payment accounts are prepared on the basis of double entry system. Under this system receipts side is always equal to the payments side.

(b) **Balance of payment in operating sense:** Practically it is not necessary that BOP may always be balanced initially. When current account is in deficit or surplus then the balance is restored with the help of capital account in form of accommodating items. In this way balance of payment is always balanced through capital account transactions. Thus from the above discussion it can be said that overall balance of payments always balances.

Or

Revenue deficit is equal to the excess of total revenue expenditure over the total revenue receipts. In short:

Revenue deficit = Total revenue expenditure – Total revenue receipts

Revenue deficit indicates the extra revenue expenditure which cannot be met by revenue receipts. If revenue expenditure increases without a corresponding increase in the revenue receipts, revenue deficit increases and this increases the liability of the government.

15. **Voluntary unemployment** refers to the situation when a person does not want to work at the prevailing wage rate in the market even though suitable work is available for him. This unemployment is not considered while estimating the unemployment in the economy.

Involuntary unemployment refers to the situation, when all the able and willing persons are willing to work but do not get work. This unemployment is considered while estimating the size of unemployment.

16. At full employment income level, when AD is higher than AS, the excess of AD over AS is called excess demand. Due to excess demand, an inflationary gap is created. Inflationary gap is the extent to which current aggregate demand is more than the aggregate demand required to achieve the full employment level of equilibrium.

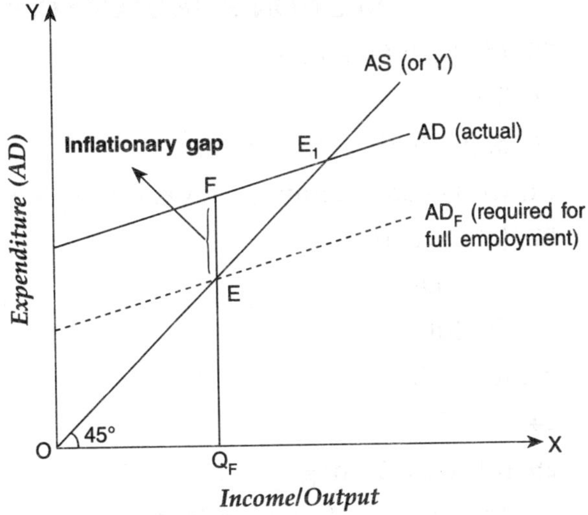

When AD is greater than AS at full employment, producers overutilise resources to meet the excess demand. As a result, demand for inputs increases, leading to rise in the price of inputs. Due to rise in costs, producers raise the prices of the products they produce. This leads to inflation in the economy.

Repo Rate (Increase in Repo Rate): Repo rate refers to the rate at which the central bank lends money to commercial banks for short-term funds as the lender of the last resort. During excess demand, the central bank increases the repo rate which raises the cost of borrowings made by commercial banks. Thus, demand for credit decreases which in turn reduces money supply by correcting excess demand in the market.

17. **National Income by income method**

NNP_{FC} = 1900 + 720 – 20

= ₹ 2600 crores

National Income by expenditure method

NNP_{FC} = 2000 + 400 + 20 + 600 + (–20) – 400

= ₹ 2600 crores

Or

(a) The statement is true. Real gross domestic product and nominal gross domestic product will be equal if price level remains constant.

(b) The statement is false. Savings are always with reference to a time period. In other words, saving is a flow.

(c) The statement is false. Butter is only a final product when purchased by households for consumption. Butter purchased by bakeries for making cakes is not a final product. Butter is an intermediate good as it is used as raw material for further production by bakeries.

SECTION B (INDIAN ECONOMIC DEVELOPMENT)

18. (d) Both (a) and (c)

19. True

20. a. (ii), b. (i), c. (iv), d. (iii)

21. (i) Global warming, (ii) Ozone depletion

22. (a) Ownership

Or

(b) Jute

23. (c) India

24. Cochin

25. (b) Mao Zedong

26. The process of moving from self employment and regular employment to casual wage work is known as casualisation of workforce.

27. (d) Bleeding nose

28.
- **Fear and skepticism:** As the green revolution strategy required a long gestation period, it almost yielded the result after a decade – there was uncertainty whether the expensive seeds bought would benefit in the requisite proportion.
- **Pest attack:** The HYV seeds were more prone to an attack by insects, pests and rodents and there always remained a risk of losing everything in the crop season to such things.
- **Regional variation:** During the course of the production activities, some regions like Punjab, Haryana and Andhra Pradesh prospered more as compared to the rest of the regions. This resulted in disparities across states.

29. Global Warming and Ozone depletion: Global warming refers to the gradual heating of the earth's surface by the greenhouse gases. Ozone depletion is the thinning of the Ozone layer caused by the action of chlorine and bromine compounds. Montreal protocol was signed to take measure against ozone depletion. Earth summit was held to reach a solution for Global Warming.

Or

According to me, following are some of the reasons:

- There is a movement of rural men from the villages to the cities in search of better employment opportunities. That is why, the women have to take care of the fields and perform the hard labour back home.
- Married women or pregnant women in urban areas can afford to discontinue work for a short while as they have the means to sustain, even without the salary of that absent period. But women in rural areas are mostly engaged in agricultural activities, which requires continuous tending or else the crop will be affected.
- Urban women look for the appropriate job to suit their qualification and comfort as there is wide variety of opportunities but in rural areas, the choices are limited. So, it has to earn a livelihood, she has to engage with it.

30.

Conventional	Non-conventional
(a) These resources have been the traditional methods of energy production and are non-renewable.	These are the new age ways of producing energy which are abundant in nature and renewable.
(b) They pollute the environment and hence a need to find non-conventional sources was realized.	They are cleaner fuels and promote sustainable development.
(c) They are relatively cheaper in monetary terms but the externalities are large. (i.e. the damage done to environment would require heavy expenditure to manage it and hence the costs are high in long term)	The installation cost is high but after that there are only returns.
Eg.– coal, petroleum and natural gas	Eg- solar energy, wind energy

Or

- Marketing and distribution are not efficient because organic food is both produced and consumed in smaller amounts. It is not a food of the masses due to the expenses.
- The shelf life of organic food is less and hence it cannot be stored for long in government granaries to meet times of crises.
- There is inadequate infrastructure to support organic farming which requires techniques such as biological pest control. The green manure or vermi-composting, which is produced at household level will take time to get commercialised.
- Production costs are higher in organic farming because farmers need more workers as compared to conventional farming. Therefore, they incur lesser profits.

31. All the 3 countries have seen improvements in the education sector. Following is an analysis of their performance:

- In adult literacy rate, which includes 15-year old's and above, China has the highest percentage, followed by Pakistan and then, India.
- China performs the best on the indicator of mean years of schooling too, followed by India and Pakistan.
- This shows that China outperforms India and Pakistan on both parameters. There is marginal difference between India and Pakistan in adult literacy rate > having 66% and 67% respectively.
- This shows that though all the countries began their development journey around the same time, China has taken over but not just economic terms but also in the field of human capital formation.

32. (a) Not a worker because people below 15 years or beyond 60 years are not considered a part of the labour pool.

(b) Not a worker because actions of love are not given remuneration and thus cannot be estimated by the statistics of India. However, it is often counted that such actions should be considered labour, and their proportional value be accounted for in GDP.

(c) Worker

(d) Worker

33. Main features of the industrial policy of 1956 were:

Categorisation of industries:

(a) **Public Sector:** Under Schedule A, 17 industries were included. These industries were to be exclusively owned by the government like arms and ammunition, atomic energy, iron and steel, heavy machinery, mineral oil, coal etc.

(b) **Public-cum-private sector:** Under Schedule B, 12 industries were given space. Industry will be state owned but private sector can also own industry in partnership. Example—aluminium, machine tools, drugs, chemical fertilizer, road and sea transport, mines and minerals.

(c) **Private sector:** Under Schedule C, all remaining industries not covered in A and B Schedule were included. These industries will be established by private sector.

- Measures were taken up to develop the cottage industries of indigenous skills like carpet making, shawls industry, basket weaving, etc.
- The backward regions would be the prime focus of the establishment of new factories and industries so regional development parity can be ensured.
- Management courses will be made part of the Indian education system by opening more universities providing qualification of the same. This was done because it was realized that efficient managers are needed to run the industries.

- Better working conditions to labour would be provided like security, protection against hazardous materials, increase in pay scale, etc.

34. Some factors leading to land degradation are:

- **Over extraction of resources:** The extraction of resources from land at a rate faster than their rate of replenishment lads to severe damage. For example—the extraction of coal through shaft mining, not only leads to pollution and displacement of people but also becomes the cause of landslides and earthquakes.
- **Ineffective agricultural practices:** Practices like crop rotation and multi cropping are still not popular which leads to the sowing of a single crop in the season. Due to this, nutrients are lost from the soil and have to be replenished by using chemical fertilisers.
- **Slash and burn agriculture:** This type of agriculture which involves abandoning the land after it is no more in use leads to significant soil erosion, as without trees and vegetation and their root systems, soil washes away during heavy rains and blows away during droughts.
- Use of **insecticides and pesticides** also alters the salinity or the alkalinity of the soil, rendering it unfit for usage.
- **Overgrazing:** This leads to a reduced growth of vegetation, thereby leading to soil erosion.
- **Deforestation:** The roots of tress hold the soil the together from getting blown away or washing down. Felling of trees is a serious cause of land degradation.

Or

- Initially, when India was in its infant stages, private sectors started acting complementary to the public sector, but in the course of time, they started sprouting their facilities across the country with affordable services.
- Today, it accounts for 82% of outpatient visits and 585 of inpatient expenditure
- Many private institutions have also come up, which provide world class training and facilities to students, alongside government universities to meet the widening ratio of doctor and patients.
- India has hence become a lucrative destination for medical tourism and people from all around the world flock here to avail the best of the facilities.
- The private healthcare providers are consistently adopting new and advanced technologies to offer better quality healthcare services to the consumers.
- Despite the suspicions of the people that many private providers of health care perform unnecessary tests and procedures, Indians are choosing private sector in overwhelming numbers.
- Today, the situation is such that private sector attracts about 75% of the population as against 23.5% in public sector in urban areas.

SAMPLE PAPER 8
(WITH SOLUTIONS)

Time allowed: 3 hours | *Maximum marks: 80*

General Instructions:

1. ***All** the questions in **both** the sections are **compulsory**. Marks for questions are indicated against each question.*
2. *Question number **1-10** and **18-27** are very short-answer questions carrying **1 mark** each. They are required to be answered in one word or one sentence each.*
3. *Question number **11-12** and **28-29** are short-answer questions caring **3 marks** each. Answers to them should not normally exceed **60-80 words** each.*
4. *Question number **13-15** and **30-32** are also short-answer questions carrying **4 marks** each. Answers to them should not normally exceed **80-100 words** each.*
5. *Question number **16-17** and **33-34** are long answer questions carrying **6 marks** each. Answers to them should not normally exceed **100-150 words** each.*
6. *Answer **should be brief** and **to the point** and the above **word limit be adhered** to as far as possible.*

SECTION A (MACROECONOMICS)

1. The minimum percentage of a bank's total deposits which is required to be kept with the RBI is called __________. **(1)**

2. Define revenue deficit in government budget. **(1)**

3. From the set of statements given in column I and Column II, match the following: **(1)**

Column I	Column II
a. Borrowings	(i) Revenue expenditure
b. Repayment of Loan	(ii) Revenue receipts
c. Payment of Interest	(iii) Capital expenditure
d. Fees and fines	(iv) Capital receipts

4. Net National Product at factor cost is also known as **(1)**

(a) Net Domestic Product (b) Gross Domestic Product
(c) National Income (d) Personal Income

Or

Indian ships operated between India and Japan are included in the domestic territory of

(a) India (b) Japan
(c) India and Japan both (d) Neither India nor Japan

5. State the relationship between exchange rate and demand of foreign exchange? **(1)**

6. If MPS is one then MPC is __________. **(1)**

7. The difference between value of visible exports and value of visible imports is called **(1)**

(a) BOP (b) BOT
(c) Balance of current account (d) Balance of capital account

8. State whether the following statement is true or false **(1)**

Fiscal deficit = Budget deficit + Borrowings

9. State two producers of money according to the concept of money supply. **(1)**

10. Average propensity to consume means **(1)**

(a) tendency of the consumer towards higher consumption
(b) ratio of total consumption to total income
(c) level of income at which consumption expenditure is equal to income
(d) additional income to be spent on consumption

11. Find National Income from the following: **(3)**

Autonomous consumption = ₹ 100
Marginal propensity to consume = 0.60
Investment = ₹ 200

Or

How should following items be treated in the estimation of National Income?

(a) Interest paid on loan taken to buy a personal car
(b) Transport expenses paid by a firm
(c) Salaries to Indian residents working in American Embassy in India

12. How can distribution of income be a limitation of using gross domestic product as an index of welfare? Explain. **(3)**

13. Explain briefly qualitative methods which a central bank may adopt for controlling the volume of credit. **(4)**

14. "Many domestic investors are likely to invest in Japanese market." How will this affect the: **(4)**

(a) foreign exchange rate (b) Current A/c deficit of India.

Or

The government of India has recently launched the 'Jan Dhan Yojna' which is aimed at every household in the country to have at least one bank account. Explain how deposits made under the plan are going to affect the national income of the country.

15. One day a shopkeeper sold goods worth ₹ 600 plus GST of ₹ 200 to a consumer. The consumer bought the good and went home. Later in the day he received a notice from the Income Tax department regarding the payment of income tax. He was confused between GST and Income Tax. Explain the different types of taxes mentioned above. **(4)**

16. Mukesh Ambani, in his receipt speech, quoted " The trend of digitalisation and the desire to end the digital poverty in India led to creation of Jio". **(6)**

Reliance Jio is the world's largest start up with initial investment of ₹ 1,00,000 crore in India.

On the basis of the above information, calculate the following by assuming the people of India have a tendency to consume ¼ portion of their additional income. Change in the level of consumption and change in the level of saving as a result of the above mentioned Initial Investment.

17. Giving reasons, explain how should the following be treated in the estimation of national income: **(6)**

(a) Expenditure by a firm on payment of fees to a chartered accountant.

(b) Payment of corporate tax by a firm.

(c) Purchase of refrigerator by a firm for its own use.

Or

Calculate GNP at FC (a) by income method, and (b) expenditure method from the following:

	(₹ in crores)
(a) Private final consumption expenditure	800
(b) Government final consumption expenditure	300
(c) Compensation of employees	600
(d) Net imports	50
(e) Gross domestic capital formation	150
(f) Consumption of fixed capital	20
(g) Net indirect taxes	100
(h) Net factor income from abroad	(–)70
(i) Dividend	150
(j) Rent	120
(k) Interest	80
(l) Undistributed profit	80
(m) Social security contribution by employees	60
(n) Corporate tax	50

SECTION B (INDIAN ECONOMIC DEVELOPMENT)

18. State any two objections of 5 year plans. **(1)**

19. _________ is the main reason for soil erosion: **(1)**

(a) Cutting trees (b) Global warming
(c) Ozone depletion (d) Watering the plants

Or

Which among the following is a renewable source of energy?

(i) solar energy (ii) wind energy (iii) natural gas

(a) Only (i) (b) Both (i) and (ii)
(c) (i), (ii) and (iii) (d) none of the above

20. From the set of statements given in column I and Column II, match the following: **(1)**

Column I	Column II
a. Unemployed people	(i) Able people not getting work
b. Open unemployment	(ii) Labour force (–) Work force
c. Disguised unemployment	(iii) Working for one self
d. Self employment	(iv) More people engaged than required

21. The newly emerging jobs are found mostly in _________ sector. **(1)**

22. The low productivity in agriculture forced India to import food grains from _________ . **(1)**

23. State whether the following statement is true or false **(1)**

'The main aim of comparing countries is to learn from the developmental experiences of other countries.'

24. Which of the following is a major source of human capital formation in a country? **(1)**

(a) Expenditure on education
(b) Expenditure on information
(c) Expenditure on national security
(d) Expenditure on makeup and grooming

25. Special Economic Zones are set up with an aim to: **(1)**

(a) Have sole areas dedicated to production
(b) To attract foreign investors
(c) To not disturb the lives of people in central country
(d) To earn more tariff on imports

26. State whether the following statement is true or false **(1)**

'The incidence of poverty is greater in rural areas.'

27. Reforms in China were introduced in the year _________. **(1)**

28. What are the Central problems of an economy which led to the need of 'PLANNING'? **(3)**

29. There is a close relationship between physical and human capital and they heavily depend on each other. How? **(3)**

Or

Describe fisheries as a non-farm activity.

30. Why is education so important if one can get a decent job without it and fend for oneself as well as the family? **(4)**

Or

What is environment? What are the various functions performed by it?

31. Explain the 'Great Leap Forward' policy of China. **(4)**

32. What is the importance of Human Capital formation? **(4)**

33.

Study the image and write a note on the concept being depicted here. **(6)**

34. Briefly explain the three-dimensional attack on poverty adopted by the government. **(6)**

Or

What are some of the ways by which electricity can be used judiciously?

SOLUTIONS TO SAMPLE PAPER 8

SECTION A (MACROECONOMICS)

1. CRR

2. It is the excess of revenue expenditure over revenue receipts of the government.

3. a. (iv), b. (iii), c. (i), d. (ii)

4. (c) National Income

Or

(a) India

5. Inverse relation

6. Zero

7. (b) BOT

8. True

9. (i) Government, (ii) The banking system

10. (b) ratio of total consumption to total income

11. Given: Autonomous consumption $(\overline{C}) = 100$

MPC (b) = 0.60

Investment (I) = 200

$\therefore$ Income (y) $= \overline{C} + by + I$

$= 100 + 0.6y + 200$

$\Rightarrow \quad y(1 - 0.6) = 100 + 200 = 300$

$\Rightarrow \quad y(0.4) = 300$

$$\Rightarrow \quad y = 300 \times \frac{10}{40}$$

$\therefore \quad y = ₹\ 750$

Therefore National Income is ₹ 750.

Or

(a) It is a part of private expenditure and therefore it is included in National Income.

(b) These are not included in National Income because these are intermediate costs.

(c) It will be included in National Income because it is factor income earned from abroad.

12. It is to be seen as to how the increase in national income is distributed. If national income rises, it is not necessary that income of each individual rises in the same proportion. Individual incomes may rise in different proportions. In some cases, it may fall. In other words, inequalities may rise. Rise in inequalities in income may adversely affect the economic welfare of the society. Therefore, for ascertaining the effect of increase in national income, it has to be seen whether it increases income inequalities or reduces income inequalities.

13. Following are the qualitative methods of credit control:

(a) **Margin requirements:** Margin is the difference between the value of security and the amount of loan. For example, if against a loan of ₹ 100 lakhs, bank keeps a security of ₹ 120 lakhs, then in this case, the margin is ₹ 20 lakhs.

If margin requirement increases, then borrowings will come down because now, the borrower has to keep more amount of security with the bank which discourages him to procure loans from the bank. In this way, the central bank can affect the volume of credit in the economy by increasing margin requirements.

(b) **Moral suasion:** In the best interests of economy, the central bank of a country may call upon commercial banks or financial intermediates to curb their loan operations. This is called as moral suasion. These requests are not directives, they are mere requests.

(c) **Credit Rationing:** In this method, the central bank can give directions to the commercial banks not to give credit for certain purposes or to a particular sector.

14. (a) As we know, the domestic investors are liking to invest in Japanese market, the demand for foreign exchange will increase which is shown by rightward shift of demand curve from DD to D_1D_1. This will further lead to increase in price of foreign exchange rate and quantity demanded of foreign exchange. This also indicates depreciation of domestic currency.

(b) As the investors would increase the investment, income from Japan will also rise which would help in reducing the current A/c deficit.

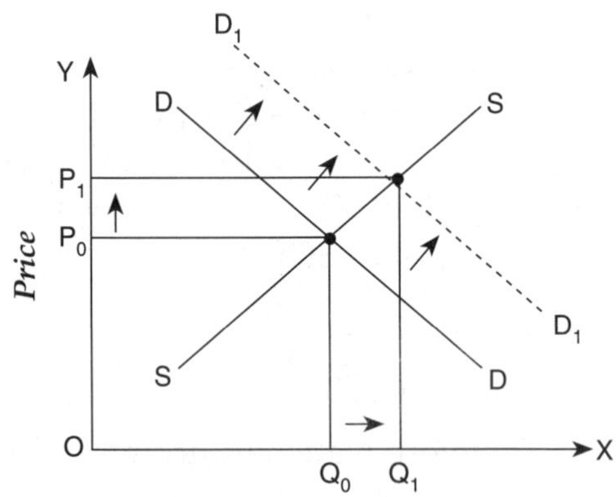

Quantity demanded and supplied of foreign exchange

Or

The Jan Dhan Yojna will result in an increase in the number of deposits with the banks. Banks in turn will be able to create more credit as shown below:

Credit creation can be explained with the help of the following illustration:

	Deposits	Loans	Cash reserves
Initial	1,000	800	200
I Round	800	640	160
II Round	640	512	128
.	.	.	.
.	.	.	.
.	.	.	.
.	.	.	.
.	.	.	.
	5,000	**4,000**	**1,000**

Let us assume that there is a fresh deposit of ₹ 1,000 by the Jan Dhan Yojna and LRR is 20%. As required, the banks keep 20% *i.e.* ₹ 200 as cash and lend the remaining ₹ 800. Those who borrow, use this money for making payments. As assumed, those who receive payments put the money back into the banks. In this way, banks receive fresh deposits of ₹ 800. The banks again keep 20% *i.e.* ₹ 160 as cash and lend ₹ 640, which is also 80% of the last deposits. The money again comes back to the banks leading to a fresh deposit of ₹ 640. The money goes on multiplying in this way, and ultimately, the total money creation is:

$$\text{Total money creation} = \text{Initial deposit} \times \frac{1}{\text{LRR}} \times 100$$

$$= 1000 \times \frac{1}{20\%} = ₹\ 5{,}000$$

Due to increase in credit creation, more investment will take place which will increase national income in the country.

15. The two types of taxes mentioned above are direct tax and indirect tax.

- GST is an indirect tax as the burden of tax and liability falls on different persons. It is imposed on goods and services.
- Income tax is a direct tax as the liability to pay and burden of tax falls on the same person. It is imposed on persons.

16. Initial investment = ₹ 1,00,000 crores

$$\text{MPC} = \frac{1}{4} \text{ or } 0.25$$

$$K = \frac{1}{1 - MPC}$$

$$K = \frac{1}{1 - 0.25} = \frac{1}{0.75} = 1.3\overline{3} \text{ i.e. } 1.34 \text{ (approx)}$$

$$K = \frac{\Delta Y}{\Delta I}$$

$$= 1.34 = \frac{\Delta Y}{1,00,000}$$

ΔY = ₹ 1,34,000 crores

ΔC = ₹ 33,500 crores

ΔS = ₹ 1,00,500 crores

17. (a) Expenditure by a firm on payment of fees to a chartered accountant will be intermediate consumption for the firm as the services of the chartered accountant are used in the process of producing the final output of the firm.

(b) Payment of corporate tax by a firm is not included in the national income as it is a transfer made from the firm to the government. However, corporate tax as a part of profits is included in finding out the income generated by the firm.

(c) Purchase of refrigerator by a firm for its own use is included as a part of gross domestic fixed capital formation in the expenditure method of measuring national income as refrigerator is a capital good for the firm.

Or

(a) GNP at FC (*Income method*)

= (c) + (f) + (h) + (i) – (j) + (k) + (l) + (n)

= 600 + 20 + (–70) + 150 + 120 + 80 + 80 + 50

= ₹ 1,030 crores

(b) GNP at FC (*Expenditure method*)

= (a) + (b) + (d) + (e) – (g) + (h)

= 800 + 300 + (–50) + 150 – 100 + (–70)

= ₹ 1,030 crores

SECTION B (INDIAN ECONOMIC DEVELOPMENT)

18. Growth and self reliance

19. (a) Cutting trees

Or

(c) (i), (ii) and (iii)

20. a. (ii), b. (i), c. (iv), d. (iii)

21. Service

22. USA

23. True
24. (a) Expenditure on education
25. (b) To attract foreign investors
26. True
27. 1978
28. The central problems of an economy are:
    - **What to produce:** This refers to the choice of goods and services to be produced and in what quantity.
    - **How to produce:** This refers to the choice of the method of production. Economies which have abundance of labour opt for labour intensive technology generally and the developed countries use capital intensive technology
    - **For whom to produce:** This refers to the section of people for whom the goods and services should be produces and it decided based upon the purchasing capacity. One can also refer to it as the distribution of output among different sections of the population.
29. - Physical capital includes the tangible resources like land, water bodies, etc. whereas human capital refers to the intellect, creativity and skills of the individual.
    - Any physical capital can run more efficiently if human resource operates on it. For example: a piece of land can develop into a factory or a park.
    - Similarly, to induce human resource in order to transform into human capital, adequate physical capital is required as infrastructure so that their potential is realized to the maximum. For example—a cricket player can polish his skills if he gets to play in a well-maintained stadium.

    Or

    Fisheries refer to the catching, processing and marketing of the fish or other aquatic animals.
    - It has emerged as a lucrative sector of employment and contributes significantly to the GDP. A lot of women also find jobs in this sector.
    - West Bengal. Kerala, Karnataka, Andhra Pradesh, Maharashtra are important centers of fishing and produce a lot of output. It is then transported to the interiors of the country.
    - Although, fish is the most consumed product of fisheries, other animals like crabs, prawns are also gaining popularity.
30. It is true that employment can be sought, without going to schools or universities. In fact, many brilliant minds have self-taught themselves or have dropped out from college.
    - It is no hidden fact that educational qualification can place you in better paying job opportunities.

- Moreover, education is necessary not just to earn a living but because it generally makes you better at the game of life. Your understanding widens and your ability to understand the changes taking place in the world increases.
- On the other hand, education is not obtained just to earn money in future. It gives you self-satisfaction and self-worth.
- It engages you in a productive activity and your time is spent fruitfully.
- It makes you meet new people when you attend schools or universities, gather new ideas, see new developments and is an enriching experience.
- Therefore, education is necessary, irrespective of the fact whether you want to be employed or not. And if one is employed, it is not only the monetary satisfaction but a lot of other things that come with it.

Or

The sum total of all surroundings of a living organism, including natural forces and other living things is called environment.

It includes the biotic and the abiotic components. Biotic component refers to the living part like human beings, animals etc. while the abiotic component refers to the non-living things like sunlight, rain and so on.

The functions of environment:

- **Source:** It provides multiple resources like oil, coal, wood, honey, medicinal plants, lac, gum, etc. A major part of the environment are plants and trees which provide the life-giving oxygen.
- **Sink:** The environment has a self-cleansing capacity like river cleans itself upto an extent. It relates to the absorption of the wastes and pollution produced by production and human life
- **Service:** Provision of the environmental or ecosystem services that support life without requiring human action, for example, climatic stability, biodiversity, ecosystem integrity and protection from ultraviolet radiation.
- **Spiritual:** The intrinsic recreational, psychological, aesthetic and spiritual value of environments

31.
- The Great Leap Forward was a campaign by the communist leader, Mao Zedong to change China from a predominantly agrarian (farming) society to a modern and industrial society.
- It was intended to reduce the dependence of China on other countries for its capita goods. That is why, people were encouraged to set up industries in their backyards.
- Communes or a collectivised system was developed. All work was shared on the communes; from childcare to cooking, daily tasks were done collectively.
- However, the ambitious campaign was not successful. Over just a few years, the Great Leap Forward also caused massive environmental damage in China.

- The backyard steel production plan resulted in households often melting useful metal items since they had to meet quotas of steel production from their backyard.
- The Great Leap Forward was supposed to be a five-year plan, but it was called off after just three tragic years, also known as the "Three Bitter Years" in China.

32. Human resource, on getting better education, health facilities, awareness and recognition transforms into human capital. The process of human capital formation is important because:

- Human capital makes use of physical capital efficiently through their skill and knowledge. This is how economies prosper, not through standing lands and abundant resources but by putting them to use judiciously.
- Education and training bring changes in the attitudes and perception of people. They acquire better problem-solving skills and the decision-making ability enhances.
- Human capital is sought by all leading firms. A country which invests in human capital formation has lower rates of unemployment as its people are demanded by employers all over the world.
- Quality of life improves. Better health leads to greater life expectancy, lower incidence of diseases and being able to lead a more fulfilling life. Moreover, human capital formation makes people more creative and this results in a life of self-worth and satisfaction.

33. The picture shown depicts the institution of small scale industries in India. Following are some of the features which characterise them:

- Essentially the small-scale industries are generally comprised of those industries which manufacture, produce and render services with the help of small machines and less manpower. They are generally defined by the maximum investment allowed on assets.
- They are also called cottage industry.
- They use labour intensive techniques and manpower for the production of goods and services. In fact, the labour is also not hired on large scale and many a times, household labour is used.
- The objectives of the small-scale industries are to generate employment opportunities and develop the rural and backward regions of the country.
- A rough figure of ₹ 1 crore can be invested in plant and machinery of the SSI.
- These enterprises account for almost 40% of the total production of goods and services in India and contribute significantly to the export basket.
- Example—small toy, papads, bindi making, etc.

34. The government has attacked on poverty from 3 different areas:

- **The trickle-down approach:** During the initial years after independence, developmental strides were made in industry and agriculture. It was thought that the benefits arising from these sectors would trickery down to the poorest of the poor. However, it was often seen that the benefits were captured by the rich and the landowning class, while the poor continued to suffer.
- **The assimilation approach:** Due to the inadequacy of the trickle-down approach to reach the target group, a more cohesive approach was adopted. This mainly included poverty alleviation programmes so that the poor can be uplifted to assimilate with the society. It included self-employment and wage employment generation schemes. Some of the very popular ones are MNREGA, Food for Work programme, Prime Minister's Rozgar Yojana etc.

  Finally, after it was believed that improvement in living conditions cannot be achieved only through providing monetary security. Therefore, social welfare was given prime importance and education, health, clean drinking water, etc., came to the force. This was based on the Capabilities approach of Amartya Sen, one of our greatest economists who stressed the importance of social indicators. This led to formulation of schemes like Right to education, Midday meal scheme and so on.

Or

Power is a very important resource for any economy to function. Following are some of the ways to save it:

- Switching off lights and fans when not in use.
- Using Compact Fluorescent lights (CFL) in place of the regular lights. Using LED bulbs in place of regular bulbs.
- Using appliances with 5 stars marking on them.
- Phantom loads, or the electricity used by electronics when they are turned off or in standby mode, are a major source of energy waste. Power strips, also known as advanced power strips, eliminate the problem of phantom loads by shutting off the power to electronics when they are not in use.
- At the community level, we can ensure that street lights are switched off in the morning as a lot of times they remain on.
- Installing solar panels in schools, colleges and homes.
- Sensitising people towards the need to save electricity.

SAMPLE PAPER 9 (WITH SOLUTIONS)

Time allowed: 3 hours *Maximum marks: 80*

General Instructions:

1. ***All** the questions in **both** the sections are **compulsory**. Marks for questions are indicated against each question.*
2. *Question number **1-10** and **18-27** are very short-answer questions carrying **1 mark** each. They are required to be answered in one word or one sentence each.*
3. *Question number **11-12** and **28-29** are short-answer questions caring **3 marks** each. Answers to them should not normally exceed **60-80 words** each.*
4. *Question number **13-15** and **30-32** are also short-answer questions carrying **4 marks** each. Answers to them should not normally exceed **80-100 words** each.*
5. *Question number **16-17** and **33-34** are long answer questions carrying **6 marks** each. Answers to them should not normally exceed **100-150 words** each.*
6. *Answer **should be brief** and **to the point** and the above **word limit be adhered** to as far as possible.*

SECTION A (MACROECONOMICS)

1. Money supply consists of **(1)**

(a) currency (b) deposit

(c) both currency and deposit (d) none of the above

2. When the burden of tax is shifted on other it is called _________. **(1)**

3. State two components of aggregate supply. **(1)**

4. Which of the following is a flow variable? **(1)**

(a) Consumption (b) Wealth

(c) Quantity of money (d) None of these

Or

GDP is greater than GNP when

(a) NFIA is positive (b) NFIA is negative

(c) Net exports is positive (d) Net exports is greater than NFIA

5. From the set of statements given in column I and Column II, match the following: **(1)**

Column I	Column II
a. Consumption (+) Savings	(i) Net factor income from abroad
b. National product (–) Domestic product	(ii) Depreciation
c. Market Price (–) Factor Cost	(iii) National Income
d. Gross investment (–) Net Investment	(iv) Net indirect tax

6. The value of MPC will be __________ if $\Delta C = \Delta Y$ **(1)**

7. Disequilibrium in balance of payments (BOP) means **(1)**
   (a) surplus balance of payments (b) deficit balance of payment
   (c) both (a) and (b) (d) none of these

8. State whether the following statement is true or false **(1)**
   'Fiscal deficit is always inflationary in nature.'

9. Credit creation means creation of **(1)**
   (a) primary deposits (b) secondary deposits
   (c) time deposits (d) none of these

10. When aggregate demand is more than aggregate supply at full employment level, the situation is called __________. **(1)**

11. Estimate the value of ex-ante AD, when autonomous investment and consumption expenditure (A) is ₹ 50 crores, MPS is 0.2 and level of income is ₹ 300 crores. **(3)**

Or

Calculate Multiplier when MPC is $\frac{4}{5}$ and $\frac{1}{2}$. From the calculations establish the relation between size of Multiplier and size of MPC?

12. Use following information of an imaginary country: **(3)**

Year	2014-2015	2015-2016	2016-2017
Nominal GDP	6.5	8.4	9
GDP deflator	100	140	125

   (a) For which year is real GDP and nominal GDP same and why?
   (b) Calculate Real GDP for the given year. Is there any year for which Real GDP falls?

13. Elaborate 'economic growth' as an objective of government budget. **(4)**

14. How will 'Reserve Repo Rate' and 'Open Market Operations' control excess money supply in an economy? **(4)**

15. 'Devaluation and Depreciation of currency are one and the same thing'. Do you agree? How do they affect the exports of a country? **(4)**

Or

What is meant by 'official reserve transactions'? Discuss their importance in Balance of Payments.

16. State whether the following statements are true or false. Give valid reasons for your answers. **(6)**

(a) Unplanned inventories accumulate when planned investment is less than planned saving.

(b) Deflationary gap exists when aggregate demand is greater than aggregate supply at full employment level.

(c) Value of APS can never be negative.

17. (a) Define Externality **(6)**

(b) Find National Income from the following using expenditure method

Items	(₹) in Crores
(a) Current transfers from rest of the world	50
(b) Net Indirect taxes	100
(c) Net Exports	–25
(d) Rent	90
(e) Private Final Consumption Expenditure	900
(f) Net Domestic Capital Formation	200
(g) Compensation of Employees	500
(h) Net Factor Income from Abroad	–10
(i) Government Final Consumption Expenditure	400
(j) Profit	220
(k) Mixed Income of Self Employed	400
(l) Interest	230

Or

Will the following factor income be included in domestic factor of India? Give reasons for your answer:

(a) Compensation of employees to the resident of Japan working in Indian embassy in Japan.

(b) Payment of fees to a Chartered Accountant by a firm

(c) Rent received by an Indian resident from Russian embassy in India.

(d) Compensation given by insurance company to an injured worker.

SECTION B (INDIAN ECONOMIC DEVELOPMENT)

18. Define the term 'Outsourcing". **(1)**

19. Livestock farming is also known as: **(1)**

(a) Animal rearing (b) Animal husbandry

(c) Grazing (d) Dairying

20. State whether the following is true or false **(1)**

'P C Mahanalobis was the man behind Green Revolution?'

21. From the set of statements given in column I and Column II, match the following: **(1)**

Column I	Column II
a. Power is generated out of coal	(i) Nuclear Power
b. Power is generated from radio active elements	(ii) Thermal Power
c. Power is generated from water	(iii) Hydro power

22. Import substitution was operationalised because: **(1)**

(a) To protect our emerging and infant industries

(b) To minimize competition

(c) To make our economy prosper by manufacturing and consuming indigenously

(d) All of the above

Or

Which of the following is an odd one out?

(a) NABARD (b) Land Development Banks

(c) Landlords (d) Co-operative credit

23. Pakistan gained independence on _________. **(1)**

24. Which of the following is a scheme to "Save electricity." **(1)**

(a) UJALA (b) UJJWALA (c) MNREGA (d) URJA

25. China, India and Pakistan: all 3 are populous countries. China has the highest population; India ranks the second highest and Pakistan is _________ **(1)**

26. CPCB stands for _________. **(1)**

27. In times of distress like droughts and famines, the government comes forth to provide loans at a very low interest rate—which are called_________ **(1)**

(a) Lichchavi (b) Taccavi (c) BHIM (d) Madad

28. Give an account of infrastructural development under the British rule. Has it improved? **(3)**

Or

India has become a favourable destination for outsourcing of services from rest of the world. List down some possible reasons.

29. While trees are a renewable resource, forests are not. Explain. **(3)**

30. Highlight the distribution of labour based on gender. **(4)**

31. How do India, China and Pakistan perform on the indicators of human development. **(4)**

32. Despite the mushrooming of the formal institutions of rural credit, the rural banking and credit facilities face challenges. Elaborate. **(4)**

Or

Briefly discuss the Mahatma Gandhi National Rural Employment Guarantee Act (MNREGA), 2005.

33. The New Economic Policy, 1991 brought significant boost to the Indian economy, however there were some areas of criticism. mention the downfalls. **(6)**

34 Describe the state of India's environment. **(6)**

Or

Describe the Indian System of Medicine (AYUSH).

SOLUTIONS TO SAMPLE PAPER 9

SECTION A (MACROECONOMICS)

1. (c) both currency and deposit
2. indirect tax
3. (i) Consumption, (ii) Savings
4. (a) Consumption

Or

(b) NFIA is negative

5. a. (iii), b. (i), c. (iv), d. (ii)
6. one
7. (c) both (a) and (b)
8. False
9. (b) secondary deposits
10. excess demand
11.

$\overline{C}$ = ₹ 50 crores I = ₹ 50 crore

MPS = 0.2 MPS = 1 –MPC = 0.8

Y = ₹ 300 crore

We know, AD = C + I

AD = [50 + 0.8 × 300] + 50 ($\because C = \overline{C} + by$)

= 290 + 50 = 340

Or

We know, $MPC = \frac{4}{5}$ and $MPC = \frac{1}{2}$

$$K = \frac{1}{1 - MPC}$$

(i) Taking MPC as $\frac{4}{5}$,

$$K = \frac{1}{1 - \frac{4}{5}} = \frac{1}{\frac{1}{5}} = 5$$

(ii) Taking MPC as $\frac{1}{2}$,

$$K = \frac{1}{1-\frac{1}{2}} = \frac{1}{\frac{1}{2}} = 2.$$

∴ There is direct relationship between value of multiplier and MPC.

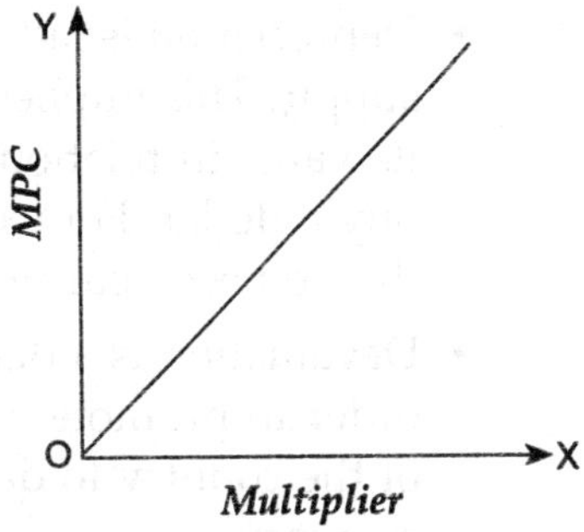

12. (a) For the base year the nominal and real GDP would be the same.

(b) $\text{Real GDP} = \frac{\text{Nominal GDP}}{\text{GDP deflator}} \times 100$

$$2014\text{–}15 = \frac{6.5}{100} \times 100 = 6.5$$

$$2015\text{–}16 = \frac{8.4}{140} \times 100 = 6$$

$$2016\text{–}17 = \frac{9}{125} \times 100 = 7.2$$

Therefore, we can observe that the Real GDP declined in the year 2015–16.

13. Economic growth means the increase in real GDP, that is, increase in value of goods and services produced in an economy. Budget helps in allocation of resources as follows:

- Government can provide subsidies to small scale manufacturers and encourage them to produce goods and services.
- Government expenditure plays at major role in creating demand and government can spend for welfare of the poor and enhance the resources of the economy.
- Government can use tax for collection of revenue so that it can be used for the welfare of the society.

14. 'Reverse repo rate' and open market operation can be used to control excess supply in the economy in the following manner:

Reverse Repo Rate: It is the rate at which RBI borrows money from commercial banks. If there is an increase in the reverse repo rate then it means that commercial banks will park more funds with RBI to earn high returns an idle cash hence, more banks will supply to central bank as it is safe and earning is more. The commercial bank will be left with less and less amount of funds to provide credit to the public. As a result, money supply will get reduced.

Open Market Operations: It is the selling and purchase of government securities by the central bank. In order to reduce the excess supply of money, the RBI sells securities and hence receive excess money from the public.

15. • I don't agree with the above statement. Devaluation and depreciation of currency are different concepts, though both imply a fall in the value of external value of currency.

- Depreciation is fall in the value of currency due to market forces of demand and supply. This implies that the domestic currency becomes less valuable and loses its value in relation to a foreign currency. An individual needs more rupees to buy a dollar. For example, If US $ exchanges for ₹ 68 instead of ₹ 65 as earlier, the domestic currency or the Indian rupee has depreciated.
- Devaluation is a deliberate fall in the value of currency done by government in order to promote exports. It is a deliberate attempt by the monetary authority of the country to decline the value of domestic currency in relation to a foreign currency.
- Thus, depreciation and devaluation promote exports in the country as the domestic goods become cheaper.

Or

- The transaction which causes a change in the official reserves of foreign exchange maintained by RBI are known as official reserve transactions.
- They are important as they help in compensating for the deficit and surplus of balance of payment.

16. (a) True, when planned savings are more then inventory will accumulate in the factory and producers will cut down production which leads to fall in income till the time AD = AS.

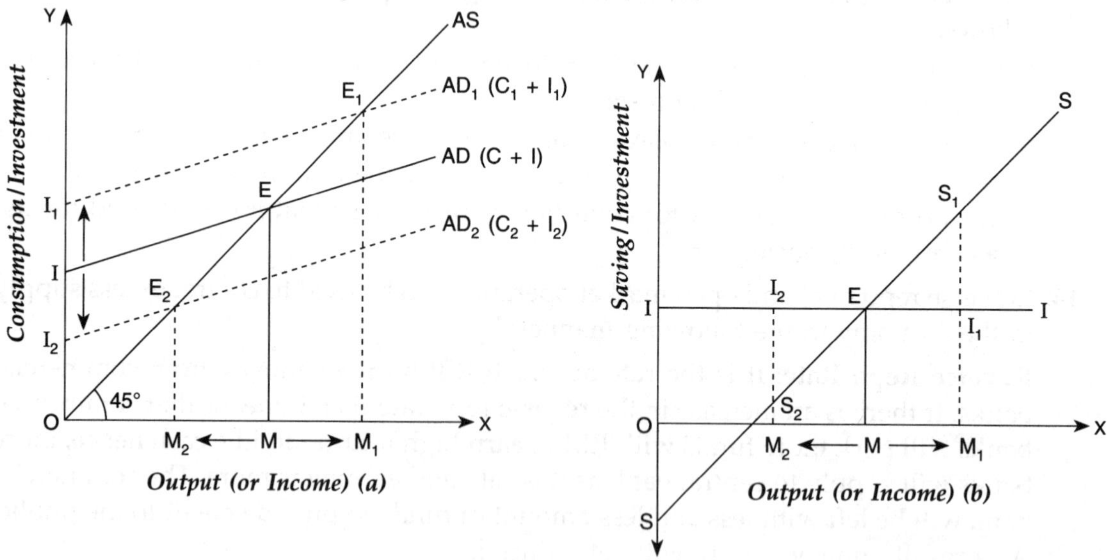

In the above figures, we suppose that level of output is greater than equilibrium level of output. Therefore, saving function lies above the investment function curve. This implies that planned savings (S_1M_1) is greater than planned investment (I_1M_1). As a result, there is more saving in the economy and less spending. This leads to accumulation of unplanned inventories.

(b) False, when AD > AS at full employment equilibrium then it is known as inflationary gap.

From the figure we can say that, to achieve full employment level of output we require only EQ_f level of aggregate demand. However, the current aggregate demand is FQ_f. Thus, there is excess demand to the extent of FE. This surplus demand gives rise to price inflation and is known as the inflationary gap.

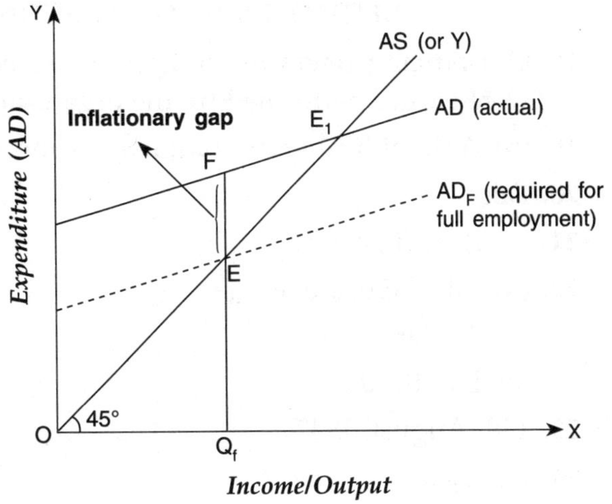

(c) False, the value APS can be negative. Average propensity to save means the ratio of total saving to total income. It is negative when at a particular level of income the saving is negative, i.e., in a situation of dissaving.

17. (a) When the economic activity provides with positive and negative side effects then it is known as externality. For e.g. production in factory causes pollution, production is backward region leads to civilized society which means construction of schools, hospitals etc.

(b)
$$\begin{aligned} GDP_{MP} &= PFCE + GFCE + GDCF + \text{Net exports} \\ &= 900 + 400 + (-)25 + (200 - 0) \\ &= 1{,}300 + 200 - 25 \\ &= ₹\ 1{,}475 \text{ crores} \end{aligned}$$

$$\begin{aligned} NNP_{FC} &= GDP_{MP} - NIT - Dep + NFIA \\ &= 1{,}475\ (-)\ 100\ (-)\ 0 + (-)\ 10 \\ &= 1{,}475\ (-)110 \\ &= ₹\ 1{,}365 \text{ crores} \end{aligned}$$

Or

(a) Yes, it will be included as they work in the domestic territory of our country.

(b) Payments of fees will not be included as it is intermediate consumption.

(c) No, it will not be included as the income does not occur in the domestic territory.

(d) No, as compensation is given by insurance company and not the employer.

SECTION B (INDIAN ECONOMIC DEVELOPMENT)

18. Outsourcing refers to lending out some of the activities to a third party which were earlier performed by the organisation.

19. (b) Animal husbandry (animal rearing is a part of animal husbandry)

20. False

21. a. (ii), b. (i), c. (iii)

22. (d) All of the above

Or

(c) Landlords

23. 14th August, 1947

24. (a) Ujala

25. The 6th most populous country of the world

26. Central Pollution Control Board

27. (b) Taccavi

28. The British built infrastructural facilities to maintain better law and order and to connect hinterlands to the interiors of the country.

- **Railways:** This was the most important development of the British era. Although this broke the cultural and geographical barriers, it was done majorly for vested interest of the British.
- **Roads:** The places where the railways could not reach had to connected by the roads and they acted as the feeder transport.
- **Telegraph:** This was an expensive yet superfast means of communication and it helped for messages to be sent across immediately.

Or

Some possible reasons are:

- **Skilled and cheap labour:** India offers a lucrative population who are willing to work at low wages and have requisite skill set.
- **Raw materials:** Resources can be procured easily as the laws are not very restricting.
- **Suitable policies:** The schemes in India, for example—the Make in India project encourage investors and companies from abroad.

29.
- Trees, when cut down can be replenished by planting more trees and restoring the balance. Many awareness campaigns like "Each one, plant one" work in this direction.
- However, when entire forests are cleared out, it cannot be gained back. This is because in the absence of trees in an entire area, the soil gets washed away by wind and water. It loses its fertility and is rendered unfit for growth again.

- Moreover, forests are home to a variety of flora and fauna, which help in maintaining the ecological balance. Once the forests are either burnt due to forest fires or are cleared for construction purposes, all the biodiversity is lost.
- For example—the burning of Amazon forests has brought much damage to the entire world.

30.

Male workers	Female workers
(a) Male workers are almost evenly spread in all the 3 sectors: primary, secondary and tertiary. They are maximum in-service sector and minimum in the industry.	Female workers are disproportionately high in the primary sector and roughly equal in the other 2 sectors.
(b) Male workers get employment opportunities in all the 3 sectors and hence the equal distribution.	Females usually dominate the agricultural sector because their men go out to cities to look for better jobs. Moreover, the lower levels of literacy rates act as a deterrence to get employed in other sectors.
(c) The overall proportion of male workers is higher than women.	The overall proportion is low. In fact, the employment rates among rural women is higher than urban women because poor economic conditions do not allow otherwise.
(d) The proportion of males is also higher because their employment in formal sector is more.	Majority of women are employed in the organised sector or are engaged in activities within the home, which are not accounted for.

31.
- Human development index is the most important indicator of Human development. Following are the ranks of China, India and Pakistan based on HDI value: 91, 130 and 148. The GDP per capita also follows the same order of decrease.
- Maternal mortality rates in India and Pakistan, though improved are still very high. On the other hand, China has made great strides in women health and only 27 women die while birthing their children.
- Infant mortality rate, which refers to number of children dying before reaching 1 year of age, also has the same story. IMR of India is 37 approximately and Pakistan touches almost the double roughly. China fares well. Life expectancy is China is about 76 years, whereas it runs in late 60s in India and Pakistan.
- Mean years of schooling is minimum in the case of Pakistan which is majorly due to the grim rates of female education and the general dismal performance on this indicator.
- Apart from these, poverty, sanitation, clean drinking water are also some indicators of human development where China takes lead, leaving the other 2 neighbours far behind.

32. Following are the problems:

- Although the credit facilities have multiplied, the rural banks still remain hesitant to grant loans to the poor because of their perceived inability to pay it back.
- A lot of times, the poor and the marginal farmers are unable to obtain credit, but the rich landlords are. The landlords then offer to lend loan to the needy of their village, which leads to more exploitation of the poor farmers as the rich landowners sell loans at very high interest rates.
- Whenever the rural folks are not able to pay their dues, they keep piling up, pushing them into debt trap. This has resulted in many farmers committing suicide.
- The amount of sanction is also small based on credit worthiness which is lent to the small farmers. Often such loans are put to secondary purposes because they are not enough for the priority ask. This dilutes the very purpose of loan.
- It is also believed that there is unawareness and lack of training to the poor about the functioning of banks and how one can efficiently repay loans.

Or

- MNREGA or the Mahatma Gandhi National Rural Employment Guarantee Act, 2005 is a scheme of government which ensures 100 days of paid work per family per year.
- These 100 days can be availed by a single member of the family or can be divided amongst many members.
- The person has to be given work within 5-6 kilometers from his place of residence, exceeding which he has to be paid extra remuneration.
- The Act provides for work of semi-skilled or unskilled nature to people living below the poverty line.
- Every person is entitled to work within 15 days of applying, which means that if he/she hasn't heard in 15 days, unemployment allowance would be provided.

33. Following were the downfalls:

- **Stiff competition from foreign exports:** The removal of barriers in the LPG policy resulted in the decline of the demand for domestic goods as they were unable to compete with the quality and prices of the foreign made goods.
- **Neglect of agriculture:** It was thought that the LPG policy will lead to a boost in the industry and services, which in turn will stimulate agricultural growth. However, this second handed strategy did not work for agriculture. Moreover, the withdrawal of subsidies and the Minimum Support prices made the condition of the farmer in India extremely vulnerable.
- **Unbalanced growth:** The growth was uneven as only a select few areas like telecommunication, information technology and the labour absorbing sectors like industry and agriculture could not cope up with the demands.

- **Social indicators like education, health, poverty took a backseat** as economic progress and the provision of basic income was the first priority. This was a noble idea but its strict focus on economy, made society suffer on many fronts and this is one of the reasons why India is the second fastest growing economy, with an increasing rich-poor divide.
- **Employment was not generated** in the proportion of the growth that we saw. The phenomenon of jobless growth was later realized as an impediment to development but at the time of economic reforms, GDP growth was an attractive indicator and all seemed good.
- **Capitalist motives:** The new economic reforms led to a culture of catering to those who can afford and the manufacture of luxury items at the expense of consumer goods began.

34. India is a dynamic country which is the cradle of natural diversity. From mountains to plateaus, flowers to animals – it is home to an enriching ecosystem. To name a few:

- The Himalayas bound the country at the north, the indo-Gangetic plains stretch over in the central India, the Deccan plateau runs towards the south-surrounded by the coastal plains. The majestic Thar desert and the island groups add beauty to the already colourful India.
- Many species of rare birds and animals like the Nilgai, tigers, rhinoceros, lions and so on live here.
- Medicinal plants, ornamental flowers, exotic plants- all find home in India.
- Many natural resources like coal, iron, petroleum, gold, copper is also found in India.

But such a rich heritage is facing a serious crisis:

- Construction activities throughout the country have meddled with the natural space. Some have resulted in massive displacement of people while others are said to have caused man-made disasters like landslides.
- The increasing levels of pollution- be it air, water or land are alarming. This is the result of both industrial activities like discharge of effluents in the water/air and human practices like not switching to cleaner fuels, etc.
- The development of the country has caused a pressure on the finite resources and hence there is a need to adopt sustainable development practices.

Or

- The system of medicines which are considered to be Indian in origin are known as Indian Systems of Medicine.
- India has the unique distinction of having six recognised systems of medicine in this category, namely-**Ayurveda, Siddha, Unani and Yoga, Naturopathy and Homoeopathy**.

- These systems are based on definite medical philosophies and represent a way of healthy living with established concepts on prevention of diseases and promotion of health.
- Yoga has become a way of life and people are practicing it all over the world. Siddha, which came from middle east and got assimilated into the Indian system of medicine, lays a great importance on 'Temperament' of a person to devise treatment. Ayurveda and naturopathy bring a person closer to nature and use indigenous ingredients to cure diseases. Homeopathy can be defined as a "dynamic and holistic system of individualistic drug therapeutics. Homeopathic remedies are used by the public for viral diseases, different forms of allergic conditions, skin disorders, behavioral problems and several chronic long-term diseases.
- In 1995, with the objective of optimal and focused development of these systems, the Department of Indian Medicine and Homeopathy was created in the Union Ministry of Health and Family Welfare. In 2003, this Department was re-named as Department of AYUSH

SAMPLE PAPER 10
(WITH SOLUTIONS)

Time allowed: 3 hours *Maximum marks: 80*

General Instructions:

1. ***All** the questions in **both** the sections are **compulsory**. Marks for questions are indicated against each question.*
2. *Question number **1-10** and **18-27** are very short-answer questions carrying **1 mark** each. They are required to be answered in one word or one sentence each.*
3. *Question number **11-12** and **28-29** are short-answer questions caring **3 marks** each. Answers to them should not normally exceed **60-80 words** each.*
4. *Question number **13-15** and **30-32** are also short-answer questions carrying **4 marks** each. Answers to them should not normally exceed **80-100 words** each.*
5. *Question number **16-17** and **33-34** are long answer questions carrying **6 marks** each. Answers to them should not normally exceed **100-150 words** each.*
6. *Answer **should be brief** and **to the point** and the above **word limit be adhered** to as far as possible.*

SECTION A (MACROECONOMICS)

1. Open market operation is a __________ measure of credit control by RBI. **(1)**

2. If fiscal deficit is Rs 35 crore and interest payment is ₹ 10 crore then primary deficit is **(1)**

(a) ₹ 25 crore (b) ₹ 45 crore
(c) ₹ 20 crore (d) none of these

3. Write the relation between MPC and MPS. **(1)**

4. A person residing in England for a business, having an Indian passport and Indian citizenship will be treated as a **(1)**

(a) resident of England (b) resident of India
(c) resident of England and India (d) non-resident

Or

Which one refers to Net Indirect Taxes?

(a) Indirect taxes + subsidies (b) Indirect taxes – subsidies

(c) Direct taxes – subsidies (d) none of the above

5. State whether the following statement is true or false **(1)**

'Devaluation of currency means reduction in the value of domestic currency in terms of foreign currency.'

6. Increase in investment expenditure leads to __________ in AD. **(1)**

7. Difference between the value of Export and import of goods is known as __________. **(1)**

8. Which of the following is not true for fiscal deficit? A fiscal deficit: **(1)**

(a) represents the borrowing of the government

(b) is the difference between total expenditure and total receipts of government

(c) is the difference between total expenditure and total receipts other than borrowing

(d) increases future liability of the government.

9. From the set of statements given in column I and Column II, match the following: **(1)**

Column I	Column II
a. NNP_{FC} (+) Depreciation	(i) NNP_{FC}
b. NDP_{FC} (+) Net factor income from abroad	(ii) GNP_{MP}
c. NDP_{FC} (+) Depreciation	(iii) GNP_{FC}
d. GNP_{FC} (+) Net indirect Taxes	(iv) GDP_{FC}

10. Excess demand leads to **(1)**

(a) increase in the level of employment (b) decrease in the level of employment

(c) increase in monetary income (d) none of these

11. Explain with the help of an example, the basis of classifying goods into final goods and intermediate goods. **(3)**

Or

Giving reasons state how the following are treated in estimation of national income:

(a) Payment of interest by banks to its depositors.

(b) Expenditure on old age pension by government

(c) Expenditure on engine oil by car service station.

12. An economy is in equilibrium. From the following data, calculate the marginal propensity to save: **(3)**

(a) Income = 10,000

(b) Autonomous consumption = 500

(c) Consumption expenditure = 8,000

13. Distinguish between direct taxes and indirect taxes. Give an example of each. **(4)**

Or

Explain how government budget can be helpful in bringing economic stabilisation in the economy.

14. Explain the "bankers' bank" function of the central bank. **(4)**

15. Distinguish between the fixed exchange rate and the floating exchange rate. If exchange rate falls, explain its effects on exports and imports. **(4)**

16. Given a consumption curve, outline the steps required to be taken in deriving a saving curve from it. Use diagram. **(6)**

Or

Given the consumption function C = 100 + 0.75Y and the autonomous expenditure as ₹ 1,100, calculate:

(a) Equilibrium level of income

(b) Consumption at the equilibrium level of income

(c) Investment multiplier

17. Calculate GNP_{MP} from the following information: **(6)**

	(₹ in crores)
(a) Compensation of employees	4,000
(b) Rent	800
(c) Profits	1,500
(d) Undistributed earnings	400
(e) Mixed income of the self-employed	1,800
(f) Net imports	30
(g) Net investment	900
(h) Gross domestic fixed capital formation	1,000
(i) Inventory investment	50
(j) Interest	900
(k) Net indirect taxes	500
(l) Net factor income to abroad	(–) 80

SECTION B (INDIAN ECONOMIC DEVELOPMENT)

18. The building of __________ led to a greater connectivity between Asia and Europe and eased the trade between India and Britain. **(1)**

19. Which among the following is not true: **(1)**

(a) Vehicles cause air pollution

(b) Sunlight causes air pollution

(c) Industries cause air pollution

(d) Burning of fossil fuels cause air pollution

20. What is land degradation? **(1)**

21. From the set of statements given in column I and Column II, match the following: **(1)**

Column I	Column II
a. Involves cultivating fruits and vegetables	(i) Information Technology
b. Involves use of computers to retrieve information	(ii) Animal Husbandry
c. Involves catching, processing or selling of aquatic animals	(iii) Horticulture
d. Involves breeding, rearing and caring for farm animals.	(iv) Fisheries

22. The NITI in NITI Ayog stands for **(1)**
(a) National Institute for Transformation of India
(b) National Institution for Transforming India
(c) National Institute for Transforming India
(d) National Institute to Transform India

Or

BPO are more commonly known as:
(a) Service centers (b) Startups (c) Call centers (d) Big hotels

23. Which country among China, India and Pakistan has the maximum percentage of people above the poverty line? **(1)**

24. State whether the following statement is true or false **(1)**
'Yoga leads to human capital formation?'

25. Which country has the highest workforce engaged in agriculture? **(1)**
(a) India (b) Pakistan (c) China (d) Canada

26. __________ institution is responsible for maintain buffer stocks in India? **(1)**

27. An establishment having 3 workers is known as: **(1)**
(a) Formal sector (b) Cottage industry
(c) Enterprise (d) Informal sector

28. What is a license? Why was it needed to be obtained for setting up industries in India? **(3)**

29. Poverty can only be eliminated when the poor themselves strive for it and do not always blame the government. Explain what all can be done at the individual level. **(3)**

Or

Write a short note on dairy farming.

30. Poverty leads to environmental degradation, but so does affluence. Explain the dichotomy. **(4)**

Or

How has the pattern of consumption of energy changed in India over the years?

31. Explain "One Child Policy" of China. Can such a policy be implemented in India? **(4)**

32. Describe the division of employment based on regions. **(4)**

33. What was the performance of demographic indicators in India under the British rule? Has it improved over the years? **(6)**

34. What are the drawbacks of the poverty alleviation programmes in India? **(6)**

Or

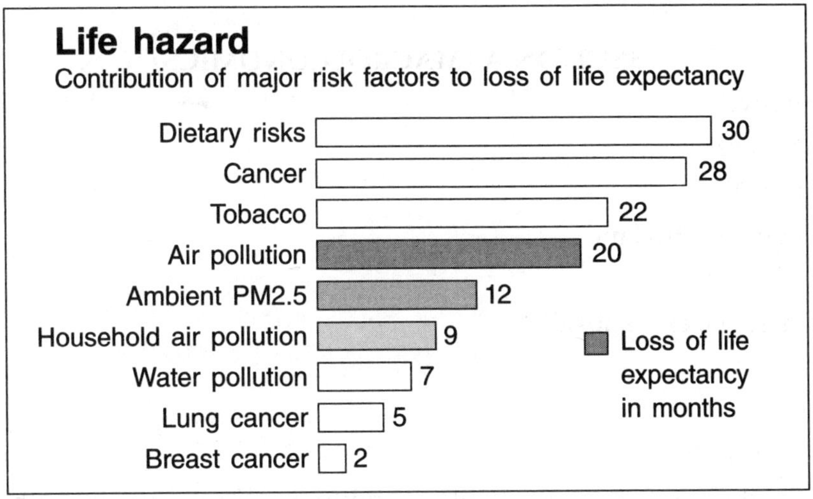

The graph above shows air pollution to be a significant cause of compromise in the life expectancy. What are some ways to curb air pollution?

SOLUTIONS TO SAMPLE PAPER 10

SECTION A (MACROECONOMICS)

1. Quantitative
2. (a) ₹ 25 crore
3. MPC + MPS = 1
4. (a) resident of England

   Or

   (b) Indirect taxes – subsidies
5. True
6. increase
7. Balance of trade
8. (c) is the difference between total expenditure and total receipts other than borrowing
9. a. (iii), b. (i), c. (iv), d. (ii)
10. (c) increase in monetary income
11. Final goods are those goods which are used for final consumption or for production of other goods. For e.g. machines, computers etc.

    Intermediate goods are those which are purchased for the purpose of resale in same period or form a part or component of the final good.

    For e.g. if rice is purchased by the household for consumption then it will be termed as final good. But if the same rice is purchased by a hotel for making their food then it will be considered as intermediate good.

    Or

    (a) Yes, it will be **included** in the national income as such interest is paid on loan taken for productive purpose. It is a factor payment by a producer.

    (b) No, it will **not be included** in national income as old age pension is a transfer payment made by the government.

    (c) No, it will **not be included** as it is a part of intermediate consumption expenditure.

12.

$$
\begin{aligned}
Y &= 10{,}000\\
\overline{C} &= 500\\
C &= 8{,}000\\
C &= \overline{C} + by\\
8{,}000 &= 500 + b(10{,}000)\\
\text{(MPC) or } b &= 0.75\\
MPS &= 1 - MPC\\
&= 1 - 0.75 = \boxed{0.25}
\end{aligned}
$$

13.

Basis	Direct Tax	Indirect Tax
Definition	It is paid by person on whom it is imposed *i.e.* shifting of burden is not possible.	It is paid by consumers *i.e.* shifting of burden is possible.
Imposition	It is imposed on persons.	It is imposed on commodities.
Nature	It is progressive in nature.	It is regressive in nature.
Burden	Real burden on rich people.	Real burden on poor people.
Example	Income tax, corporate tax.	Sales tax, service tax.

The **role of government budget** can in **influencing allocation of resources** is explained below.

(a) Government aims to allocate resources to maintain a balance between maximisation of welfare as well as profits.

(b) Private sector of economy usually ignores social welfare. Government budget allows the government to intervene in the economy so as to increase social welfare.

(c) For example, government levies taxes on socially harmful goods such as tobacco, cigarettes etc. and provides subsidies on essential commodities such as LPG, food grains etc.

Or

Economic stability is one of the important objectives of budgetary policy of the government. The policy of the surplus or deficit budgeting is adopted as and when the government is required to control inflation and deflation. During the period of depression, the government adopts the policy of deficit budgeting, while on the other hand during the period of inflation government adopts the policy of budgeting.

14. **Banker of the Government**

(a) **Banking business:** As the government's bank, the central bank accepts deposits, makes payments, and carries out exchange and remittances on behalf of the government.

(b) **Extends loans:** It provides short-term credit to the government by printing money against its security and bills to finance government deficit.

(c) **Agent:** A central bank also provides various services as an agent of the government. It manages public debts. It undertakes payment of interest on this debt and all sorts of other services relating to public debt.

(d) **Advisor:** The central bank gives advice to the government regarding taxation, interest rates, credit expansion, etc.

15.

Basis	Fixed exchange rate	Floating exchange rate
Determination of exchange rates	It is officially fixed in terms of gold or any other currency by government.	It is determined by forces of demand and supply of foreign exchange.
Government control	There is complete government control as only government has the power to change it.	There is no government intervention and it fluctuates freely according to market conditions.
Stability in exchange rate	The exchange rate generally remains stable and only a small variation is possible.	The exchange rate keeps on changing.

- To explain the effects of fall in exchange rate on imports and exports let us take the following example:

  Earlier 1\$ = ₹ 70

  1\$ = ₹ 65

∴ Foreign exchange rate decreases. This is known as **currency appreciation.**

- Currency appreciation means increase in value of domestic currency in terms of foreign currency. As a result:

  (i) Imports increases as foreign goods become cheaper.

  (ii) Exports decreases because domestic goods become costlier

16. In the diagram $\overline{C} + bY$ is the consumption curve. The 45° line is the aggregate supply curve.

At point A, consumption = income i.e (Y = C)

$\overline{C}$ represents the autonomous consumption *i.e.* consumption at zero level of income.

Steps for derivation of savings curve from consumption curve as follows:

(a) Corresponding to $\overline{C}$ in the consumption function we have $-\overline{C}$ in the saving function. That is, there are negative savings equal to autonomous consumption at Y = 0. This is represented by S on the negative axis in the lower panel.

(b) Point A implies that all the income is spent on consumption expenditure *i.e.* Y = C. Thus, savings equal to zero. This is shown as S = 0 in lower panel. This point is also known as the Break-even point.

(c) Beyond the break-even point, by connecting points S and B we derive the straight upward sloping saving curve.

(d) SS is the required saving curve.

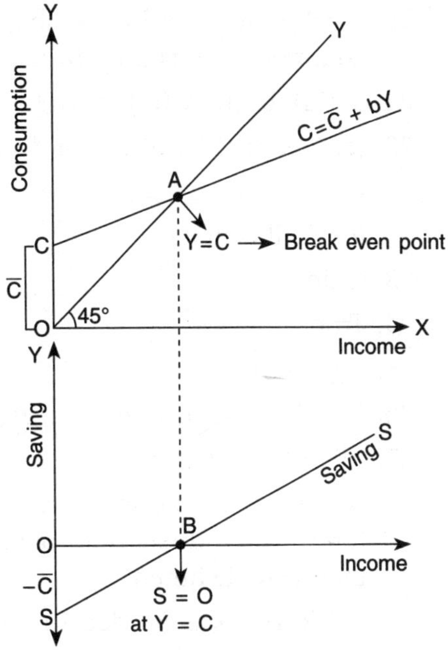

Or

(a)
$$C = 100 + 0.75\ Y \text{ (given)}$$
$$\overline{A} = 1100 \text{ (given)}$$
$$\overline{A} = \overline{C} + \overline{I}$$
$$1100 = 100 + \overline{I}$$
$$\Rightarrow \quad I = 1000$$
$$Y = C + I$$
$$Y = 100 + 0.75Y + 1000$$
$$Y(1 - 0.75) = 1100$$
$$Y = \frac{1100}{0.25} = \boxed{₹\ 4,400}$$

(b)
$$C = 100 + 0.75Y$$
$$= 100 + 0.75 \times 4,400$$
$$= 100 + 3,300 = \boxed{₹\ 3,400}$$

(c)
$$K = \frac{1}{1 - MPC}$$
$$= \frac{1}{1 - 0.75} = \frac{1}{0.25}$$
$$= \boxed{K = 4}$$

17. $GNP_{MP} = a + b + c + e + j - l + h + i - g + k$

$= 4,000 + 800 + 1,500 + 1,800 + 900 - \{-80\} + 1,000 + 50 - 900 + 500$

= ₹ 9,730 crores

SECTION B (INDIAN ECONOMIC DEVELOPMENT)

18. Suez Canal

19. (b) Sunlight causes air pollution

20. It refers to a decline in the overall quality of soil, water or vegetation condition, commonly caused by human activities.

21. a. (iii), b. (i), c. (iv), d. (ii)

22. (c) National Institute for Transforming India

Or

(c) Call centers

23. China

24. True

25. (a) India

26. FCI (Food Corporation of India)

27. (d) Informal sector

28. According to the Industries (Development and regulation) Act, it was mandatory for all the industries to obtain a written permission by the government to set up their establishment.

- License was needed to set up new industries. It was easier to obtain licenses in cases the industry was to come up in backward areas and promote development. In such cases, tax benefits were also provided.
- License was needed to expand the existing unit, in terms of both acquiring more area or increase in production.
- License was needed to diversify the production and include new products. The permission was granted only when the government saw the need for such products in the economy.

29. The poor, just like anybody else have the ability to break away from the cycle of poverty. It is true that may not have all the required material resources but they definitely have the inner strength.

- The most important step at the individual level is to limit the production of more and more children. The poor feel that more kids would mean more hands at work, but it also means more mouths to feed.
- Another very significant way is to educate your children and encourage them to read and write. It might not lead to immediate gratification and some money would initially have to be spared for education, but it will lead to a much better quality of life.
- Moreover, it is healthy to accept your economic deprivation but unwise to settle with it. If one keeps fighting it with his hard work and determination, there will be ways to move out of the family occupation or earn a better livelihood.

Or

- Dairy Farming or Dairying is the breeding, rearing and milking of cows, sheep, goats, camels and other animals who produce milk.
- The milk is used to produce and process other dairy products as well like cheese, paneer, curd etc.

- The dairy industry received a huge boost after the milk revolution, post which the cooperative culture was developed like Amul and Mother Dairy.

30. - Poor living conditions force people to depend heavily on the natural resources for their survival. For example—firewood for cooking, bathing in rivers, etc. These activities degrade the environment.
    - Encroachment in the forest land, orchards and vineyards is a very common practice and people of the nearby villages procure essential products like fruits, vegetables, medicinal plants from here.
    - Rise in the living standards has also led to damage to the environment. The increase in vehicles for both need and status has increased pollution levels considerably.
    - Affluence has also given rise to consumerism which generates excessive waste, more than the absorbing capacity of the environment.
    - This is how the dichotomy presents itself.

Or

- In India. About 75% of the energy used is commercial energy which is obtained from coal, natural gas, hydel etc. The non-commercial energy is produced by using domestic waste, agricultural leftovers, cow dung and is used for meeting household purposes only.
- The consumption of all the sectors within India has increased. However, the increase in agricultural sector has been the smallest. This is because majority of farmers are still dependent on the traditional methods of farming.
- The household consumption has also increased with the advent of technology and the popularity of machine led chores.
- The transport sector, however, witnesses a reduction in energy consumption because of effective methods of commuting like the metro lines and cleaner fuels such as CNG.

31. A voluntary program was announced in late 1978 that encouraged families to have no more than two children, one child being preferable. In 1979 demand grew for making the limit one child per family by 1980 the central government sought to standardise the one-child policy nationwide.

Although this was the norm, some exceptions were made such as the parents whose first born was a handicapped or ethnic minorities whose cult was nearly extinct.

The fertility rate of China came down by a large magnitude, about 2 births per woman.

However, such a policy is very stringent in nature and cannot be implemented in India because:

- One child policy resulted in skewed sex ratio as a male offspring was desirable if only one child was allowed. India already has an uneven sex ratio because of practices like female feticide, infanticide, honor killings, etc. Therefore, such a policy is highly undesirable.

- India is a human resource rich country. It has one of the youngest population pools among all the countries of the world. Restrictive birth control measures would result in an ageing population after few years down the line.
- Moreover, illegal practices would emerge, whereby people will have more than one child but not document it. It is these undocumented children who will face hardships later in life.

32. • The rural areas have a greater proportion of self-employed workers as majority of the farmers are cultivating on their own lands.
- In urban areas, regular salaried employment dominates due to presence of companies and factories. Moreover, the level of education and skills makes it easier for urban people to find jobs.
- Cities like Bangalore, Chennai, Pune, Delhi, Mumbai and Kolkata have a higher incidence of employment opportunities. Many MNCs have set up their establishments in these cities and service sector has become a lucrative area of interest.
- States like Punjab, Haryana and Andhra Pradesh have people engaged in agricultural activities as they have been traditionally rich farming areas since the green revolution. A major chunk of crops come from these states.

33. • **Birth rate and Death rate:** Both these indicators were very high during the British rule. It was because nothing was done to improve the living conditions of the people, they were only used as a means to an end.
- **Literacy rate:** It was extremely low, a mere 16% and 7% among women. The only people who were expected to be educated were the ones who were required to serve as translators for British. The introduction of English language as compulsory medium of instruction also made people averse to the idea of getting themselves enrolled in schools to learn foreign ways of life.
- **Poverty:** It was rampant and people lived at the mercy of exploitative landlords and British rulers.
- **Infant mortality rate:** This was a very disturbing figure of approximately 220 per thousand.
- **Life expectancy** was also very low due to no investment in health facilities.
- **Sanitation, clean drinking water** adequate infrastructure was all provided only for the British Lords. The common people lived at whatever little they could get.

Yes, all the indicators improved considerably since India became an independent nation. The life expectancy has reached upto 69 years as against 45 years. The Swachh Bharat Abhiyan has laid great importance on sanitation.

The literacy rate is 74.04%. however, a lot of work still needs to be done.

34. The poverty alleviation programmes in India face the following problems:

- Identification of target group remains a key issue. The benefits of such schemes are availed by the rich landowning class and the trickle-down approach could not lend its benefits to the poorest of the poor.
- Corruption and inefficiency of the government officials in implementing the schemes also causes hurdles. The funds sanctioned by the central government are often not sent to the village panchayats and there is a close nexus of the rich farmers and the authorities.
- Lack of awareness in the poor people about the prevailing schemes and benefits they could avail. The lower levels of awareness stem from illiteracy and also the fact that enough measures are not taken to popularise government initiatives.
- Lack of infrastructure in terms of roads, buildings, offices also act as a detriment in the proper functioning of the schemes and the active participation of the poor people.
- The resources sanctioned for poverty alleviation are less in comparison to the alarming number of people who are in need of protection through such schemes.
- A lot of times, poverty alleviation initiatives are only taken up during the time of elections after which the promises are long gone and forgotten.

  Nevertheless, the situation is changing. There is increase in awareness among the poor people and they hold their representatives more accountable.

Or

Air pollution refers to the addition of contaminants into the air by human activities like burning of fossil fuels or natural processes like forest fires.

It can be prevented in the following ways:

- Using cleaner fuels like CNG in place of petroleum in vehicles as they cause more carbon emissions.
- Getting regular pollution checks of the vehicles done.
- Filtering the waste before emitting it out from the chimneys into the air.
- Promotion of healthy practices like cycling, carpooling and using public transport. The metro services in NCR are very popular.
- Avoid burning leaves and trash. Instead bury them.
- Recycling and reusing products because each stage of the manufacture process is accompanied by emissions of polluting particles, heavy metals, chemicals and greenhouse gases.
- Plant trees. They are natural cleansing agents of the environment and absorb a lot of waste.

SAMPLE PAPER 11
(FOR PRACTICE)

Time allowed: 3 hours *Maximum marks: 80*

General Instructions:
Same as given in Sample Paper 1.

SECTION A (MACROECONOMICS)

1. Barter system means exchange of _________ for _________. **(1)**

2. Define Surplus Budget. **(1)**

3. What is the value of APC at break even point? **(1)**

4. With the rise in real national income, welfare of the people: **(1)**

(a) Rises (b) Falls
(c) Remains unchanged (d) None of the above

Or

Market value of all the final goods and services produced within the domestic territory of a country during a year is called

(a) GDP_{MP} (b) GDP_{FC}
(c) GNP_{MP} (d) NNP_{MP}

5. The rate at which demand for and supply of foreign exchange becomes equal is called **(1)**

(a) equilibrium rate of exchange (b) unequal rate of exchange
(c) equal rate of exchange (d) all of these

6. Complete the given: $K \times \Delta I =$ _________ **(1)**

7. State whether the following statement is true or false:

'Depreciation in currency means fall in value of domestic currency in terms of foreign currency'. **(1)**

8. Budget is **(1)**

(a) financial statement (b) political statement
(c) monetary statement (d) all of the above

9. Match the alternatives given in Column II with respective terms in Column I. **(1)**

Column I	Column II
a. Recovery of loan	(i) Revenue expenditure
b. Interest received	(ii) Capital receipt
c. Construction of bridges	(iii) Revenue receipt
d. Subsidies given	(iv) Capital expenditure

10. Excess demand may be caused due to **(1)**

(a) increase in supply of money (b) increase in taxes
(c) decrease in government expenditure (d) decrease in export demand

11. In an economy, only the following transactions take place. Firm A sells all of its product worth 4,000 to the firm B. Firm B sells its entire output for 8,000 to firm C. Firm C sells its goods for final demand at 14,000. Calculate: **(3)**

(a) Value added by each firm.
(b) Indirect tax of 20% is levied on A's product. This burden of tax is shifted on to the consumers. Find market price of good for each firm.

12. If national income is 90 and consumption expenditure is 81, find out average propensity to save. When income rises to 100 and consumption to 88, what will be the marginal propensity to consume and marginal propensity to save. **(3)**

Or

From the following information calculate consumption level in the economy:

(a) Wages and salaries	250
(b) Autonomous consumption	25
(c) MPS : MPC	29 : 87
(d) Dividend	110
(e) Net factor income from abroad	100
(f) Mixed income	400
(g) Rent, Interest and Profit	350

13. As per news headlines, "RBI future cuts the repo rate to 5%." What is the implication of the statement with reference to Indian economy. **(4)**

14. A rise in the foreign exchange rate adversely affects the imports in the country. How can this rise be managed and by whom in the interest of general public? **(4)**

Or

With the given information answer the following questions:

Earlier 1$ = ₹ 60 and now 1$ = ₹ 65

(a) What does the above indicate?
(b) Some economists say the reason behind this is change in balance of payment. Do you agree?

15. From the following data find: **(4)**

(a) Primary deficit

(b) Revenue deficit

(i) Capital receipts net of borrowings	₹ 950
(ii) Salary paid to government employees	₹ 1,000
(iii) Interest payments	₹ 100
(iv) Goods & Services tax	₹ 500
(v) Purchase of machinery by government	₹ 1,110
(vi) Wealth tax	₹ 300

16. Giving reasons, state whether the following statements are true or false: **(6)**

(a) If the ratio of marginal propensity to consume and marginal propensity to save is 4 : 1, the value of investment multiplier will be 4.

(b) The value of marginal propensity to save can never be negative.

(c) Sum of average propensity to consume and marginal propensity to consume is always equal to 1.

(d) When marginal propensity to consume is greater than marginal propensity to save, then the value of multiplier will be greater than 5.

17. Distinguish between factor income and transfer income. Giving reason classify the following into factor income or transfer income: **(6)**

(a) Pension paid at time of retirement

(b) Interest on loan taken by Rakesh for purchase of car

(c) Bonus given to the employees by employer

Or

From the following information calculate National Income:

	(₹ in Crores)
(a) Compensation of employees	1,200
(b) Rent	400
(c) Interest	250
(d) Consumption of fixed capital	300
(e) Net indirect taxes	350
(f) Mixed income of self-employed	1,000
(g) Net imports	60
(h) Net factor income to abroad	50
(i) Profit	800

SECTION B (INDIAN ECONOMIC DEVELOPMENT)

18. __________ industries was particularly well known before the British came. **(1)**

19. Which of the following is not a form of self-employment? **(1)**

(a) Businessman (b) Farmer cultivating on own land

(c) Shopkeeper (d) Travelling ticket examiner

20. How many member countries does WTO have presently? **(1)**

21. Match the alternatives given in Column II with respective terms in Column I and identify the one which was of prime importance for the British during their colonial rule in India: **(1)**

Column I	Column II
a. Panama Canal	(i) connectivity between Atlantic Ocean and Pacific Ocean
b. Palk Strait	(ii) trade route between Tamil Nadu and Sri Lanka
c. Cape of good hope	(iii) sea way through Egypt connecting Europe and Asia
d. Suez Canal	(iv) Far end of South Africa

22. Which of the following is not an employment related scheme: **(1)**

(a) MNREGA (b) Prime Minister's Rozgar Yojana

(c) Antyodaya yojana (d) Swarna Jayanti Shahri Rozgar Yojana

23. State whether the following is true or false: **(1)**

'First five year plan was from 1961 to 1966.' **(1)**

24. Why is the minimum support price fixed by the government? State one reason. **(1)**

25. __________ programme/s was/were started in China to undertake rapid industrialisation. **(1)**

(a) One child policy (b) Great leap forward

(c) Cultural revolution (d) All of the these

26. In order to monitor water and air pollution, the GOI set up __________ Board. **(1)**

27. Which of the following is not a source of energy? **(1)**

(a) Jatropha plant (b) Hydrogen gas

(c) Biomass (d) Plastics

Or

Disguised unemployment refers to:

(a) Persons hiding at the workplace

(b) More people employed than are needed

(c) People with no jobs

(d) People trying to encroach on other's jobs

28. Explain the type of land reforms implemented in the agricultural sector. **(3)**

29. How does illiteracy lead to poverty? **(3)**

Or

List down a few problems faced by the workers of the informal sector.

30. What do you understand by environment. What are the various functions served by it? **(4)**

31. compare the demographic indicators of India, China and Pakistan. **(4)**

32. Although the GDP of the country is increasing the level of employment is not proportional to it. What do you think is the reason? **(4)**

Or

The use of chemical fertilizers, insecticides and pesticides are extremely beneficial at one hand but they lead to degradation of soil and environment at the same time. Do you agree?

33. Explain the policy of Liberalisation, Privatisation, Globalisation (LPG). **(6)**

34. **(6)**

Particulars	Gender	1990 (%)	2000 (%)	2005-10 (%)
Adult Literacy Rate	Male	61.90	68.4	76.7
	Female	37.9	45.4	54.9
Primary Completion Rate	Male	78	85	96
	Female	61	69	95
Youth Literacy Rate	Male	76.6	79.7	88
	Female	54.2	64.8	74

Analyse the data given above and comment on the condition of education in India. Also show the link between education and economic growth.

Or

What are the various ways through which Human Capital Formation takes place?

SAMPLE PAPER 12
(FOR PRACTICE)

Time allowed: 3 hours *Maximum marks: 80*

General Instructions:
Same as given in Sample Paper 1.

SECTION A (MACROECONOMICS)

1. State whether the following statement is true or false: **(1)**
   'Money is what money does.'
2. Direct tax is a __________ tax. **(1)**
3. Deficient demand leads to __________ employment equilibrium. **(1)**
4. Income earned by an NRI living in America will **(1)**
   (a) form a part of national income of India
   (b) form a part of national income of America
   (c) not form a part of national income of America
   (d) be divided between America and India

   Or

   As a result of double counting, national income is
   (a) over-estimated
   (b) under-estimated
   (c) correctly estimated
   (d) not estimated for the entire year of accounting
5. State the relationship between exports and balance of trade. **(1)**
6. Propensity to save means **(1)**
   (a) rate of saving to income
   (b) level of income at which saving is equal to income
   (c) additional income that is not to be saved
   (d) none of these
7. A systematic record of all economic transactions between residents of a country and the rest of the world during a year is called the __________. **(1)**

8. Capital expenditure is that estimated expenditure of the government by which: **(1)**

(a) assets are increased
(b) liability is decreased
(c) both (a) and (b)
(d) assets and liabilities do not change

9. Match the alternatives given in Column II with respective terms in Column I: **(1)**

Column I	Column II
a. Net exports	(i) Gross Investment (–) Net Investment
b. Net imports	(ii) Exports > Imports
c. Inventory investment	(iii) Imports > Exports
d. Consumption of fixed capital	(iv) Closing stock (–) Opening Stock

10. State whether the following statement is true or false: **(1)**
'AD Curve starts from the point below the origin.'

11. Calculate operating surplus: **(3)**

Gross value of output at market price	₹ 9,000
Consumption of fixed capital	₹ 700
Wages & Salaries	₹ 4,000
Indirect taxes	₹ 500
Subsidies	₹ 200
Intermediate consumption	₹ 1,000
Mixed Income of self-employed	Nil
Profits	₹ 250

12. Given C = 40 + 0.8Y. Find **(3)**
(a) Dissavings
(b) Marginal propensity to save
(c) Investment multiplier
(d) Average propensity to consume given that income level is ₹ 4,000.

Or

Giving reasons state whether the following are true or false
(a) There is inverse relationship between MPS and multiplier.
(b) When MPC is zero, multiplier will be zero.
(c) When APS is negative then MPS is also negative.
(d) Value of APC can never be zero.

13. In the government budget, the Finance Minister proposed to raise the excise duty on cigarettes. He also proposed to increase income tax on individuals earning more than one crore per annum. Is the objective only to earn tax revenue? What possible welfare objective can you think of from these proposals? Explain. **(4)**

14. What are the various categories of economic transactions which are recorded in balance of payment account? **(4)**

Or

Explain the meaning and two merits of fixed exchange rate?

15. Explain briefly two components of capital account and two components of current of balance of payment. **(4)**

16. When is an economy in equilibrium? Explain with the help of saving and investment functions. Also explain the changes that takes place in an economy when the economy is not in equilibrium. Use diagram. **(6)**

17. Calculate (a) National income and (b) Indirect tax **(6)**

	(₹ in Crores)
(a) Compensation of employees	2,000
(b) Subsidy	40
(c) Exports	100
(d) Factor income from abroad	60
(e) Profits	800
(f) Inventory investment	40
(g) Imports	200
(h) Net fixed investment	300
(i) Rent	500
(j) Gross domestic capital formation	440
(k) Gross national Product at market price	3,900
(l) Factor income to abroad	60
(m) Royalty	300

Or

Calculate (a) GDP_{FC} and (b) Factor income to abroad

	(₹ in Crores)
(a) Compensation of employees	800
(b) Profits	200
(c) Dividends	50
(d) Gross national product at market price	1,400
(e) Rent	150
(f) Interest	100
(g) Gross domestic capital formation	300
(h) Net fixed capital formation	200
(i) Change in stock	50
(j) Factor income from abroad	60
(k) Net indirect taxes	120

SECTION B (INDIAN ECONOMIC DEVELOPMENT)

18. Who was the first chairman of the Planning Commission? **(1)**

19. State whether the following statement is true or false **(1)**

'One of the major causes of unemployment in India is Population growth.'

20. More than 50% of the trade of India was confined to: **(1)**

(a) Ceylon (b) Burma (c) Britain (d) Korea

21. Organic farming does not make use of which of the following? **(1)**

(a) Vermi-compost (b) Chemical pesticides

(c) Crop rotation (d) Green manure

22. Match the alternatives given in Column II with respective terms in Column I: **(1)**

Column I	Column II
a. horticulture	(i) Rearing and breeding of animals for eggs, wool etc.
b. Fisheries	(ii) Producing and distributing milk/milk products
c. Dairying	(iii) Catching, processing, selling of fish and other aquatic animals
d. Animal husbandry	(iv) Cultivating fruits and vegetables

23. Pakistan has the second largest Muslim population in the world, followed by __________. **(1)**

24. What is the calorie intake estimated for rural and urban areas? **(1)**

25. Which of the following countries have the lowest density of population? **(1)**

(a) Pakistan (b) China

(c) India (d) None of the above

26. The income of a barber working in a shop in Lucknow gets accounted in which of the following? **(1)**

(a) GDP (b) GNP

(i) Only(a)

(ii) Only (b)

(iii) Both (a) and (b)

(iv) Neither (a) or (b)

Or

Sustainable development can be achieved by:

(a) Recycle products (b) Reduce wastage

(c) Afforestation (d) All of the above

27. State one non-commercial source of energy? **(1)**

28. Discuss the land settlement policy of the British. **(3)**

29. Mukesh Ambani inherited a lot of wealth from his father. A lot of people like him do. Then why do you think people work? **(3)**

Or

Women have a lower life expectancy as calculated by the statisticians and are more disadvantaged as compared to the men in India. What do you think are the possible reasons?

30. What is sustainable development? What are its aims? **(4)**

31. List down some similarities in the path of development adopted by China, India and Pakistan. **(4)**

32. What are the challenges to organic farming? **(4)**

Or

What do you understand by the Food for Work Programme?

33. **(6)**

The cartoon is designed by a Western artist and has a satirical take on the quantum of jobs being outsourced to India. Do you think India has benefitted from it?

34. A 2% education cess is levied on all Union taxes. What else has the government done to make education available to all? **(6)**

Or

What are the main problems of Human Capital Formation in India?

SAMPLE PAPER 13
(FOR PRACTICE)

Time allowed: 3 hours *Maximum marks: 80*

General Instructions:
Same as given in Sample Paper 1.

SECTION A (MACROECONOMICS)

1. Define Money supply. **(1)**

2. Repayment of loan is __________ expenditure. **(1)**

3. Result of excess demand is **(1)**
(a) inflation
(b) deflation
(c) underemployment equilibrium
(d) losses to producers

4. Value added method measures the contribution of which of the following within the domestic territory of a country? **(1)**
(a) One producing enterprise only
(b) All producing enterprises
(c) A few producing enterprises
(d) None of these

Or

State which one of the following statements is not true:
(a) citizen of a country is necessarily the resident of that country.
(b) citizen of a country is not necessarily the resident of that country.
(c) citizen and resident are two different concepts.
(d) a person can be a citizen as well as a resident.

5. State whether the following is true or false: **(1)**
'Balance of trade is measured as difference between all exports and all imports.'

6. Match the alternatives given in Column II with respective terms in Column I: **(1)**

Column I	Column II
a. Slope of consumption curve	(i) MPC
b. Slope of savings curve	(ii) MPS
c. Consumption / Income	(iii) APC
d. Savings / Income	(iv) APS

7. Capital A/c and Current A/c are components of __________. **(1)**
8. State one implication of fiscal deficit. **(1)**
9. When RBI acts as a banker to the government, what does it do? **(1)**
   (a) It carries out government transactions.
   (b) It advises on monetary and financial matters.
   (c) It keeps account of the government.
   (d) All the above.
10. State four components of Aggregate demand. **(1)**
11. What monetary measures should be taken by RBI to correct excess demand? **(3)**

Or

Define investment. Explain national income equilibrium through savings and investment function.

12. Calculate Subsidy: **(3)**

(a) NNP_{MP}	25,000
(b) Wealth tax	1,000
(c) Net factor income to abroad	(–) 14,100
(d) Operating surplus	2,500
(e) Mixed income of self-employed	1,000
(f) Sales tax	500
(g) Profits	2,500
(h) Compensation of employees	7,500

13. Foreign exchange rate in India is on a rise. How does this affect the balance of trade of India? **(4)**

Or

Differentiate between devaluation and depreciation of domestic currency.

14. What are the consequences of fiscal deficit in government budget? **(4)**
15. Explain the concept of CRR and SLR. How do they affect the credit created by commercial bank. **(4)**
16. (a) Only one product X is produced in the country. Its output during the year 2012 and 2013 was 1000 units and 1200 units respectively. The market price of

the product during the year was ₹ 10 and ₹ 15 per unit respectively. Calculate percentage change in real GDP in the year 2013 and also calculate GDP deflator for 2013. **(6)**

(b) Find net value added at factor cost from the following:

(i) Sale of rice by farmer in domestic market	3,40,000
(ii) Purchase of tractor by farmer	1,50,000
(iii) Procurement of rice by government from the farmer	10,000
(iv) Consumption of rice by farmer for his family consumption	3,000
(v) Subsidy received by farmer	1,000
(vi) Expenditure on maintenance of existing capital stock	8,500

Or

Calculate GNP_{MP} by (a) Income method and (b) Expenditure method

	(₹ in lakhs)
(a) Personal consumption expenditure	350
(b) Wages and salaries	340
(c) Contribution to S.S. scheme	200 (25% by employer)
(d) Gross business fixed investment	30
(e) Inventory Investment	10
(f) Profits	50
(g) Government Purchase of goods & services	100
(h) Rent	25
(i) Net imports	(–) 10
(j) Gross residential construction investment	30
(k) Interest	20
(l) Mixed Income	50
(m) Net factor income to abroad	5
(n) Depreciation	15
(o) Gross public investment	20

17. In an economy, actual level of income is 500 whereas the full employment level of income is a bit more than this. Three-fourth of the income is consumed in the economy. If there is an increase in investment in the economy by 75, calculate: **(6)**

(a) new income level at full employment level

(b) change in savings

(c) change in consumption

SECTION B (INDIAN ECONOMIC DEVELOPMENT)

18. The concept of 5-year plans was borrowed from ________. **(1)**

19. Which organisation collects data on poverty in India? **(1)**

20. Trade between more than 2 countries is called: **(1)**

(a) Multilateral trade (b) Bilateral trade

(c) Multinational trade (d) Multiple partner trade

Or

The first crop that saw a boom after Green Revolution:

(a) Rice (b) Wheat (c) Maize (d) Bajra

21. The number of people who are actually employed at a given point of time is known as ________ force. **(1)**

22. TISCO stand for: **(1)**

(a) Tata iron and steel company (b) Tata institute of cooperatives

(c) Tata iron and steel corporation (d) Tata iron and steel consignment

23. Match the alternatives given in Column II with respective terms in Column I: **(1)**

Column I	Column II
a. LPG	(i) used for cooking in rural areas
b. dung cakes	(ii) reduces household pollution
c. Global warming	(iii) respiratory diseases
d. Water pollution	(iv) climate change

24. A worker is somebody who is paid by an employer. **(1)**

(a) True (b) False

25. The national language of Pakistan is ________ and the official language is ________. **(1)**

26. Mention the objective of introducing The Right to Education Act. **(1)**

27. The magnitude of Water contamination caused is highest in: **(1)**

(a) Discharging of untreated waste by the factories into the water bodies

(b) Bathing in rivers

(c) Washing clothes alongside the river

(d) Immersing of Lord Ganesha's idol during Ganesh Chaturthi

28. Give one word for the following: **(3)**

(a) Defining the size of land that an individual/ family can own—

(b) Taxes levied on imported goods—

(c) Financial aid/support extended by the government for production—

Or

Mention the characteristics of Globalisation when it was undertaken as a strategy

29. What are the 3 main sources of electricity in India? **(3)**

30. How do the following factors contribute to the environmental crisis in India? **(4)**
    (a) Rising population (b) illiteracy
    (c) Urbanisation (d) Poaching

Or

State the functions of pollution control boards.

31. Explain the distribution of labour based on 'gender'. **(4)**

32. Differentiate between conventional and non-conventional sources of energy. **(4)**

33. Explain the Industrial Policy Resolution, 1956. **(6)**

Or

What were some of the positive contributions of the British rule to the Indian economy?

34. "Poverty begets poverty". Explain the relation between poverty as a cause and as a consequence. **(6)**

SAMPLE PAPER 14
(FOR PRACTICE)

Time allowed: 3 hours *Maximum marks: 80*

General Instructions:

Same as given in Sample Paper 1.

SECTION A (MACROECONOMICS)

1. Which items are not included in M_1? **(1)**

(a) Inter bank deposits (b) Other deposits with RBI

(c) Currency and coins with public (d) Net demand deposits with banks

2. Borrowing is a capital receipt because __________. **(1)**

3. What is excess demand. **(1)**

4. Fishing vessels operated by Indian fishermen in international waters are the parts of the economic territory of **(1)**

(a) India (b) UNO

(c) International territory (d) None of these

Or

In estimation of the national income, we include

(a) value of an old woolen suit

(b) commission of the traders in the trading of old articles

(c) value of an old TV

(d) purchase of an old houses

5. State the following is true or false: **(1)**

'Balance of Trade always balances.'

6. Break-even point is achieved when consumption __________. **(1)**

7. Autonomous items in BOP are related to those transactions which: **(1)**

(a) are determined by motive of profit

(b) are not concerned with the equilibrium status of BOP

(c) both (a) and (b)

(d) none of these

8. State two examples of revenue receipt of government. **(1)**

9. Match the alternatives given in Column II with respective terms in Column I: **(1)**

Column I	Column II
a. MPC = 0.2	(i) K = 2
b. MPS = 0.5	(ii) K = 1.25
c. MPC = 0.8	(iii) K = 5
d. MPS = 0.4	(iv) K = 2.5

10. Propensity to consume means **(1)**
    (a) tendency of the consumer towards higher consumption
    (b) ratio of consumption to income
    (c) level of income at which consumption expenditure is equal to income
    (d) additional income to be spent on consumption

11. Calculate value added by Firm A & B from the following data: **(3)**

(a) Purchase by Firms B from Firm A	40
(b) Sales by Firm B	80
(c) Imports by Firm B	10
(d) Rent Paid by Firm B	05
(e) Opening stock of Firm B	15
(f) Closing stock of Firm B	20
(g) Purchase by Firm A from Firm B	20
(h) Closing Stock of Firm A	20
(i) Opening stock of Firm A	10

Or

Calculate (a) GVA_{MP} for A and B and (b) National Income

Sales by A	1,000
Sales by B	2,000
NFIA	20
Change in stock of B	(–)200
Closing stock of A	50
Opening stock of A	100
Consumption of fixed capital	180
Indirect taxes	120
Purchase of raw material by A	500
Purchase of raw material by B	600
Exports by B	70

12. Derive the savings curve with the help of consumption curve. **(3)**

13. Explain the meaning of deficit in balance of payment account. **(4)**

Or

Explain the meaning and two merits of flexible foreign exchange rate.

14. There is a wide gap between rich and poor in the country, how can the government through its budget help to reduce this gap? **(4)**
15. Explain two types of tax receipts and two types of non-tax receipts of government. **(4)**
16. Distinguish between full employment equilibrium and under employment equilibrium. Also explain two measures by which full employment equilibrium can be reached from under employment equilibrium situation. **(6)**
17. Calculate compensation of employees **(6)**

	(₹ in Crores)
(a) Value of output of primary sector	2,000
(b) Sales tax	400
(c) Gross National Product at Market Price	6,000
(d) Net factor income to abroad	200
(e) Net domestic capital formation	60
(f) Purchase of raw material by all sectors	5,800
(g) Rent	600
(h) Value of output of secondary sector	4,000
(i) Subsidy	100
(j) Interest	700
(k) Import of machinery by all sector	1,000
(l) Gross investment	300
(m) Value of output of territory sector	6,000
(n) Profits	640
(o) Mixed income of self-employed	1,660

Or

Explain the problem of double counting in estimating national income with the help of an example. Also explain two alternative ways of avoiding the problem.

SECTION B (INDIAN ECONOMIC DEVELOPMENT)

18. Occupational structure in India during the British rule revealed that Indian economy was: **(1)**

(a) Underdeveloped (b) Developing

(c) Stagnant (d) Both (a) and (c)

19. Give One example of social infrastructure. **(1)**

20. __________ means increasing the role of private sector in the economy: **(1)**

21. Which of the following is false? **(1)**
   (a) LPG reduces household pollution
   (b) In rural areas, dung cakes are used for cooking
   (c) Water pollution causes respiratory diseases
   (d) Global warming is caused due to climate change

Or

Sunlight can be converted into Solar Energy using:
   (a) Photo-Voltaire cells (b) Light cells
   (c) Photo voltaic cells (d) Uranium battery

22. Define Miracle seeds. **(1)**

23. Population per square kilometer of land area denotes __________. **(1)**

24. In year 1969, Nationalisation of banks was carried out under which __________ banks were nationalised. **(1)**

25. Match the alternatives given in Column II with respective terms in Column I: **(1)**

Column I	Column II
a. White revolution	(i) Crops
b. Green revolution	(ii) Milk
c. Yellow revolution	(iii) Organic farming to curb soil degradation
d. Brown revolution	(iv) Oil Seeds

26. __________ policy of the government includes Expenditure by government and Tax and revenue policy. **(1)**

27. midday meals are provided to: **(1)**
   (a) develop a sense of taste among small children
   (b) develop a feeling of community eating
   (c) attract children from poor sections to attend school
   (d) give a relief to mothers from cooking by providing food at school

28. Decline of handicraft industry adversely affected the Indian economy. Comment. **(3)**

29. Explain the areas where absolute poverty is useful and those where relative poverty is useful as a standard of measure. **(3)**

Or

Differentiate between commercial and non-commercial sources of energy.

30. Write a short note on Montreal protocol. **(4)**

31. Compare the GDP growth of China, India and Pakistan. **(4)**

32. Women health has become a matter of great concern. Elucidate. **(4)**

Or

The informal sector of employment poses a threat to the idea of a "decent job" as proposed by the ILO. List down the detriments.

33. **(6)**

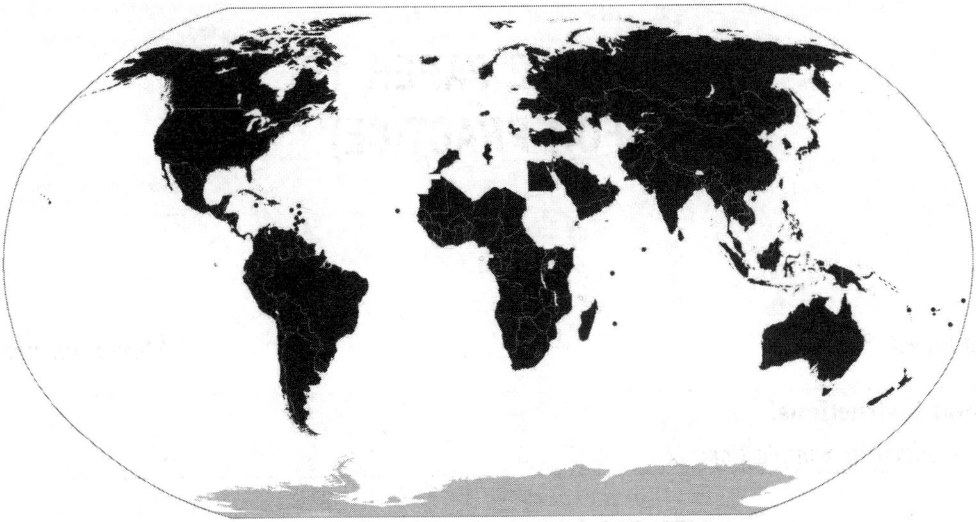

The above given map shows the number of countries who are a part of World Trade Organisation (WTO) in dark black colour. As you can see a majority of counties are members of the WTO, however a lot of developing countries feel that WTO is partial towards the major power states. Would it then be more beneficial for India or continue being a part or leave it?

Or

Discuss the achievements of Green Revolution

34. Discuss the various institutional sources of rural credit. **(6)**

SAMPLE PAPER 15 (FOR PRACTICE)

Time allowed: 3 hours *Maximum marks: 80*

General Instructions:
Same as given in Sample Paper 1.

SECTION A (MACROECONOMICS)

1. M_1 measure of money supply is also known as __________. **(1)**

2. In the Constitution of India, Union budget is known as **(1)**
(a) Balance sheet of government
(b) Annual financial statement
(c) Summary of taxes
(d) Profit and loss account of government

3. __________ in taxes lead to increase in aggregate demand. **(1)**

4. Sales of an old car is not included in National Income because **(1)**
(a) it has become obsolete being an old car
(b) it does not form part of the current production process
(c) its exact value cannot be estimated
(d) a good amount of expenditure has to be incurred on its maintenance

Or

Which of the following is included in the economic territory of a country?
(a) political frontiers of a country
(b) ships and aircrafts operated by the residents between two countries
(c) embassies operated in other countries
(d) All of the above

5. State two components of current account of BOP. **(1)**

6. Value of MPC lies between __________ and __________ (both inclusive). **(1)**

7. Identify the correct sequence of alternatives given in Column II by matching them with respective terms in Column I: **(1)**

Column I	Column II
a. Import of Furniture	(i) Increases balance of invisibles
b. Export of Machine	(ii) Decreases balance of invisibles
c. Import of Insurance service	(iii) Increases balance of trade
d. Export of transport service	(iv) Decreases balance of trade

8. State whether the following statement is true or false **(1)**
'Primary deficit is equal to difference between Fiscal deficit and interest payment.'

9. Which one is not the instrument of monetary policy? **(1)**
(a) Open market operation
(b) Bank rate
(c) Selective credit-control
(d) Government spending

10. Define Average propensity to consume. **(1)**

11. What is Net factor income from abroad? What are its components? **(3)**

12. Explain the relation of slope of consumption curve with investment multiplier with the help of diagram and schedule. **(3)**

Or

Explain the "consumption function" with the help of a schedule and diagram.

13. What are the implications of large revenue deficit? Give two measures to reduce it. **(4)**

14. State giving reasons which of the following items constitute demand or supply of foreign exchange: **(4)**
(a) Shah Rukh Khan going to Canada for medical treatment.
(b) Salman Khan purchased a bungalow in Dubai
(c) Bill Gates donated \$100 million to flood affected region in India.

Or

Explain briefly the functions of foreign exchange market.

15. Distinguish between "Statutory Liquidity Ratio" and "Cash Reserve ratio". **(4)**

16. Given C = 40 + 0.8Y. Find **(6)**
(a) Dissaving's
(b) Marginal propensity to save
(c) Investment multiplier
(d) Average propensity to consume given that income level is ₹ 4,000.

17. Calculate "Gross National Product at Market Price" by production method and income method. **(6)**

	(₹ in Crores)
(a) Value of output of primary sector	1,000
(b) Indirect tax	200
(c) Compensation of employees	780
(d) Net factor income to abroad	100
(e) Intermediate purchase by all sectors	2,900
(f) Rent	300
(g) Value of output of secondary sector	2,000
(h) Subsidy	50
(i) Interest	600
(j) Consumption of fixed capital	120
(k) Value of Output of territory sector	3,000
(l) Profits	320
(m) Mixed income of self employed	830

Or

Calculate NNP_{MP} by (a) Income method and (b) Expenditure method.

	(₹ in Crores)
(a) Personal consumption expenditure	700
(b) Wages and salaries	680
(c) Employer's contribution to S.S. scheme	100
(d) Gross business fixed investment	60
(e) Gross residential construction investment	60
(f) Gross public investment	40
(g) Inventory Investment	20
(h) Profits	100
(i) Government Purchase of goods & services	200
(j) Rent	50
(k) Net exports	20
(l) Interest	40
(m) Mixed Income	100
(n) NFIA	(–) 10
(o) Depreciation	20
(p) Net indirect taxes	10

SECTION B (INDIAN ECONOMIC DEVELOPMENT)

18. State two commercial Indian banks. **(1)**

19. __________ refers to the cultivation of fruits, flowers, aromatic plants, spices. **(1)**

20. Persia is the old name of __________. **(1)**

21. Potential labour force of India consists of: **(1)**

(a) People in a particular age group (b) Those who are fit to work
(c) Those who are willing to work (d) All of the above

22. Crops raised using the HYV seeds were prone to __________ attacks. **(1)**

23. Which of the following countries has the lowest Adult Literacy Rate? **(1)**

(a) China (b) Pakistan (c) India (d) All equal

24. If White revolution: Milk; Green revolution: Crops, then Yellow revolution? **(1)**

(a) Corn (b) Oil seeds (c) Flowers (d) Pulses

Or

The institutional credit approach in rural areas was undertaken from the year:

(a) 1969 (b) 1970 (c) 1971 (d) 1975

25. State whether the following statement is true or false: **(1)**

'life expectancy in China is 76 years.'

26. Following are the events which led to Green Revolution. Identify the correct sequence of alternatives given in Column II by matching them with respective terms in Column I: **(1)**

Column I	Column II
a. Low Agricultural Productivity	(i) High production of wheat and rice
b. Initial years after Independence	(ii) Use of HYV seeds and irrigation facilities
c. Green Revolution	(iii) 75% population dependent on agriculture
d. Boom in Agricultural produce	(iv) Dependence on Monsoon and Outdated Technology

27. Which of the following is not a communicable disease? **(1)**

(a) Hepatitis (b) AIDS (c) Salmonella (d) Cancer

28. What measures were taken after the independence to improve the condition of agriculture which had become stagnant under the British Raj. **(3)**

Or

Why did India opt for a mixed economy?

29. How does fishing lead to pollution? **(3)**

30. What were the features of "Food for Work" programme? **(4)**

31. What are the various means by which countries are trying to strengthen their domestic economies? **(4)**

32. An Odd-Even policy was carried out by the Delhi government to improve the alarming situation of the capital city in India. What other measures have been taken by the government to curb pollution? **(4)**

Or

Trace the relationship between human capital and economic growth.

33. **(6)**

Retain the edge with FINANCIAL EXPRESS

INDIAN EXPRESS

SCREEN — India's largest selling film weekly

New Delhi, Tuesday, July 2, 1991

RV influenced Punjab poll postponement

By Prabhu Chawla

RV's invitation

RV's interests

Mr Chandra Shekhar told the President that postponing Punjab elections at this stage would be worse than "Operation Bluestar" decision of June 1984.

Sharp depreciation of rupee

Express News Service

RBI spot exchange rates	JUNE 28	JULY 1	Depreciation in Re value
Pound Sterling	Rs 34.36	Rs 37.37	−8.05%
US Dollar	Rs 21.05	Rs 23.04	−8.63%
Deutsche Mark	Rs 11.61	Rs 12.71	−8.58%
Yen	Paise 15.22	Paise 16.69	−8.83%

* The percentage was worked out prior to the second revision of rupee value

Top officials among 14 kidnapped in Assam

Express News Service

Pandey demands arrest of Chandraswami

Express News Service

A look at the front page of the Indian Express on July 2, 1991, announcing the devaluation which set in motion an irreversible process. What is it that the article is talking about. Give the reasons for the introduction of the process?

34. Human capital can be improved by incurring expenditure on Education, Health, On-the– job training, migration and information. Explain in detail. **(6)**

Or

What are the pros and cons of organic farming?

SAMPLE PAPER 16
(FOR PRACTICE)

Time allowed: 3 hours *Maximum marks: 80*

General Instructions:
Same as given in Sample Paper 1.

SECTION A (MACROECONOMICS)

1. Barter system economy was also known as ________ to ________ economy. **(1)**

2. Fiscal deficit signifies **(1)**
(a) Revenue deficit (b) Borrowings and other liabilities
(c) Primary deficit (d) None of these

3. Define autonomous expenditure. **(1)**

4. Increase in national income due to increase in current market prices is **(1)**
(a) increase in real national income
(b) increase in nominal national income
(c) increase in national income based on the prices of base year
(d) decrease in per capita income

Or

Real national Income means
(a) National income at current prices
(b) National income at factor prices
(c) National income at constant prices
(d) National income at average prices of the past 10 years

5. If balance of trade is (–) ₹ 600 crore and value of exports is ₹ 500 crore, then the value of imports will be ________. **(1)**

6. AD curve is a parallel to ________ curve. **(1)**

7. Transfer of payment may be **(1)**
(a) grants in cash from foreign government
(b) contribution from international organisation
(c) donations
(d) all of these

8. State whether the following is true or false: **(1)**
'Income tax is not a direct tax.'

9. Match the alternatives given in Column II with respective terms in Column I: **(1)**

Column I	Column II
a. Value of output	(i) National Income
b. Value added	(ii) Sales + inventory investment
c. Net value added at factor cost from all production units.	(iii) Value of output (–) Value of input
d. Net National Product at factor cost	(iv) Domestic income

10. Aggregate demand refers to the **(1)**
(a) total demand of all the consumers in the economy
(b) total demand of all the producers in the economy
(c) total demand for final goods and services in an economy during a year
(d) total demand for consumption and exports in the economy

11. Explain "Composition and distribution of GDP" as limitation of Real GDP to be considered as welfare of index. **(3)**

12. What does "Zero savings" in the economy indicate? Explain with the help of schedule and diagram. **(3)**

Or

What are the two types of unemployment and also explain the concept of under employment equilibrium?

13. Recently government increases the slab of direct tax being paid by higher income group people, explain the objective and significance behind this step of government. **(4)**

14. How does balance of payments affect the foreign exchange rate of a country? **(4)**

Or

How do depreciation and appreciation of currency affect exports and imports of the country?

15. How will the following changes will affect the money supply (increase or decrease) in the economy. State with reasons: **(4)**
(a) Rise in repo rate from 5% to 7.5%
(b) Margin requirement increases by 2%
(c) RBI reduces statutory reserve ratio.
(d) Purchase of government securities by RBI

16. Find gross domestic product at market price with the help of income and expenditure method using the following data: **(6)**

	(₹ in Crores)
(a) Final consumption expenditure	6,500
(b) Final consumption expenditure of non-profit organisations serving households	1,500
(c) Wages and salaries	9,000
(d) Operating surplus	2,000
(e) Mixed income	5,000
(f) Net indirect tax	1,500
(g) Depreciation	2,500
(h) Net occupational fixed investment	4,000
(i) Net house construction investment	1,200
(j) Net government investment	800
(k) Stock investment	2,000
(l) Net factor income from abroad	1,000
(m) Government final consumption expenditure	2,000
(n) Net exports	2,000

Or

What are the steps taken for calculating national income by expenditure method? Also give two precautions while calculating national income by this method.

17. (a) Given S = (–) 200 + 0.25Y. Find **(6)**

(i) Consumption when income is ₹ 1,000

(ii) Investment multiplier

(b) In an economy investment expenditure is increased by 400 crore and marginal propensity to consume is 0.8. Calculate increase in income and increase in savings.

SECTION B (INDIAN ECONOMIC DEVELOPMENT)

18. The classification of industries in group A under Industrial Policy Resolution, 1956 did not include: **(1)**

(a) Heavy and core industries (b) Atomic energy

(c) Railways (d) Fertilizers

19. ICMR stands for: **(1)**

(a) International Council of Medical Research

(b) Indian Council of Medical Resources

(c) Indian Council for Medical Research

(d) International Cooperative Medical Sciences

20. State the main objective of Great Leap Campaign of China. **(1)**

21. Established in 1982, __________ is an apex institution of Rural Banking **(1)**

(a) RBI (b) Land Development Bank

(c) Food corporation of India (d) None of the above

Or

Which of the following is not a way to meet power crisis?

(a) Increase in production capacity

(b) Reduction in distribution losses

(c) Increase use of non-renewable resources

(d) Increased role of private sector

22. Construction of ____________________ by the British ensured a check on famines as food could to be transported to the affected areas in case of crisis. **(1)**

23. Match the alternatives given in Column II with respective terms in Column I: **(1)**

Column I	Column II
a. Disguised unemployment	(i) Able and willing; but fail to get work
b. Seasonal unemployment	(ii) More people are engaged than what are required
c. Self employment	(iii) Available only for certain period of time
d. Open unemployment	(iv) Using own resources for a living

24. What is the meaning of Casualisation of workforce? **(1)**

25. State whether the following is true or false: **(1)**

'India and Pakistan both have adopted the Mixed Economic system.'

26. "Land to the tiller" was: **(1)**

(a) A land reform measure

(b) An employment generation scheme

(c) A campaign against droughts

(d) A campaign to save crops from pests

27. __________ is an abiotic component of the environment. **(1)**

28. Choose answers from the following: Liberalisation, Privatisation, Globalisation. **(3)**

An Apple phone, the components of which are manufactured in China and Korea and finally integrated in USA.

Dilution of stakes of the Indian government in Maruti Udyog.

Mc Donald's coming to India and setting up its chain.

29. List down some sources from where the data on unemployment is obtained. **(3)**

Or

Has the employment opportunities for women increased with the emergence of diversified agricultural activities?

30. What are the vital functions of the environment? **(4)**

Or

Explain the functioning of Self-Help Groups as an entity of rural credit source.

31. How is China's experience to its developmental path different from that of India and Pakistan? **(4)**

32. What is the relation between Poverty line and Minimum Calorie intake? **(4)**

33. Highlight the reforms done in the Indian economy under the liberalisation policy with focus on tax reforms, financial sector reforms and industrial sector reforms. **(6)**

34. How is expenditure on information and On-the–Job training an investment to Human Capital Formation? **(6)**

Or

Following is the data published by World Economic Forum which shows a comparative position of India's infrastructure. Give reasons for the low trends and illustrate the importance of infrastructure for the growth of any economy.

Quality of infrastructure in India and in peer countries

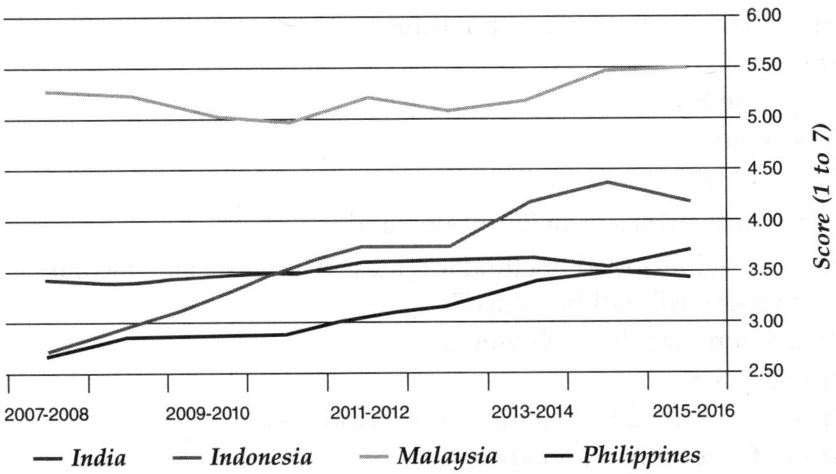

Source: World Economic Forum

SAMPLE PAPER 17
(FOR PRACTICE)

Time allowed: 3 hours *Maximum marks: 80*

General Instructions:

Same as given in Sample Paper 1.

SECTION A (MACROECONOMICS)

1. The value of credit multiplier will be high when cash reserve ratio is __________. **(1)**

2. Which of the following is not an indirect tax? **(1)**

(a) Sales tax
(b) Corporate tax
(c) Service tax
(d) Excise duty

3. State one consequence of deficient demand. **(1)**

4. As per the value-added method of measuring national income which of the following items will not be added? **(1)**

(a) Production for self-employment
(b) Imputed rent
(c) Brokerage earned by selling second hand goods
(d) Sales of second hand goods

Or

Which one is not a transfer payment?

(a) Interest on national debt
(b) Pension
(c) Old age pension
(d) Donations

5. If balance of trade (BOT) deficit is (–) ₹ 5,000 crores and the value of imports is ₹ 9,000 crores then the value of exports will be __________. **(1)**

6. If it is given that: C = 20 and Y = 100 then APS is equal to __________. **(1)**

7. How will the exports of domestic country gets affected by appreciation of foreign currency. **(1)**

8. Which of the following is not a revenue receipt? **(1)**
   (a) Income from sale of equity (b) Special assessment
   (c) License fee (d) Custom duty

9. Match the alternatives given in Column II with respective items in Column I: **(1)**

Column I	Column II
a. Increase in demand of foreign exchange	(i) Leads to Currency appreciation
b. Decrease in demand of foreign exchange	(ii) Leads to Currency depreciation
c. Increase in supply of foreign exchange	
d. Decrease in supply of foreign exchange	

10. State whether the following statement is true or false: **(1)**
    'If MPS = 1 and increase in National Income is ₹ 500 crore then the increase in investment is 50 crore.'

11. Classify the following into "Fixed capital formation" or "Inventory investment" giving reasons **(3)**
    (a) New railway engines manufactured by Indian railways
    (b) Increase in number of goats in a poultry farm.
    (c) New residential building constructed by a builder.

12. What is investment multiplier? Explain the relationship between marginal propensity to consume and investment multiplier. **(3)**

    Or

    How can you derive consumption curve from savings curve? Elaborate.

13. Comment on the statements:
    "RBI can control the money supply in the market through Repo and Reverse Repo Rate." **(4)**

14. Explain the concept of "Surplus" in the balance of payment account. How does central bank use this surplus? **(4)**

    Or

    Recently more foreign investors are investing in India which leads to a rise in foreign direct investment. How does this affect the price of foreign exchange?

15. Distinguish between surplus budget and deficit budget. How is deficit budget used to correct deficient demand in the economy. **(4)**

16. Distinguish between inflationary gap and deflationary gap. Show deflationary gap on diagram. Can this gap exist at equilibrium level of income? Explain. **(6)**

17. Calculate (a) GDP_{FC} and (b) Factor income to abroad **(6)**

	(₹ in Crores)
(a) Compensation of employees	1600
(b) Profits	400
(c) Dividends	100
(d) Gross national product at market price	2800
(e) Rent	300
(f) Net indirect taxes	240
(g) Gross capital formation	600
(h) Net fixed investment	400
(i) Change in inventory	100
(j) Factor income from abroad	120
(k) Interest	200

Or

(a) Find net value added at factor cost from the following:

(i) Sale of rice by farmer in domestic market	3,60,000
(ii) Purchase of tractor by farmer	1,75,000
(iii) Procurement of rice by government from the farmer	12,000
(iv) Consumption of rice by farmer for his family consumption	4,000
(v) Subsidy received by farmer	1,500
(vi) Expenditure on maintenance of existing capital stock	7,500

(b) Distinguish between gross investment and net investment.

SECTION B (INDIAN ECONOMIC DEVELOPMENT)

18. At the time of independence, there were only two well-managed iron and steel firms. One was TISCO in Jamshedpur, the other was in __________. **(1)**

19. The Mahatma Gandhi National Rural Employment Guarantee Act, provides for: **(1)**

(a) 100 days of paid work
(b) 50 days of paid work
(c) one year of paid work
(d) 3 months of paid work

20. __________ mode of economy rests on the principle of Profit Making. **(1)**

21. Give two examples of a physical resource. **(1)**

22. Rupee was devalued in 1991 as part of the economic reforms in order to: **(1)**

(a) Stimulate exports and discourage imports
(b) To integrate with USA and thereby not compete with Dollar
(c) Both (a) and (b)
(d) None of the above

Or

GATT was established in 1948 with how many member nations?

(a) 21 (b) 22 (c) 23 (d) 24

23. State whether the following statement is true or false **(1)**

'Reforms in China were introduced in 1978.'

24. Population explosion is one of the basic reasons for rampant poverty. **(1)**

(a) True (b) False

(c) Maybe (d) Cannot be determined

25. Since the introduction of One Child Policy, fertility rate in China has fallen from over 3 births to __________. **(1)**

26. Match the alternatives given in Column II with respective terms in Column I: **(1)**

Column I	Column II
a. Wind Energy	(i) Non-Commercial Source
b. Petroleum	(ii) Non-Conventional Source
c. Agriculture Waste	(iii) Nuclear Fission and Fusion
d. Atomic Energy	(iv) Traditional Source

27. A system in which marketing societies are formed by producers to sell the output are called: **(1)**

(a) Self-help groups

(b) Collective marketing

(c) Wholesale markets

(d) Ghettos

28. What do you understand by Self-Reliance as a goal of the economy? **(3)**

29. A recent report by the World Bank suggests that India should make a transition to a Knowledge Economy as it has all the key ingredients. What are they? **(3)**

Or

Why is it necessary to generate employment in the formal sector, so that the influx of informal sector is absorbed?

30. Explain the trends in poverty across states of India. **(4)**

31. Give reasons for the sluggish growth of Pakistan on both economic as well as social indicators? **(4)**

32. Why do farmers need credit? **(4)**

Or

The opportunity costs of negative environmental impacts or what are known as environmental externalities are very high. Explain.

33. (a) The rate of growth of GDP in India has been on the increase from 5.6% during 1980-90 to 7% in the 1993-2001 period.

(b) The foreign exchange reserves were $39 billion in 2000-01, $107 billion in 2003-04, $145 billion 2005-06 and $180 billion in 2007.

If these are the positive effects of Globalisation for India, then what are its dark sides, if any? **(6)**

Or

What are the achievements of the LPG policy?

34. What are the various factors which lead to poverty? **(6)**

SAMPLE PAPER 18
(FOR PRACTICE)

Time allowed: 3 hours *Maximum marks: 80*

General Instructions:
Same as given in Sample Paper 1.

SECTION A (MACROECONOMICS)

1. Difference between M_3 and M_1 is ________. **(1)**

2. Which of the following is not a characteristic of revenue receipts? **(1)**
(a) Recurring nature
(b) No repayment burden
(c) Non-recurring nature
(d) None of these

3. What does Full employment means? **(1)**

4. Factor cost is equal to **(1)**
(a) Market price – Indirect tax
(b) Market price – Net indirect tax
(c) Market price + Indirect tax
(d) Market price + NIT

Or

When indirect taxes are subtracted from NNP_{MP} and subsidies are added, then it will be equal to
(a) NNP_{FC}
(b) Domestic income
(c) GNP_{MP}
(d) NNP_{MP}

5. Which of these measures will reduce deficit on the current account of BOP? **(1)**
(a) Export promotion
(b) Import substitution
(c) Reducing inflation
(d) All of the above

6. MPC is expressed as __________. **(1)**

7. State whether the following statement is true or false **(1)**

'Devaluation of currency leads to decrease in imports.'

8. Which of the following is not a capital expenditure? **(1)**
   (a) Repayment of loans
   (b) Loans given to state governments and union territories
   (c) Expenditure on construction of school building
   (d) None of these

9. Buying and selling of government securities by the central bank from the public and banks is known as? **(1)**

10. If disposable income is ₹ 100 and consumption expenditure is ₹ 80, find out APS. **(1)**

11. From the following information calculate consumption level in the economy: **(3)**

(a) Wages and salaries	250
(b) Marginal propensity to consume	0.75
(c) Net factor income from abroad	100
(d) Rent, Interest and profit	350
(e) Autonomous consumption	25
(f) Mixed income	400
(g) Dividend	110

12. What is investment multiplier? Also calculate MPC if as a result of increase in investment by 60, national income rises by 240. **(3)**

Or

What is aggregate demand? Also explain its components in Keynesian's theory.

13. When the price of foreign currency rises, its supply also rises. Explain why? **(4)**

14. What is a balanced budget? Mention any two demerits of balanced budget. **(4)**

Or

State any three sources of capital receipts of government.

15. How is exchange rate determined in foreign exchange market? Explain. **(4)**

16. Do you agree with the following statements? Give reasons: **(6)**
   (a) When planned investment falls short of planned saving, then planned inventory falls.
   (b) An increase in the stock of goods held by consumer will contribute to capital formation.
   (c) Market rate of interest tends to be positively related to the bank rate.
   (d) Margin requirement is raised by central bank with a view to increase money supply.

17. Find (a) National income from product method, (b) Gross national product at factor cost from income method. **(6)**

	(₹ in Crores)
(a) Value of output at market price	
Primary sector	15,000
Secondary sector	8,000
Tertiary sector	6,000
(b) Depreciation of fixed capital	1,000
(c) Excise duty	1,700
(d) Sales tax	1,300
(e) Subsidies	1,500
(f) Value of intermediate consumption	
Primary sector	6,000
Secondary sector	4,000
Tertiary sector	2,000
(g) Income from property and enterprise	4,000
(h) Mixed income of the self-employed	6,500
(i) Compensation of employees	5,000
(j) Contribution of employers in social security	2,000
(k) Net factor income from abroad	(–)2,000

Or

Find national income with income and expenditure method—

	(₹ in Crores)
(a) Retirement pension	500
(b) Wages and salaries	6,500
(c) Contribution of employers' in social security	1,400
(d) Income from property and enterprise	1,500
(e) Mixed income of self-employed	2,500
(f) Old age pension	700
(g) Private final consumption expenditure	3,000
(h) Payment of compensation of employees by the Government	3,000
(i) Direct purchase of non-durable goods from abroad by the Government	1,800
(j) Net purchase of goods and services by the Government in domestic market	1,200
(k) Net factor income from abroad	(–)400
(l) Gross domestic capital formation	6,000
(m) Net domestic capital formation	3,000
(n) Net indirect tax	600
(o) Net exports	1,000

SECTION B (INDIAN ECONOMIC DEVELOPMENT)

18. British era was infused with feudal relations. Feudal here means ________ relationship. **(1)**

19. One of the major reasons for educated unemployment is: **(1)**
(a) Dullness among the youth
(b) Lack of vocational training
(c) Out dated books
(d) Inability of the firms to realize the potential of the youth

20. Inward looking strategy is more commonly known as? **(1)**

21. State whether the following statement is true or false: **(1)**
'Health is defined as Mental, physical and social well- being.'

22. Which of the following was not an exploitative policy of the British? **(1)**
(a) Reducing India to a mere exporter of raw materials
(b) Divide and rule
(c) Genocide of all those who were not fair skinned
(d) Compulsory imposition of English

23. Match the alternatives given in Column II with respective terms in Column I: **(1)**

Column I	Column II
a. Highest density of population	(i) China
b. Highest population	(ii) India
c. Sixth Most populous country	(iii) Pakistan
d. Growth rate of GDP	(iv) Human Development Indicator
e. GDP per capita	(v) Economic Indicator

24. Which of the following is not an alternative to using Chemical fertilizers and pesticides: **(1)**
(a) Producing pesticides from neem
(b) Using owls, peacocks, lizards to clear insects
(c) Using worms in pit to manure
(d) Using bats to scare away birds

25. PPP US$ is also called? **(1)**

26. ________ refers to transforming local farm produce into value added products for sale. **(1)**

27. The challenges before Organic farming are: **(1)**
(a) Lack of popularity
(b) Limited choice of crops
(c) Shorter shelf life
(d) All of the above

Or

Organic farming requires cheaper agricultural inputs.
(a) True
(b) False
(c) Maybe
(d) Cannot be determined

28. Partition of the country on the eve of independence amputated not just the social relations, but also the economy. Explain. **(3)**

Or

Before the advent of the British India was known for a handsome number of things. Mention a few of those things.

29. Greenhouse effect multiplies itself. How? **(3)**

30. List down some recent steps which have been taken in the field of education to improve both its quality and access. **(4)**

31. **(4)**

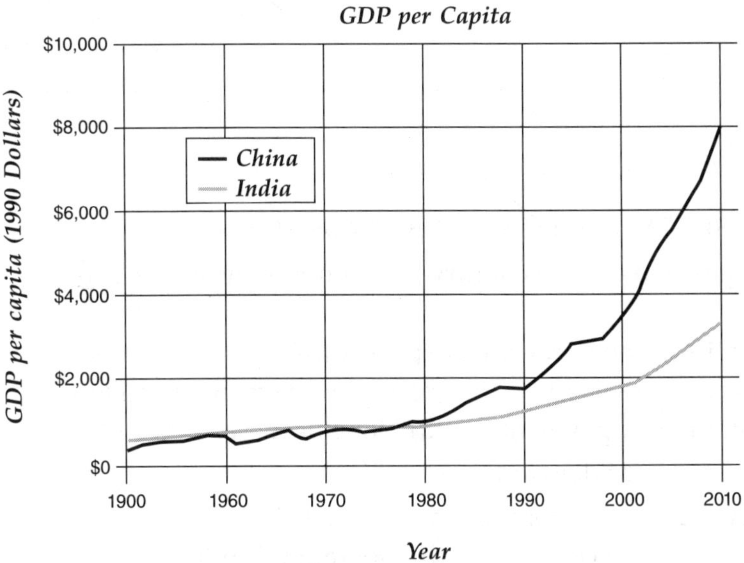

Study the given figure and answer the following questions:

(a) Which is a steeper line graph and what does it indicate?

(b) In which year, according to the graph did China make a huge jump against India?

(c) What are the measures that China undertook for its economic reform?

32. Explain the trends in poverty across states of India. **(4)**

Or

Mention a government scheme which is targeting poverty by improving the condition of women and safeguarding children.

33. 15th August 1947 was the beginning of a new era in Indian history. How were the imprints of British rule visible on it? **(6)**

34. Explain how do people become a resource by citing examples. **(6)**

Or

Cooperative Agricultural and Rural Developmental Bank (CARDB) in each state give long term credit to rural people. List some of the problems with the arrangement.

SAMPLE PAPER 19
(FOR PRACTICE)

Time allowed: 3 hours *Maximum marks: 80*

General Instructions:
Same as given in Sample Paper 1.

SECTION A (MACROECONOMICS)

1. __________ is an apex bank of the country that controls the entire banking system of the country. **(1)**

2. Which of the following is not a revenue expenditure? **(1)**

(a) Expenditure on defence capital (b) Expenditure on tax collection
(c) Expenditure on interest payment (d) None of these

3. State two causes of deficient demand? **(1)**

4. Which of the following is not a component of domestic income? **(1)**

(a) Compensation of employees (b) Operating inputs
(c) Mixed income (d) NFIA

Or

Which of the following items will be included in National Income?

(a) Interest paid by one firm to another
(b) Interest received on debenture by shareholders.
(c) Money received by people from their family members who are permanently settled abroad.
(d) Gains from the sale of shares

5. The Current account balance of payment includes **(1)**

(a) Direct investment
(b) Portfolio investment
(c) Unilateral transfer receipts
(d) All of the above

6. State whether the following is true or false **(1)**

'AD and AS become equal at full employment level of output.'

7. Match the alternatives given in Column II with respective terms in Column I. **(1)**

Column I	Column II
a. GDP_{MP} – Net indirect taxes – Depreciation	(i) NNP_{MP}
b. NNP_{FC} + Net indirect taxes + Depreciation	(ii) GNP_{MP}
c. NDP_{MP} + Net factor income from abroad – Net indirect taxes	(iii) Domestic Income
d. GNP_{FC} – Depreciation + Net indirect taxes	(iv) National Income

8. Define Balanced budget. **(1)**
9. In India, suppliers of money are **(1)**
   (a) government of the country
   (b) banking system of the country
   (c) both (a) and (b)
   (d) none of these
10. Relation between MPC and multiplier is __________. **(1)**
11. Explain "Composition and distribution of GDP" as limitation of Real GDP to be considered as welfare of index. **(3)**
12. What does "Zero savings" in the economy indicate? Explain with help of schedule and diagram. **(3)**

Or

Distinguish between "Statutory Liquidity Ratio" and "Cash Reserve Ratio".

13. What are the implications of large revenue deficit? Give two measures to reduce it. **(4)**
14. Distinguish between autonomous transactions and accommodating transactions in balance of payments. What is the significance of this distinction? **(4)**
15. Why does a rise in foreign exchange rate causes rise in its supply? **(4)**

Or

Explain the concept of "Managed floating" and why it is adopted.

16. Given C = 40 + 0.8Y. Find **(6)**
    (a) Dissavings
    (b) Marginal propensity to save
    (c) Investment multiplier
    (d) Average propensity to consume given that income level is ₹ 4,000.
17. What are the steps taken for calculating national income by expenditure method? Also give two precautions while calculating national income by this method. **(6)**

Or

Calculate NNP_{MP} by (a) Income method and (b) Expenditure method.

	(₹ in Crores)
(a) Personal consumption expenditure	700
(b) Wages and salaries	680
(c) Employer's contribution to S.S. scheme	100
(d) Gross business fixed investment	60
(e) Gross residential construction investment	60
(f) Gross public investment	40
(g) Inventory Investment	20
(h) Profits	100
(i) Government Purchase of goods & services	200
(j) Rent	50
(k) Net exports	20
(l) Interest	40
(m) Mixed Income	100
(n) NFIA	(–) 10
(o) Depreciation	20
(p) Net indirect taxes	10

SECTION B (INDIAN ECONOMIC DEVELOPMENT)

18. Due to poor agricultural technology, farmers in India depended on ________. **(1)**

19. Urban areas suffer most from: **(1)**

(a) Seasonal unemployment
(b) Open unemployment
(c) Disguised unemployment
(d) Chronic unemployment

20. What is Occupational structure. **(1)**

21. Give one example of man-made capital. **(1)**

22. Which of the following does not belong to secondary sector? **(1)**

(a) Food processing (b) Oil refinery
(c) Energy production (d) Quarrying

Or

During the initial years of development, private sector was skeptical to take up capital goods industries because:

(a) Lack of capital
(b) Lack of demand
(c) Both (a) and (b)
(d) Neither (a) *Or* (b)

23. India, China and Pakistan have made a considerable progress in the area of GDP but they must learn from their neighbour, __________ which gives equal importance to Happiness Index. **(1)**

24. State whether the following is true or false **(1)**

'Rickets is not a disease caused by Air pollution.'

25. Among India, Pakistan and China, __________ has the highest life expectancy at birth: **(1)**

26. Match the alternatives given in Column II with respective terms in Column I. **(1)**

Column I	Column II
a. Human Resources	(i) Electricity, Irrigation, Marketing etc.
b. Land Reforms	(ii) Education and Health facility
c. Infrastructure	(iii) Alleviation of poverty
d. Targeting social evils	(iv) Land to the tiller

27. Human capital comprises of: **(1)**

(a) Startup entrepreneurs
(b) Whole population
(c) Workers
(d) Both (a) and (c)

28. What was the 2-fold motive of the British? **(3)**

Or

What were the factors which did not let the goal of equity to be fully realised?

29. How does Human Capital Formation lead to economic development? **(3)**

30. Which is the form of unemployment in which a person is visibly unemployed but is not required at the job. State the name and give its characteristics. **(4)**

Or

Name and explain 4 schemes to improve the power situation in India.

31. Explain the development path of India and its performance trajectory. **(4)**

32. Write a note on medical tourism in India. **(4)**

33. Explain the taxation reforms under the New Economic Policy. **(6)**

34. What do you understand by the worker- population ratio? Give its characteristics. **(6)**

Or

Pollutants Entering the Oceans

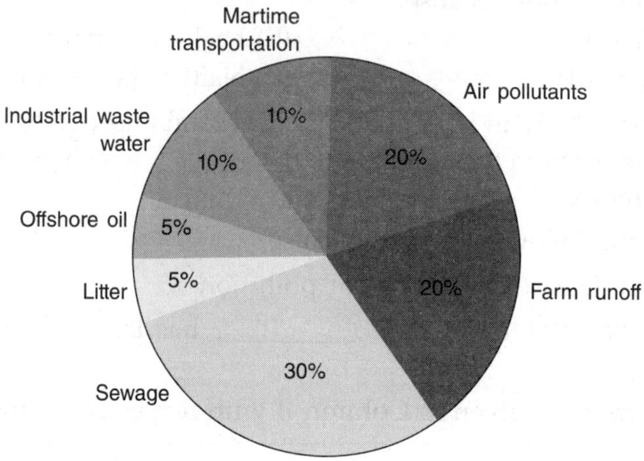

Refer to the image and answer the questions that follow:

(a) If the amount of waste produced by the industries is 20,000 kg, then what is the quantity of water pollution accruing to litter?

(b) Explain Water pollution with special reference to agricultural activities.

SAMPLE PAPER 20
(FOR PRACTICE)

Time allowed: 3 hours *Maximum marks: 80*

General Instructions:
Same as given in Sample Paper 1.

SECTION A (MACROECONOMICS)

1. Central Bank ________ credit. **(1)**

2. Any deficit in revenue budget can be met by **(1)**
(a) Imposing more indirect taxes
(b) Imposing more direct taxes
(c) Withdrawing money from capital receipts
(d) None of these

3. When planned investment is equal to planned savings, there will be ________. **(1)**

4. National product – Domestic product is equal to **(1)**
(a) Factor cost (b) Depreciation
(c) Net exports (d) NFIA

Or

Net capital formation causes
(a) increase in production capacity (b) increase in depreciation
(c) increase in profits (d) increase in cost

5. Define Balance of trade. **(1)**

6. Multiplier = **(1)**
(a) $\frac{\Delta Y}{\Delta S}$ (b) $\frac{\Delta Y}{\Delta I}$ (c) $\frac{\Delta I}{\Delta Y}$ (d) $\frac{\Delta Y}{\Delta C}$

7. Flexibility in foreign exchange rate **(1)**
(a) Promotes world trade
(b) Is a barrier to world trade
(c) Flexibility does not matter in world trade
(d) None of the above

8. Match the alternatives given in Column II with respective terms in Column I. **(1)**

Column I	Column II
a. Export of furniture	(i) Credit Side of Current A/c of BOP
b. Gifts sent to Canada	(ii) Debit Side of Current A/c of BOP
c. Investment in shares of foreign company	(iii) Debit Side of Capital A/c of BOP
d. Borrowings	(iv) Credit Side of Capital A/c of BOP

9. Money multiplier is denoted by __________. **(1)**

10. If the value of MPC = 0.9 find the value of multiplier. **(1)**

11. Classify the following into "Fixed capital formation" or "Inventory investment" giving reasons **(3)**
    (a) New railway engines manufactured by Indian railways
    (b) Increase in number of goats in a poultry farm.
    (c) New residential building constructed by a builder.

12. What is investment multiplier? Explain the relationship between marginal propensity to consume and investment multiplier. **(3)**

Or

How can you derive consumption curve from savings curve? Elaborate.

13. Distinguish between "Floating exchange rate system" and "Dirty floating exchange rate system". **(4)**

14. Explain the concept of "Surplus" in the balance of payment account. How does central bank use this surplus? **(4)**

Or

Recently more foreign investors are investing in India which lead to a rise in foreign direct investment. How does this affect the price of foreign exchange?

15. Recently government increases the slab of direct tax being paid by higher income group people, explain the objective and significance behind this step of government. **(4)**

16. (a) Given S = (–) 200 + 0.25Y. Find **(6)**
    (i) consumption when income is ₹ 1,000
    (ii) Investment multiplier.

    (b) In an economy investment expenditure is increased by 400 crore and marginal propensity to consume is 0.8. Calculate increase in income and increase in savings.

17. Calculate (a) GDP_{FC} and (b) Factor income to abroad **(6)**

	(₹ in Crores)
(a) Compensation of employees	1600
(b) Profits	400
(c) Dividends	100
(d) Gross national product at market price	2800
(e) Rent	300
(f) Net indirect taxes	240
(g) Gross capital formation	600
(h) Net fixed investment	400
(i) Change in inventory	100
(j) Factor income from abroad	120
(k) Interest	200

Or

(a) Find net value added at factor cost from the following:

(i)	Sale of rice by farmer in domestic market	3,60,000
(ii)	Purchase of tractor by farmer	1,75,000
(iii)	Procurement of rice by government from the farmer	12,000
(iv)	Consumption of rice by farmer for his family consumption	4,000
(v)	Subsidy received by farmer	1,500
(vi)	Expenditure on maintenance of existing capital stock	7,500

(b) Distinguish between gross investment and net investment.

SECTION B (INDIAN ECONOMIC DEVELOPMENT)

18. In order to increase the performance of the PSUs, the government handpicked 9 of them as the __________. **(1)**

19. The absolute number of poor in rural areas have declined and their urban counterparts have increased because: **(1)**

(a) The poor in villages are practicing birth control
(b) Migration of poor rural folk to cities in search of jobs
(c) The rich in the urban areas losing their jobs and becoming poor
(d) None of the above

20. __________ is a form of agriculture in which a landowner allows a tenant to use the land in return for a share of crops produced at the land. **(1)**

21. The education pyramid of India is: **(1)**

(a) Broader at the base and converging at the top
(b) Broader at the top and converging at the base
(c) Broader in the middle and converging from both the ends
(d) Uniform throughout

Or

Read the five sentences and arrange them in a sequence:

(i) Wheat chapattis are cooked at home

(ii) Wheat is distributed to poor families through these ration shops

(iii) The government sets a Minimum Support Price at which it buys any amount of wheat from the farmers

(iv) The Public Distribution System works through a mechanism of fair price shops

(v) Food Corporation of India purchases wheat at the procurement prices to maintain the Buffer stock. Thereafter, the wheat is ready for distribution.

(a) v, iv, iii, ii, i (b) i, ii, iii, iv, v (c) iii, v, iv, ii, i (d) ii, iv, iii, v, i

22. State two causes of unemployment. **(1)**

23. At the time of economic reforms, which led India to a developmental path, __________ was the Prime Minister of the country. **(1)**

24. Identify the correct sequence of alternatives given in Column II by matching them with respective terms in Column I and under which heading from Column 1 would you categorize Swach Bharat Abhiyan campaign: **(1)**

Column I	Column II
a. Preventive Medicine	(i) Provision of Clean Drinking Water
b. Curative Medicine	(ii) Vaccination
c. Social Medicine	(iii) Drugs and Pills

25. In which year were the reforms introduced in China? **(1)**

26. What is hydel power? **(1)**

27. If Gujarat is a success story for Milk cooperative, then Maharashtra is known for which cooperative arrangement? **(1)**

(a) Wheat production (b) Lijjat papad

(c) Dabbawalla (d) None of the above

28. Were the economic reforms of 1991 necessary? What would have been the condition of India had they not occurred? **(3)**

29. The only reason why poverty levels in India seem reduced is the manipulation of statistical data to arrive at the results. Do you agree? **(3)**

Or

What does the difference in male and female literacy indicate?

30. What do you understand by Rural Development? What needs to be done to ensure that? **(4)**

Or

Differentiate between labour force and work force.

31. The following table shows the annual GDP growth in two time periods: 1980-90 and 2011-15. Critically analyse it by giving reasons for the observations. **(4)**

Years	India	China	Pakistan
1980-90	5.7	10.3	6.3
2011-15	6.7	7.9	4.0

32. Write a note on the conventional sources of energy. **(4)**

33. Discuss India's foreign trade during colonial rule. **(6)**

34. **(6)**

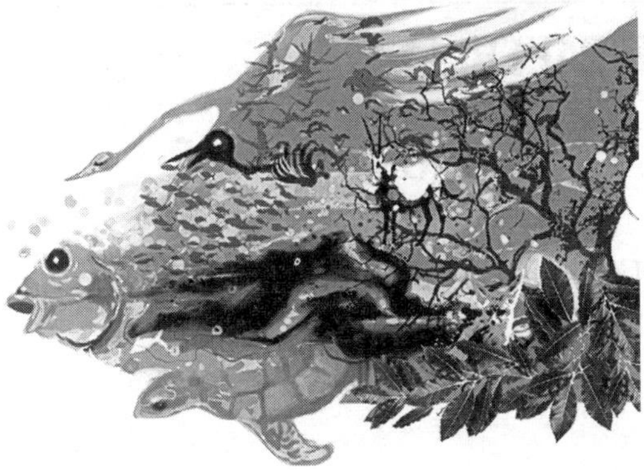

The above image depicts flora and fauna against black background, which indicates them being endangered. The phenomenon is known as biodiversity.

Name any 3 animals which are declared endangered in India. List down some methods to curd down biodiversity loss.

Or

Elaborate upon some of the employment generation schemes taken up by the government.

HINTS AND ANSWERS TO SAMPLE PAPERS 11–20

SAMPLE PAPER 11

SECTION A (MACROECONOMICS)

1. Goods

2. Estimated total receipts > Estimated total expenditure.

3. APC = 1

4. (a)

Or

(a)

5. (a)

6. ΔY

7. True

8. (b)

9. a. (ii), b. (iii), c. (iv), d. (i)

10. (a)

11. (a) ₹ 4,000, ₹ 4,000, ₹ 6,000

(b) ₹ 4,800, ₹ 8,800, ₹ 14,800

12. 0.1; 0.7; 0.3

Or

₹ 850 crores

13. This will lead to increase in money supply.

14. It can be managed by RBI by selling of foreign exchange in market.

Or

(a) Currency depreciation for rupees

(b) Yes, BOP somewhere tells about the demand and supply of foreign exchange.

15. (a) ₹ 360 crores (b) ₹ 300 crores

16. (a) False

$$\frac{MPC}{MPS} = 4$$

Let $MPC = x$

$$\frac{x}{1-x} = 4$$

$$x = 4 - 4x$$

$$5x = 4$$

$$x = \frac{4}{5} = 0.80$$

$$K = \frac{1}{1 - MPC} = \frac{1}{1 - 0.80} = \frac{1}{0.20} = 5$$

(b) True (c) False (d) False

17. (a) Transfer income (b) Transfer income (c) Factor income

Or

National income = ₹ 3,600 crores

SECTION B (INDIAN ECONOMIC DEVELOPMENT)

18. Handicraft

19. (d)

20. 164

21. i, ii iv, iii Suez Canal was used for trade between Britain and India

22. (c)

23. False

24. To safeguard the interest of farmers.

25. (b)

26. Central pollution control board

27. (d)

Or

(b)

28. Abolition of Zamindari, land ceiling, consolidation of fragmented land

31. Population, density of population, sex ratio, fertility rate, level of urbanisation, etc.

32. Discuss the concept of 'Jobless Growth.' Capital intensive techniques have reduced the need for labour, producing results at the same time.

Or

Yes, I agree. Highlight the practice of vermicomposting, organic farming etc. although it was necessary at the time of green revolution to boost agricultural production.

Similarly, you can refute the statement also, if you have justifiable reasons for the same.

34. (First Part) Investment in education sector leads to economic growth

SAMPLE PAPER 12

SECTION A (MACROECONOMICS)

1. True
2. Progressive
3. Under
4. (b)

   Or

   (a)
5. Higher exports lead to favorable balance of trade and vice versa.
6. (a)
7. Balance of payment.
8. (c)
9. ii, iii, iv, i
10. False
11. ₹ 3000 crores
12. (a) (–) 40 (b) 0.2
    (c) 5 times (d) 0.81

    Or

    (a) True
    (b) False, multiplier will be 1
    (c) False, MPS can never be negative
    (d) True, as consumption can never be zero.
13. The government aims at improving health and also aims at reducing the inequality of income and wealth.
14. (a) Visible items (b) Invisible items
    (c) Unilateral transfers (d) Capital transfers

    Or

    Foreign exchange rate fixed by the Government is known as the fixed foreign exchange rate. Its two merits are:
    (a) Stability of currency (b) Promotes international trade

15. Two components of Capital A/c are:

(a) Private transaction (2) Official transaction

16. Economy is in equilibrium when S = I.

17. ₹ 3,600 crores; ₹ 240 crores

Or

₹ 1,300 crores; ₹ 80 crores

SECTION B (INDIAN ECONOMIC DEVELOPMENT)

18. J.L. Nehru

19. True

20. (c)

21. (b)

22. iv, iii, ii, i

23. Indonesia

24. 2400 & 2100

25. (b)

26. (c)

Or

(d)

27. Agricultural waste.

29. Hint: Work is not done just for monetary value, it is also done for self-satisfaction, self-work and to keep oneself busy.

Or

Hint: Female feticide, infanticide; problems during pregnancy, no special laws at workplace for pregnant or lactating mothers, etc. Add more points as you see fit.

31. Hint: Started developing almost at the same time.

Had planning in place, as a periodic vision

In china and India, SEZs were established and they both opened the doors of their economy to the rest of the world.

Pakistan and India, gave enough importance to the public sector

33. Yes, it has been advantageous as it provided international credibility, employment, brought newer technology and improvement in living standards.

34. (Second Part) Insufficient resources, brain drain, population influx leading to crunch of resources, etc.

SAMPLE PAPER 13

SECTION A (MACROECONOMICS)

1. Amount of money held by public at a particular point of time.

2. Capital

3. (a)

4. (b)

Or

(a)

5. False

6. i , ii , iii , iv

7. Balance of Payment

8. Debt Trap

9. (d)

10. Consumption expenditure, Investment expenditure, Government expenditure and Net Exports

11. (a) Increase in Repo rate (b) Increase in Marginal requirement
(c) Increase in CRR/SLR (d) Selling of government securities

Or

The money that is put in something which gives future benefits or helps in wealth creation is called investment.

Equilibrium level = $\boxed{S = I}$

12. ₹ 600 crores

13. BOT = Export (–) Import

Rise in foreign exchange rate will increase exports and will lead to a favourable BOT.

Or

Devaluation is deliberate rise in price of foreign exchange and depreciation is caused by market forces of demand and supply.

14. (a) Debt trap (b) Dependency on foreign exchange (c) Inflation

15. Net deposit and time liabilities to be kept with RBI is CRR and the one kept with the bank itself is SLR.

16. (a) 20%; 150 (b) ₹ 3,45,500 crores

Or

₹ 545 crores

17. (a) 800 (b) 75 (c) 225

SECTION B (INDIAN ECONOMIC DEVELOPMENT)

18. USSR

19. NSSO: National Sample Survey Organisation

20. (a)

Or

(b)

21. Work

22. (a)

23. ii , i , iv , iii

24. (b) (even self-employed people are workers)

25. Urdu, English

26. Free and compulsory education for 6 – 14 years group people and to make education a fundamental right.

27. (a)

28. (First Part) Land Ceiling

Tariff

Subsidy

29. Hint: Thermal, hydro and nuclear

31. Hint: Demographic indicators measure the population size, sex ratio, density and dependency ratio

34. Hint: Illiteracy, unemployment lead to poverty and poverty leads to the inability to acquire education, feed oneself etc.

SAMPLE PAPER 14

SECTION A (MACROECONOMICS)

1. (a)

2. It creates liability.

3. Excess of AD over AS at full employment level.

4. (a)

Or

(b)

5. False

6. is equal to income

7. (c)

8. Escheat, Taxes

9. ii , i , iii , iv

10. (b)

11. ₹ 30 crores; ₹ 30 crores

Or

(a) ₹ 450 crores; ₹ 1,200 crores (b) ₹ 1,370 crores

12.

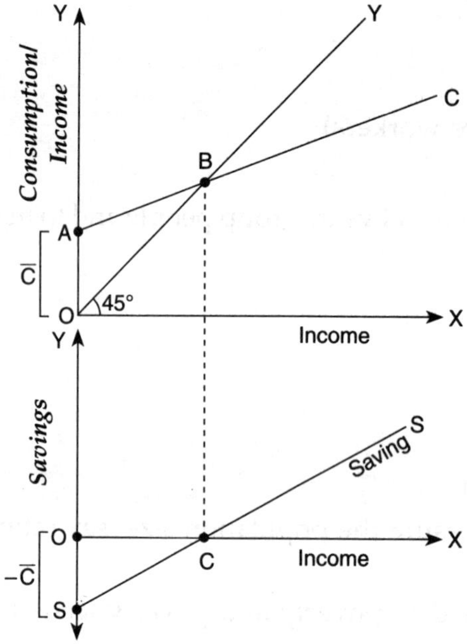

13. When outflow of foreign exchange > inflow of foreign exchange, then there is deficit.

Or

Foreign exchange rate is fixed by market forces of demand and supply. Merits:

(a) No Government intervention

(b) No fear of under or over estimation

14. Increase of taxes on rich and more expenditure on poor will help in reducing inequality.

15. Direct and indirect tax receipts. Non-tax receipt are:

(a) Special assessment (b) Fees and fines

16. When AD = AS at full employment output level then it is called full employment equilibrium and when AD = AS below full employment output level, then it is known as under employment equilibrium.

17. ₹ 1,060 crores

Or

Calculating the value of output more than once, while calculating national income is called double counting. Two ways to avoid it are:

(a) Take value added

(b) Final value of goods and services.

SECTION B (INDIAN ECONOMIC DEVELOPMENT)

18. (d)

19. Ports

20. Privatisation

21. (c) (Air pollution causes respiratory diseases like Asthma)

Or

(c)

22. Miracle seeds refer to high yielding varieties (HYV) seeds which raised agriculture yield per acre to incredible heights.

23. Population Density.

24. 14

25. ii, i, iv, iii

26. Fiscal

27. (c)

28. Hint: Handicraft was a major industry before British advent, stiff competition from foreign imports led to its decline- leading to widespread unemployment.

32. Hint: (First Part) Maternal mortality, miscarriage, sex ratio, nutritional deficiency, marriage at early age, abortion and surrogacy.

33. Hint: (First Question 2nd Part) India and many other developing countries have lifted their trade barriers, following the WTO guidelines. But the developed countries like USA, still continue to impose some form or the other of import restrictions. The powerful countries easily get away with this because of their significant contribution to the funds of WTO.

You can choose any direction from this point, either it is good for India to continue being a part because of its growing trade relations and increasing demand of Indian goods. You can say it's better to leave and foster regional trade through bodies like SAARC, ASEAN, etc.

SAMPLE PAPER 15

SECTION A (MACROECONOMICS)

1. Narrow Money

2. (b)

3. Decrease

4. (b)

Or

(d)

5. Balance of trade and Balance of invisibles

6. 0 and 1

7. iv, iii, ii, i

8. True

9. (d)

10. Ratio of consumption to income.

11. NFIA = FIFA (–) FITA

12. Direct relationship.

Or

C = f(y)

13. (a) Inability of government to meet its regular and recurring expenditure.
(b) Disability of government
(c) Inflation

Measure to reduce Revenue deficit:
(a) Reduce expenditure (b) Increase revenue

14. (a) demand (b) demand (c) supply

Or

Credit, transfer and Hedging

15. Statutory Liquidity Ratio are net demand and time liabilities kept by commercial banks with themselves and that kept with the RBI is Cash Reserve Ratio.

16. (–) 40; 0.2; 5 times; 0.81

17. ₹ 3,000 crores

Or

₹ 1,070 crores

SECTION B (INDIAN ECONOMIC DEVELOPMENT)

18. ICICI Bank and Punjab National Bank

19. Horticulture

20. Iran

21. (d)

22. Pest

23. (b)

24. (b)

Or

(a)

25. True

26. iv, iii, ii, i

27. (d)

28. Hint: (First question) Land reforms and green revolution were the most important developments.

29. Hint: Oil and liquid spills, chemical and solid elements discharged into the water by fishing boats, vessels and trawlers often hurt marine life.

31. Hint: Regional associations, engaging in more trade, inviting FDI etc.

32. Hint: (First Part) Swachh Bharat (NDA) and Nirmal Bharat (UPA), governance agencies and tribunals-Green Tribunal, pollution control boards, India's recently released National Clean Air Program (NCAP)- provides a roadmap to prevent, control and reduce unhealthy air pollution, etc.

33. Hint: This refers to the opening up of the economy by devaluating the Rupee, i.e. the Economic Reforms of 1991

SAMPLE PAPER 16

SECTION A (MACROECONOMICS)

1. Commodity to commodity

2. (b)

3. Summation of autonomous consumption expenditure and autonomous investment expenditure is known as autonomous expenditure.

4. (b)

Or

(c)

5. ₹ 1100 crore

6. Consumption

7. (d)

8. False

9. ii, iii, iv, i

10. (c)

11. Real GDP does not show 'Composition and distribution of GDP'.

12. Zero saving indicate break even point i.e. Y = C.

Or

Voluntary and involuntary unemployment

13. It will help in reducing in equalities of income and wealth.

14. It affects demand and supply of foreign exchange through outflow and inflow of foreign exchange.

Or

Depreciation: X ↑ M ↓

Appreciation: X ↓ M ↑

15. (a) Reduction in money supply (b) Reduction in money supply
(c) Increase in money supply (d) Increase in money supply

16. (First Part) GDP_{MP} using expenditure method = ₹ 20,000
GDP_{MP} using income method = ₹ 20,000

17. (a) (i) 950 (ii) 4 times
(b) ₹ 2,000 crores; ₹ 4,000 crores

SECTION B (INDIAN ECONOMIC DEVELOPMENT)

18. (d)

19. (c) Indian Council for Medical Research

20. To transform agrarian economy into modern economy through the process of rapid industrialisation.

21. (d) (It is NABARD)

Or

(c) (use of renewable resources will meet power crisis)

22. Roads or Railways

23. ii, iii, iv, i

24. The process of moving from regular salaried employment to casual wage work

25. True

26. (a)

27. Water

28. (a) Globalisation: This is an example of outsourcing whereby Apple has lent out its manufacturing process to different countries. The reasons could be many like cheap labour, skills etc.
(b) Privatisation: The government has transferred part of its ownership.
(c) Globalisation: This is an example of removal of entry and exit barriers on MNCs and encouraging them to invest in the country. It shows integration of the world.

(please note that outsourcing refers to contracting out of services, i.e. hiring a third party but an MNC which is controlled by its headquarter and only increases its presence in different countries is an example of opening up of doors of the economy.)

29. Hint: (First Question) Census of India, NSSO, Directorate General of Employment and Training.

31. Hint: Power concentrated with the centre as opposed to India which follows democratic processes, therefore delay in decisions and accounting of every opinion. Public services and provision of literacy and health were given foremost importance which led to human capital formation. These are fronts which India and Pakistan are still struggling with. (include any other reason you think fit).

32. Hint: In India, poverty line is determined by computing the per capita expenditure on minimum calories that are required to be consumed per day for survival.

SAMPLE PAPER 17

SECTION A (MACROECONOMICS)

1. Low

2. (b)

3. fall in level of output

4. (d)

Or

(a)

5. ₹ 4,000 crores

6. 0.8

7. Exports will increase since domestic goods becomes cheaper.

8. (a)

9. (a) & (d) both (ii) and (b) & (c) both (i)

10. False, ₹ 500 crore

11. (a) Inventory investment (b) Inventory investment (c) Fixed capital formation

12. It is the ratio of change in income (ΔY) to change in investment (ΔY)

$$K = \frac{\Delta Y}{\Delta I} \text{ or } K = \frac{1}{1 - MPC}$$

There is direct relationship between K and MPC.

Or

Step 1: When S = –C then C = $\overline{C}$ which is the starting point.

Step 2: When S = O then Y = C which gives us the second point.

Joining the two points and extending them further we get the consumption curve.

13. The given statement is true.

14.

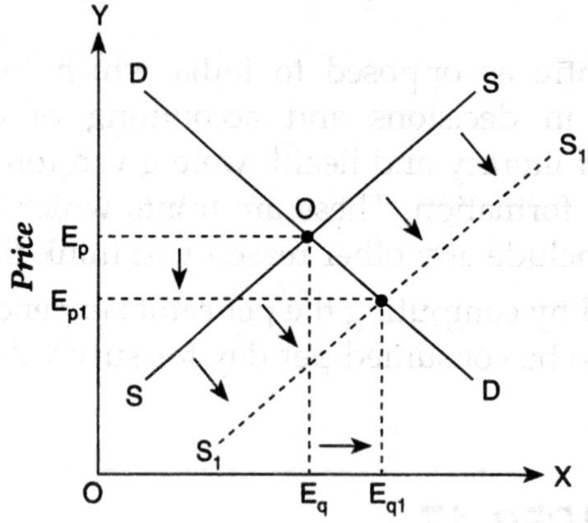

Quantity demanded and supplied of foreign exchange

Or

When total inflow of foreign exchange is more than the outflow of foreign exchange. Central bank creates reserves out of this surplus for future.

Due to increase in supply the equilibrium price of foreign exchange will fall.

15. Surplus budget = Total Receipts > Total Expenditure

Deficit budget = Total Receipts < Total Expenditure

16. When AD > AS at full employment equilibrium then it creates inflationary gap.

When AD < AS at full employment equilibrium level then it creates deflationary gap.

17. ₹ 2,600 crores; ₹ 160 crores

Or

(a) ₹ 3,70,000 crores (b) ₹ 5,12,000 crores

SECTION B (INDIAN ECONOMIC DEVELOPMENT)

18. Kolkata

19. (a)

20. Capitalist

21. School, Playgrounds

22. (a)

Or

(c)

23. True

24. (a)

25. 1.6 births

26. ii, iv, i, iii

27. (b)

29. Hint: (First question) Skilled workers, infrastructure for R & D and democratic environment.

Or

(Second question) Social security, healthy working conditions, pay above the minimum wage rate, etc.

31. Military takeovers, international meddling by other nations, terrorist activities blooming in the name of religion, etc.

32. Hint: (First Part) To buy inputs like fertilizers, seeds. Apart from their profession, they need credit for human and societal necessities like marriages, deaths, etc.

SAMPLE PAPER 18

SECTION A (MACROECONOMICS)

1. Time Deposits

2. (c)

3. Zero involuntary employment

4. (b)

Or

(a)

5. (d)

6. $\frac{\Delta C}{\Delta Y}$

7. False

8. (d)

9. Open market operations

10. 0.2

11. ₹ 850 crores

12. (First Part) $K = \frac{\Delta Y}{\Delta I}$

$K = Y$

$$Y = \frac{1}{MPS}$$

$$MPC = 0.75$$

13. This is because it leads to increase in exports.

14. When total receipts is equal to total expenditure demerits.

(a) Restricts freedom of action on part of government.

(b) Hampers process of economic growth.

Or

(a) Sale of asset

(b) Loan taken from any institution

(c) Disinvestment

(d) Deficit financing

15. It is determined by intersection of demand and supply of foreign exchange.

16. (a) False (b) False (c) True (d) False

17. (a) NNP_{FC} from output method

$$GDP_{MP} = 29{,}000\ (-)\ 12{,}000$$
$$GDP_{MP} = ₹\ 17{,}000$$

$$\begin{aligned} NNP_{FC} &= GDP_{MP} - \text{Dep.} + NFIA - NIT \\ &= 17{,}000 - 1{,}000 + (-)\ 2{,}000 - 200 \\ &= 14{,}000 - 200 \\ &= ₹\ 13{,}800 \end{aligned}$$

(b) GNP_{FC} from income method

$$\begin{aligned} NDP_{FC} &= 5{,}000 + 6{,}500 + 4{,}000 \\ &= ₹\ 15{,}500 \end{aligned}$$

$$\begin{aligned} GNP_{FC} &= NDP_{FC} + \text{Dep.} + NFIA \\ &= 15{,}500 + 1{,}000\ (-)\ 2{,}000 \\ &= 13{,}500 + 1{,}000 \\ &= ₹\ 14{,}500 \end{aligned}$$

Or

₹ 12000 Crores

SECTION B (INDIAN ECONOMIC DEVELOPMENT)

18. Owner-tenant relationship

19. (b)

20. Import Substitution

21. True

22. (c)

23. ii, i, iii, v, iv

24. (d)

25. GDP per capita

26. Agro processing

27. (d)

Or

(a)

28. Hint: (First question) Shortage of raw materials since a lot of fertile area went to Pakistan, example—the jute growing areas. Migration of people across borders resulted in massive movement of tangible goods and liquid money, communal tensions led to people losing their jobs, etc.

Or

(Second question) handicrafts, cloth print like tie and dye and muslin, spices, precious gems etc.

29. Hint: Leads to melting of sow laden mountains and glaciers which have Carbon dioxide trapped within the ice. Molten ice raises sea level-areas get submerged and the adverse effects only keep growing

31. Hint:

(a) The red line is a steeper graph and it shows that the GDP per capita has increased at a faster pace as compared to India

(b) 1980.

32. Hint: (Second question) Integrated Child Development Scheme (ICDS) is one such scheme. Provides nutrition to pregnant women, education to children from 0 to 6 years of age, immunization to school children, etc.

33. Hint: It is a differently worded question for What was the state of Indian economy on the eve of independence.

34. Hint: (Second part) Overdues, lack of proper follow up, faulty lending policy, lack of awareness, dearth of staff, lack of supervision and check on corruption.

SAMPLE PAPER 19

SECTION A (MACROECONOMICS)

1. Central Bank

2. (a)

3. Decrease in Consumption expenditure, decrease in investment expenditure

4. (d)

Or

(b)

5. (c)
6. False
7. iii, ii, iv, i
8. budgeted expenditure of government is equal to total budgeted receipts of government
9. (c)
10. Direct
11. Real GDP does not show 'Composition and distribution of GDP'.
12. Zero saving indicate break even point i.e. Y = C.

Or

Statutory Liquidity Ratio are net demand and time liabilities kept by commercial banks with themselves and that kept with the RBI is Cash Reserve Ratio.

13. (a) Inability of government to meet its regular and recurring expenditure.

(b) Disability of government

(c) Inflation

Measure to reduce Revenue deficit:

(a) Reduce expenditure (b) Increase revenue

14. Autonomous Transaction are undertaken for Profit Motive.

Accommodating Transaction are undertaken to cover deficit of BOP.

This distinction helps in fixing the real deficit or surplus in BOP.

15. This is because domestic goods become cheaper and export increases or import decreases leads to rise in increase of supply of foreign exchange.

Or

Exchange rate is determined by market forces of demand and central bank influences exchange rate.

16. (–) 40; 0.2; 5 times; 0.81
17. (Second Part) ₹ 1,070 crores

SECTION B (INDIAN ECONOMIC DEVELOPMENT)

18. Rainfall
19. (b)
20. The distribution of working force into primary, secondary and tertiary occupations is known as occupation structure.
21. Machinery
22. (d) (this is mining activity which is primary because it is extraction of resources)

Or

(c)

23. Bhutan
24. True
26. ii, iv, i, iii
27. (d)
30. Hint: (First question) Disguised unemployment
34. Hint: (First question)

$$\text{Worker-population ratio} = \frac{\text{Numer of workers}}{\text{Population}} \times 100$$

Highlight the worker-population ratio using gender, education level, urban–rural divide, etc.

Or

Hint: Second Part

(a) 10,000 kg

(b) Pesticides and fertilisers get washed away into water bodies during rains. Oil, degreasing agents, metals and toxins from farm equipment cause health problems when they get into drinking water.

SAMPLE PAPER 20

SECTION A (MACROECONOMICS)

1. restricts
2. (c)
3. Equilibrium in economy
4. (d)

   Or

   (a)
5. Balance of trade is the difference between export and import of merchandise transactions
6. (b)
7. (a)
8. i, ii, iii, iv
9. 1/LRR
10. 10 times
11. (a) Inventory investment
    (b) Inventory investment
    (c) Fixed capital formation

12. It is the ratio of change in income (ΔY) to change in investment (ΔY)

$$K = \frac{\Delta Y}{\Delta I} \text{ or } K = \frac{1}{1 - MPC}$$

There is direct relationship between K and MPC.

Or

Step 1: When S = –C then C = $\overline{C}$ which is the starting point.

Step 2: When S = O then Y = C which gives us the second point.

Joining the two points and extending them further we get the consumption curve.

13. Floating exchange rate is fixed by market forces of demand and supply Dirty floating exchange rate is influence by the RBI.

14.

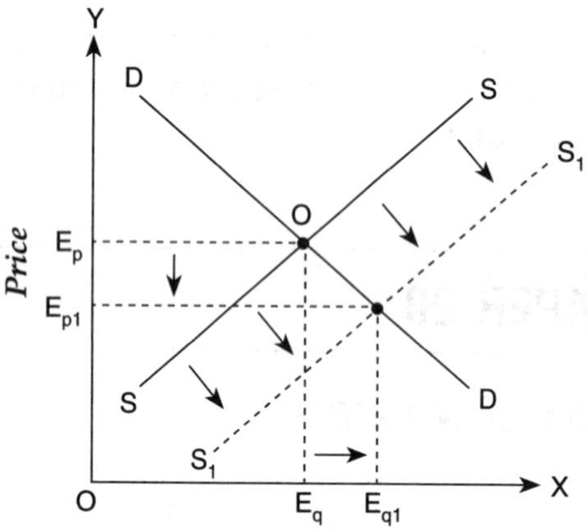

Quantity demanded and supplied of foreign exchange

Or

When total inflow of foreign exchange is more than the outflow of foreign exchange. Central bank creates reserves out of this surplus for future.

Due to increase in supply the equilibrium price of foreign exchange will fall.

15. It will help in reducing in equalities of income and wealth.

16. (a) (i) 950 (ii) 4 times

(b) ₹ 2,000 crores; ₹ 4,000 crores

17. ₹ 2,600 crores; ₹ 160 crores

Or

(a) ₹ 3,70,000 crores

(b) ₹ 5,12,000 crores

SECTION B (INDIAN ECONOMIC DEVELOPMENT)

18. Navratans

19. (b)

20. Share Cropping

21. (a) (because lesser and lesser number of people reach the higher level of education)

Or

(c)

22. Slow rate of economic growth and Population explosion

23. P V Narasimha Rao

24. ii, iii, i

Social Medicine due to the creation of toilets and a strive towards clean, hygienic surroundings.

25. 1978

26. Power generated from water is called hydel power

27. (c)

28. Hint: Yes, the economic reforms were necessary because the country was under severe crisis.

- Famines
- Debt-repayment of loan taken by the World Bank
- Rising poverty
- Overall stagnation of the economy, etc.

29. (First question) No, that is incorrect. Poverty has reduced in India. There has been improvement in the income levels due to job creations and emphasis on education + skill-based training. Mention a few government schemes.

31. Hint: Only India saw an increase in the GDP growth, hence often referred to as the fastest growing economy. This was due to the successful implementation of the 1991 reforms. India has always seen a huge percentage of GDP as savings by the people. It is these savings which prevent fluctuations during inflationary conditions – for example: India was very less affected by the 2008 financial crisis.

